DRAGON'S JAW

DRAGON'S JAW

AN EPIC STORY OF COURAGE AND TENACITY IN VIETNAM

STEPHEN COONTS
& BARRETT TILLMAN

Da Capo Press

Cover design by Kerry Rubinstein.
Cover image United States Air Force.

Excerpts from *Rampant Raider* by Stephen Gray used by permission of the United States Naval Institute.

Da Capo Press
Hachette Book Group
1290 Avenue of the Americas, New York, NY 10104
www.dacapopress.com
@DaCapoPress

Printed in the United States of America

First Edition: May 2019

Published by Da Capo Press, an imprint of Perseus Books, LLC,
a subsidiary of Hachette Book Group, Inc.

Editorial production by Christine Marra, *Marra*thon Production Services.
www.marrathoneditorial.org

Book design by Jane Raese
Set in 12-point Dante

Library of Congress Control Number: 2018958070

ISBN 978-0-306-90347-2 (hardcover)
ISBN 978-0-306-90346-5 (ebook)

LSC-C

10 9 8 7 6 5 4 3 2 1

TO ALL THOSE AMERICAN MILITARY AIRMEN,

PAST, PRESENT, AND FUTURE,

WHO HAVE BEEN OR WILL BE CALLED UPON

TO FIGHT IN THE DEFENSE OF FREEDOM.

CONTENTS

PROLOGUE
FULL THROTTLE

The telephone rang in the wee hours. It was the duty officer in the ready room.* Time to rise and shine for a predawn launch, still two hours away. D. D. Smith's roommate merely grunted and turned over in his berth. As usual, Smith staggered off to the head, came back, donned his dirty flight suit—he could get another day out of it—and steel-toed boots, and retrieved his pistol and shoulder holster from the tiny safe in his desk. He closed the door to the safe and spun the combination.

The ship was quiet—just the usual groans and creaks as she rode the back of the sea. Everyone who could grab some sack time was doing it; Smith was the only one in the passageways as he made his way to the wardroom, which was of course closed. But the stewards were cooking in the kitchen, and there was coffee—in the Navy there was always coffee. He grabbed a roll or two and coffee and headed for his squadron ready room.

Smith's wingman was there—unshaven, with tousled hair, sucking a cigarette and drinking coffee from the pot near the duty desk. The squadron Air Intelligence officer (AI) was chatting with the duty officer. In minutes both pilots were seated in the front row by the blackboard, learning about their mission.

That's the way it usually went. But one morning there was a new wrinkle.

---

*Adapted from *Above Average, an Autobiography*, by Commander D. D. Smith, USN (Ret) 2012, unpublished, used by permission of the author.

On the flight schedule their mission was armed recce—road reconnaissance: rocket and strafe anything moving on North Vietnam's north-south main highway, Route One.

The AI dropped the bomb. "A few hours ago during the night the Air Force hit the Thanh Hoa Bridge. They think they did some real damage and want the Navy to do some BDA [bomb damage assessment] at first light. You guys get the look."

"Why us?"

"You're the eyes of the fleet."

"How come the air farce doesn't do their own BDA?"

"As if I knew."

Smith, the flight lead, immediately foresaw serious problems with this assignment. Just amble over the Thanh Hoa Bridge? No jammers or flak suppressors? There were a hundred guns around that bridge that would shred the two A-4E Skyhawks if they got anywhere *near* the bridge!

Well, they punched off the front end of the big gray boat in the predawn darkness, rendezvoused, and proceeded toward the beach. Smith had no plan on how this was going to go down. His mind was still fixated on a nice, peaceful road recce where they might shoot up a truck or maybe a road grader. His mind refused to think about getting anywhere near that bridge in their two little A-4Es. The Dragon's Jaw Bridge at Thanh Hoa was the most heavily defended structure on the planet, surrounded by antiaircraft artillery (AAA) pieces manned by five battalions of gunners who got lots of practice. And above the envelope of the AAA were the SAMs—surface-to-air missiles.

SAMs could be brutally effective and very lethal. The only way to avoid them was to maneuver, and that would bleed off energy and drive the target aircraft down into the flak envelope, where North Vietnamese gunners could pick them off. The old tactic of cruising into bad-guy country at sixteen to twenty thousand feet was history.

Facing the problem, Smith decided to ingress at six to eight thousand feet, which allowed them to execute a quick dive for the deck in case of a missile launch. Yes, they were in range of flak guns at that altitude, but, hey, life's a compromise.

The aircraft had been retrofitted with missile-detection gear that sounded an alert when the plane was acquired by search radar, when the SAM-fire-control radar locked up an individual airplane, and when a missile was in the air being guided toward it. The sounds that came through the pilot's earphones as each of these evolutions took place were unique—and they couldn't have been worse if a Hollywood horror–film composer had arranged them.

The beam of the sweeping search radar made a chirp each time it illuminated the plane, so these chirps were regular and a few seconds apart as the radar antennae made its circle on its mount. When the missile-fire-control radar locked on, the tone became loud and steady. As the pilot's adrenaline level went into medical emergency overload, he waited . . . and waited . . . and then there it was: the tone began to cycle, a deedle or warble, indicating that the fire-control radar had been switched to a higher pulse repetition frequency (PRF) so as to locate you, the target, more precisely in three-dimensional space. Red lights, one on each side of the bombsight, illuminated on the glare shield above the instrument panel and said MISSILE, just in case the pilot was terminally stupid or humming an Elvis tune.

The finale occurred when the missile had been in the air for six seconds and the first stage dropped away: the earphone tone went to a screaming warble as the detection gear picked up the actual guidance commands that the fire-control radar was sending to the missile. The red MISSILE lights on the glare shield began flashing: the SA-2 missile was supersonic now and on its way to kill *you*.

That was a moment!

To make matters worse, it was not unusual for the North Viets to launch multiple missiles or, if they wanted to kill you badly enough, multiple missiles from different launch sites, which meant the deadly things came from different directions. The defense against a missile, whether one or many, was to outmaneuver it, which cost the planes' energy and soon had them headed for the dubious safety of Mother Earth waiting below.

That miserable morning the two Skyhawks began their jinking routine as they approached the coast while listening to the chirp of the search radars. The dawn revealed the usual Vietnam soup-like haze: they couldn't see crap in the early light. There was no way they could make out the details of the bridge from a reasonable distance, and overflying the bridge at three or four thousand feet would just get them killed.

Smith could see only one option. He figured swooping out of the haze with the rising sun at his back in his corkscrewing little A-4 gave him his best chance. Maybe he could surprise the North Vietnamese gun crews while they ate their breakfast of rice balls and fish heads or whatever. This was probably not a very bright idea, as the bridge defenders were undoubtedly on alert, waiting for an American plane to come motoring by to assess the effect of last night's strike. The Americans were as predictable as the tides—they *always* sent a plane or two after an attack to do damage assessment. The Viet gunners had only to wait until the sucker showed up.

Yet that was the only idea Smith had. He gulped down a deep breath, detached his wingman, and told him to keep him in sight. He pitched off at about eight thousand feet and headed downhill at full throttle. About a mile or so short of the bridge he leveled at fifty feet above the Ma River while going about 650 miles per hour. So far, so good.

Uh oh, some tracers. Holy Crap! Lots of tracers—and some geysers in the water ahead of him! He was jinking as best he could while flat on the deck, and the bridge was coming up fast.

Smith pitched the nose up, rolled inverted, and flew over the bridge for a good look—leaning his head back and getting an unobstructed view of the bridge through the top of the canopy. *The Dragon's Jaw was still standing in all its majesty.* He saw no damage at all.

Jinking like a wild man, he flew his adrenalin-drenched, pounding heart out of there as the guns hammered. Muzzle flashes and tracers strobed the gray morning haze like hot embers ejected from hell. Only every sixth or seventh shell was a tracer, so there were six or seven times more explosive shells in the air than he saw. Any one of them could finish him, send him on to whatever was afterward. Then . . .

Miraculously, he was out of it.

Out over the ocean his wingman was waiting.

Later, at the flight debrief back on the big gray boat, Smith asked him if he had had any trouble keeping lead in sight. "Oh," he said, "I lost you right away in the haze, but I could tell exactly where you were by watching the tracers converge."

The United States should not, under any circumstances, get involved in land warfare in Southeast Asia.

—GENERAL DAVID M. SHOUP
USMC, COMMANDANT OF THE MARINE CORPS,
AFTER A 1962 VISIT TO VIETNAM

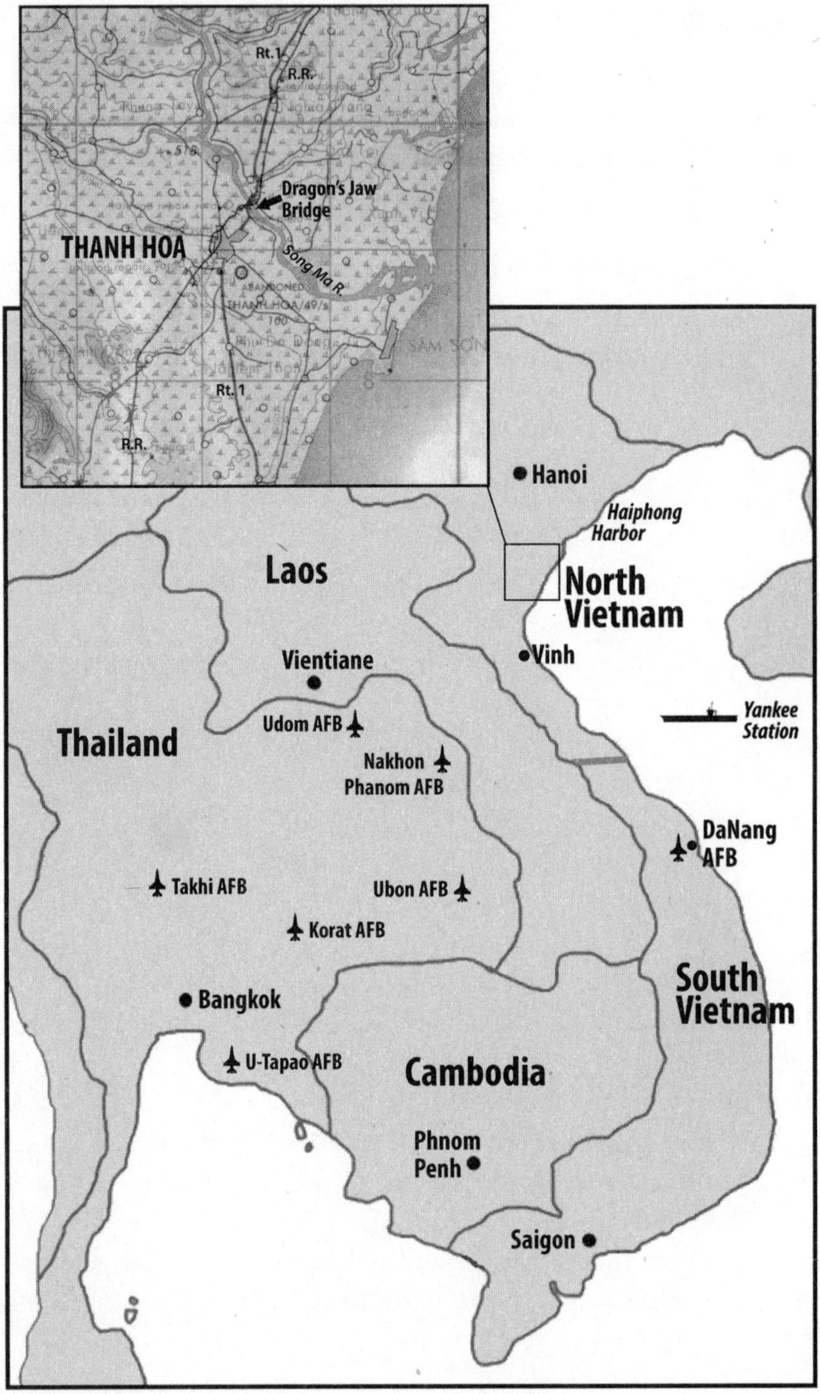

Rt. 1
R.R.
Dragon's Jaw
Bridge
THANH HOA
Song Ma R.
Rt. 1
R.R.
Hanoi
Haiphong
Harbor
Laos
North
Vietnam
Vinh
Vientiane
Udom AFB
Thailand
Nakhon
Phanom AFB
Yankee
Station
DaNang
AFB
Takhi AFB
Ubon AFB
Korat AFB
South
Vietnam
Bangkok
U-Tapao AFB
Cambodia
Phnom
Penh
Saigon

CHAPTER 1

"WE WILL PAY ANY PRICE . . ."

Bridges are the tangible products of the advance of a civilization that urges people to pool their resources and join together to construct a permanent way over a watercourse or chasm not only for their use but also the use of those who will come after them. When war comes, as it often does, bridges become the focal point of military strategy to exploit, defend, or destroy.

Military history is full of bridges: Xerxes' boat bridge across the Hellespont in 480 BC, Horatius at the Tiber bridge, Scottish hero William Wallace at Stirling in 1297, the Old North Bridge at Concord, Burnside's Bridge at Antietam, "the bridge too far" across the lower Rhine at Arnhem, the Ludendorff Bridge across the Rhine at Remagen—to mention just a few. Battles for bridges have determined the outcomes of campaigns and the fate of empires.

French colonial administrators in what was then French Indochina in the late nineteenth century were determined to build a rail network in Vietnam to tie the country together, and bridges were a key part of that plan. The Long Bien Bridge in Hanoi was named after the French colonial administrator Paul Doumer (Du-MAY), under whose administration the work was begun. It was completed in 1902, and for a time its mile-long cantilever design was the longest span in Asia.

Eighty miles south of that the French built another bridge across the Ma River (Song Ma) that, from time immemorial, people and livestock had crossed in small boats, or *sampans*. French engineers decided that the best place to bridge the river was nine miles inland from the Tonkin Gulf, a site three miles northeast of the provincial capital of Thanh Hoa, where the river flowed between a jagged limestone ridge on its west side and a small hillock on the east. The river gorge was about fifty feet deep. The Vietnamese who lived nearby thought these geological features looked like bones on the sides of a dragon's jaw, so that became the popular name for the location and where the French built their bridge. Completed in 1904, the Cau Ham Rong, or the Dragon's Jaw Bridge, was a single span of 532 feet, a double-steel arch with vertical beams supporting the deck.

After France surrendered to Germany in World War II, a pro-Axis Vichy French regime took over in Indochina, one that cooperated with the Japanese. Japanese troops occupied the country, which they probably would have done regardless of whether the French cooperated.

In 1945 the Vietnamese resistance, the Viet Minh, looking for a way to interrupt Japanese-Vichy logistics, decided to destroy the bridge at Thanh Hoa. Popular legend has it that they hijacked two locomotives, loaded them with explosives, and set them racing to crash head-on in the center of the bridge. Whatever the truth may be, an explosion did indeed destroy the bridge.

After World War II a new French government sent administrators and troops to reclaim their lost colony, only to run into a whirlwind of Vietnamese partisans. The war dragged on until 1954, when the French army was massively defeated at Dien Bien Phu. In 1954 a multination Geneva Convention divided Vietnam at the 17th parallel of latitude. President Diem refused to recognize the division, claiming that fair elections were impossible in the Communist north, a claim that was indubitably true. An estimated one million Vietnamese moved south of the 17th parallel, and Hanoi began supporting Communist guerillas in the south.

The fact that the Vietnamese partisans in the north were avowed Communists, led by a longtime Communist named Ho Chi Minh and supported by the Communist governments of China and the Soviet Union, was political poison in the United States. Despite the fact that Vietnam, a tropical backwater of rice paddies and mosquitos with a subsistence economy, was literally on the other side of the world from the United States, the conventional wisdom in the Eisenhower and Kennedy administrations was that its fate was tied to all of Indochina and, ultimately, Indonesia and Australia. At the height of the Cold War no administration, Democrat or Republican, could afford to be called "soft on Communism." The Eisenhower and then Kennedy administrations gave money and military assistance to the South Vietnamese government after the Geneva agreements of 1954.

In 1957, twelve years after World War II ended and three years after Vietnam's partition into North and South, the Communist regime in Hanoi decided to rebuild the Thanh Hoa Bridge across the Ma River. The decision to rebuild the rail and road network along the coast that linked the nation—north or north-and-south combined—together was absolutely inevitable. The new structure was built in precisely the same location, the Dragon's Jaw, as the old bridge destroyed by the Viet Minh in 1945. It was largely designed by Nguyen Dinh Doan, a structural engineer.

Some Westerners considered the bridge overengineered and overbuilt; certainly it was up to the task. Two steel truss spans met in the middle of the river on a massive, oval-shaped, reinforced concrete pier measuring sixteen feet across at the narrowest point. The cantilever spans from both banks were affixed to concrete abutments anchored against the bridge's limestone ridge on the west and the hillock on the opposite bank, and the "free ends" met on the concrete pier. These free ends were moveable due to the stresses and natural flexing of the structure. Fifty-six feet wide, the bridge supported a narrow-gauge railway track with concrete roadways on either side. The bottom of the structure measured about fifty feet above the surface of the river at normal flow. The French design had been elegant; the Vietnamese was practical and designed to carry more traffic. Like the French bridge, the structure was oriented east and west, a location dictated by the natural channel of the river. The railroad approaches on both ends were about two miles in length.[1]

The North Vietnamese worked on the bridge for seven years, finishing it in 1964. Although the first train had crossed on May 15, the bridge was dedicated on President Ho Chi Minh's seventy-fourth birthday, May 19. The Dragon's Jaw Bridge represented North Vietnam's emerging status in the region and was a source of national pride above the 17th parallel. Although President Ho was not there, the Vietnamese politburo was well represented at the dedication ceremonies. The luminaries included Prime Minister Pham Van Dong, Deputy Prime Minister Le Thanh Nghi, and other Communist officials, including the ministers of transportation and heavy and light industry and the first secretary of the youth central committee. Communist propaganda organs pulled out all the stops: newspapers all over the North trumpeted the brilliant work of engineers, factory workers, laborers, and, above all, the superb leadership of the Communist Party in bringing this grand national achievement to fruition.

The same month the Dragon's Jaw was dedicated, the Americans began frequent reconnaissance flights over Laos, supporting the Laotian government in Vientiane, which was also under attack by Communist guerillas. Frequently the jets were fired upon, and in June Communist Pathet Lao shot down two US Navy planes. Both pilots were eventually recovered, but tensions between the United States and North Vietnam increased.

★

While the North Vietnamese were building a bridge on the Ma River, John F. Kennedy was elected president of the United States.* In his inaugural address on January 20, 1961, he said, "Let every nation know, whether it wishes us well or ill, that we will pay any price, bear any burden, meet any hardship, support any friend, oppose any foe in order to assure the survival and success of liberty." Fine rhetoric, but even the most optimistic must have wondered just how far Kennedy would push it.

Behind that rhetoric was a policy dilemma with which the Kennedy administration was soon grappling. The Eisenhower administration had relied heavily on nuclear deterrence to keep world peace and allowed America's military conventional war capability to atrophy from lack of investment. The Korean War, which lasted three years and ended in a stalemate, revulsed the American public, which was thoroughly sick of wars. Was there a compromise, some way between these two extremes to militarily resist Communist aggression? The Bay of Pigs incident at the start of the Kennedy administration, followed by the Cuban Missile Crisis, made these policy choices the subject of great debate in Washington.

Kennedy brought into his administration highly educated young men from the northeastern US establishment, the New Frontiersmen. Robert S. McNamara, the new secretary of defense, had been president of Ford Motor Company for five weeks and was a disciple of quantitative analysis. He staffed the defense department with his "Whiz Kids," young men who believed wholeheartedly in quantitative analysis and distrusted senior military officers, whom they regarded as intellectually inferior fossils who relied upon "military experience,"

*It is not our purpose in this book to write a history of the Vietnam War but to illuminate Americans' efforts to destroy and, to the extent we can, North Vietnamese efforts to defend just one bridge, the Dragon's Jaw at Thanh Hoa. Still, to understand the battles over the bridge, we must see them in context, so a brief discussion of America's involvement is in order.

which these Whiz Kids distrusted instinctively. The Whiz Kids were arrogant, condescending, and inclined to ignore the advice of military professionals, if they asked for it at all.

Kennedy's national security adviser was former Harvard dean McGeorge Bundy, another tweedy elitist with self-confidence oozing from every pore.

Kennedy and McNamara found an ally in retired General Maxwell Taylor, former Army chief of staff, and they brought him back to active duty and again installed him as chairman of the Joint Chiefs of Staff (JCS). Taylor had written a book—always a door opener with JFK—in which he argued that the policy of massive nuclear response to Communist aggression was obsolete and needed to be replaced with one of flexible response. Taylor reveled in the role of the administration's military Richelieu.* He gradually took over the function of the JCS and often failed or refused to pass the Chiefs' policy positions to the White House, preferring instead to rely upon McNamara's civilian staffers and his own infallible judgment.

There were civilian staffers who urged Kennedy to get more militarily involved in Vietnam—against the advice of the uniformed professionals. Army chief of staff General George H. Decker said bluntly that "we cannot win a conventional war in Southeast Asia," so he was forced to retire after his first two-year term.

In his seminal work, *Dereliction of Duty*, H. R. McMaster wrote, "Already predisposed to distrust senior military officers he had inherited from the Eisenhower administration, the Bay of Pigs Cuban incident and the Laotian Crisis motivated the president to seek a changing of the guard at the Pentagon. After the Bay of Pigs, an unsatisfactory diplomatic settlement in Laos, confrontation with the Kremlin over a divided Berlin, and Soviet Premier Nikita Khrushchev's bullying rhetoric

---

*Cardinal Richelieu was the powerful minister of France who basically ran the country during the Thirty Years' War (1618–1648) and drastically curtailed the power of the aristocracy. Taylor did the same to the JCS.

persuaded Kennedy that the United States needed to 'make its power credible.'

"'Vietnam,' Kennedy concluded, 'is the place.'"[2]

So more money and military assistance flowed to the South Vietnamese regime in Saigon.

Yet during the Kennedy administration the South Vietnamese, even with American help, were losing the war with the Viet Cong. The Diem regime was blatantly corrupt and militarily incapable. It was obvious to Washington decision-makers that unless something changed, the Viet Cong, backed by North Vietnam, would eventually conquer the South. That truth was not shared with the American public.

South Vietnam was not a modern nation in any sense of the word. There was no concept of a loyal opposition or open and free debate on public issues. The government was venal and corrupt. So-called sects—or armed gangs—existed by shaking down the population. Military units were tied to the area from which their personnel were recruited and could not be used for offensive thrusts elsewhere in the country. The generals in charge of the military could be compared to feudal warlords. South Vietnam in the 1960s resembled England in the fourteenth century.

Several months before he died, hoping for a more stable government in Saigon, Kennedy authorized the CIA to arrange a coup, one that resulted in the murder of President Diem and his brother by South Vietnamese army officers on November 1, 1963. The situation in Saigon got no better, and in the ensuing months seven coups followed, one after another.

The assassin's bullet that killed Kennedy on November 22, 1963, a mere three weeks after Diem's murder, dropped Vietnam into Lyndon B. Johnson's lap.

★

Big, blustery, and quick-tempered, Lyndon Johnson's political style tended toward intimidation more than leadership. Even his most ardent fans admit that Johnson had neither the intellectual capacity nor the executive experience to understand the consequences, intended and unintended, resulting from policy choices. Nor did he have the moral courage to be a war leader.

McMaster noted, "Both Lyndon Johnson's self-doubt and his willingness to forego the truth would color his relationship with his principal military advisers and shape the way that the United States became more deeply involved in the Vietnam War."[3] Baldly, Johnson had a real propensity for lying for his own political benefit. In Robert S. McNamara he found a soul mate.

McNamara later stated that on his ascendency to the presidency,

> Johnson was left with a national security team that, although it remained intact, was deeply split over Vietnam. Its senior members had failed to face up to the basic questions that had confronted Eisenhower and then Kennedy: Would the loss of South Vietnam pose a threat to U.S. security serious enough to warrant extreme action to prevent it? If so, what kind of action should we take? Should it include the introduction of air and ground forces? Launching attacks against North Vietnam? Risking a war with China? What would be the ultimate cost of such a program in economic, military, political, and human terms? Could it succeed? If the chances of success were low and the costs high, were there other courses—such as neutralization or withdrawal—that deserved careful study and debate?
>
> Lyndon Johnson inherited these questions (although they were not presented clearly to him), and he inherited them without answers. They remained unanswered throughout his presidency, and for many years afterward.[4]

McNamara, although nominally only secretary of defense, became President Johnson's principal adviser on Vietnam. "McNamara would dominate the policy-making process because of three mutually reinforcing factors: the Chiefs' ineffectiveness as an advisory group, Johnson's profound insecurity, and the president's related unwillingness to entertain divergent views on the subject of Vietnam. Above all

President Johnson needed reassurance. . . . McNamara could sense the president's desires and determined to do all he could to fulfill them. He would become Lyndon Johnson's 'oracle' for Vietnam."[5] And he would not raise these basic policy questions with the president that he identified in his apologia, *In Retrospect: The Tragedy and Lessons of Vietnam.*[6]

CHAPTER 2

A DAMNED TOUGH NUT TO CRACK

On the afternoon of August 2, 1964, the US Navy destroyer USS *Maddox* (DD-731) engaged three hostile torpedo boats off the North Vietnamese coast in the Gulf of Tonkin. The ship was monitoring North Vietnamese radio traffic and South Vietnamese commando raids against the north.

Due to intercepted communications, *Maddox* officers believed the Communist PT boats intended to attack, and so they retreated from several miles off the coast to about twenty-eight miles out. *Maddox* was capable of making twenty-eight knots at top speed, yet the enemy boats were capable of fifty. *Maddox*'s commanding officer (CO), Captain John J. Herrick, ordered his gunners to fire three warning shots when the enemy boats closed to ten thousand yards.

They did so, opening the battle.

The Vietnamese launched torpedoes that *Maddox* evaded as the enemy boats zipped along at high speed with machine guns hammering as the destroyer's three- and five-inch batteries blasted away. It would have been quite a feat for the American gunners to hit tiny targets skittering along at fifty knots, and they didn't, even though they whanged off 280 shells at the enemy. Still, it was a dilly of a little sea battle. Yet the Americans had backup. While the American destroyer and Vietnamese boats exchanged torpedoes and gunfire, four F-8 Crusader fighters from USS *Ticonderoga* (CVA-14)—the *"Tico"*—arrived and dove into the fight. The fighters shot up the boats with 20-mm cannon and rockets as the Vietnamese retreated toward the coast.

Four North Vietnamese sailors were killed and six wounded in the incident. The *Maddox* sustained one small hole from a North Vietnamese machine gun bullet. Interestingly, the Johnson administration conveniently forgot about the warning shots that *Maddox* fired and always insisted that the North Vietnamese fired the first shots.

Two days later the USS *Turner Joy* (DD-951) joined the *Maddox* to reinforce right of passage in international waters. With darkness falling, US shipboard radar detected a distant contact, prompting a hasty conclusion that the Vietnamese were attacking again. But they weren't. The nervous sailors on the sonars and radars were seeing echoes, or ghosts. Once more, *Tico* Crusaders were summoned, and for more than two hours the Americans shelled and strafed the area.

Leading the fighters was Commander James B. Stockdale, who was asked by an intelligence officer when he trapped back aboard the *Tico* if he saw any boats. "Not a one," Stockdale replied. "No boats, no wakes, no ricochets off boats, no boat gunfire. For goodness' sake, I must be going crazy. How could all of that commotion have built up without something being behind it?"*[1]

Although evaluation of radar and sonar records produced no confirmation of hostile action on August 4, President Lyndon B. Johnson seized the hilt of the sword with both hands and jerked it free of the

*Thirteen months later Stockdale would be shot down and became one of the senior prisoners of war in Hanoi. For more than seven years he lived in dread that his captors would stumble on the fact that he had witnessed the nonevent on August 4 that Lyndon Johnson used as justification to escalate America's involvement in Vietnam, but his secret remained unknown.

stone. With a presidential election barely ninety days away, Johnson was not going to risk being called "pink" in contrast to his hawkish conservative opponent, Senator Barry Goldwater. Johnson was the moderate candidate, but he saw the possibility of armed retaliation against the North Vietnamese as a gift from heaven, allowing him a political masterstroke. Johnson wanted to win the election "bigger than anyone had ever won."[2]

Johnson ordered retaliatory air strikes against North Vietnam the next day, August 5, resulting in two planes shot down, with one US pilot killed, Lieutenant Richard C. Salter, and one captured, Lieutenant Edward Alvarez Jr. As a prisoner of the Communists, Alvarez would be subjected to torture and physical abuse for eight and a half years.

On August 7, 1964, Congress passed a joint resolution authorizing military action without a declaration of war.* There was almost no opposition; only two Democratic senators dissented. During the debate Wayne Morse of Oregon said, "I believe that history will record that we have made a great mistake in subverting and sabotaging the Constitution of the United States." Although defeated for reelection in 1968, Morse would remain a leading Democrat dove for the rest of the war.[3]

The die was cast. The storm had been gathering for years. The Johnson administration was determined to escalate the conflict, and the fanatic ideologues in Hanoi had no intention of giving up their ambition to reunite the country under Communist leadership. An armed cataclysm with the United States, the most powerful nation on the planet, was inevitable.

★

At first the American plan was to use air power gradually against North Vietnam, then the United States would increase pressure slowly. Robert McNamara's "graduated response" was supposed to force the

*Known as the Gulf of Tonkin Resolution, Johnson signed it into law three days later.

North Vietnamese Communists to abandon their goal of reuniting Vietnam while ensuring that Red China did not send troops across the border to prevent North Vietnam's military collapse.

McMaster noted in his seminal work, *Dereliction of Duty*, "Graduated pressure depended on the assumption that the limited application of force would compel the North Vietnamese to the negotiating table and exact from them a favorable diplomatic settlement. There was no need to pursue military victory because negotiations would achieve the same political objectives with only the threat of more severe military action. The only question was when, not if, the enemy would be induced to negotiate."[4]

It was a prescription for military and political failure.

Cyrus Vance, McNamara's deputy secretary of defense during the Johnson years, said in 1970 that "we had seen the gradual application of force applied in the Cuban Missile Crisis and had seen a very successful result. We believed that, if this same gradual and restrained application of force were applied in South Vietnam, that one could expect the same result."[5] Of course, US troops were not fighting in Cuba, a fact that made the Cuban Missile Crisis and the Vietnam War incomparable, nor was the Soviet Union engaged in total war to unify the nation. Sadly, this flawed premise was the intellectual foundation for how the United States conducted the war in Vietnam during the Johnson administration.

As journalist David Halberstam said of McNamara, "He was—there is no kinder or gentler word for it—a fool."[6]

★

So the air-power storm was coming, and Thanh Hoa Bridge, that strategic target on Route One, was doomed. Or was it? The Americans soon learned that they lacked the air power weapons necessary to destroy the bridge, and the Vietnamese learned that they could bleed American air forces with guns, fighters, and missiles.

In 1964 there were 23,000 American military personnel in South Vietnam and 6,500 in Thailand. The numbers soon skyrocketed. In

1965 nearly 185,000 American servicemen were in Vietnam, 26,000 of them Air Force personnel; in Thailand, where the Americans had built air bases, there were another 9,000 Air Force servicemen.[7]

By June of 1965, ten months after Lyndon Johnson threw down the bloody gauntlet and seven months after he was reelected, the US Air Force had moved 460 aircraft to Southeast Asia, yet fighter-bombers were few: seventy-nine F-105 Thunderchiefs and eighteen F-4 Phantoms. The F-105s had been designed to deliver nuclear weapons in the event of total war with China or the Soviet Union. Both these airplanes had an air-to-air capability if they weren't carrying bombs under their wings. They lacked any computer or radar that would simplify the pilot's job of dropping bombs. This meant that conventional high-explosive bombs were delivered the same way they had been delivered since the 1920s, with the pilot looking through an optical-mechanical bombsight as he dove at the target and then pushing a button to release the weapons.

The F-105 Thunderchief had a single engine and single pilot and, thanks to a large afterburner, was supersonic—but not while carrying external weapons. The Air Force's policy of demanding that all tactical aircraft be supersonic meant that the wings were not optimized for carrying bombs, so subsonic performance suffered. Still, the Thud, as it was called by those who flew and maintained it, could escape the target area at supersonic speed after the bombs were gone, an advantage Thud drivers came to appreciate.

The F-4 Phantom II was a Navy design and, thanks to the idiocy of the admirals, lacked guns. It was designed as an interceptor to protect the fleet. It was touted as a Mach 2 fighter and carried missiles—heat-seeking Sidewinders and radar-guided Sparrows. The two crewmen, seated in tandem, could also use the raw power of two internal engines and afterburners to haul bombs for visual delivery, then escape at supersonic speeds if fuel was not a concern. Air Force Phantoms were not intended to launch from and land aboard aircraft carriers, but they had the same landing gear, tailhook, and beefed-up airframe of the Navy versions. Amazingly, they were supposedly several hundred pounds heavier than the Navy version, the F-4J.

Twenty years after the end of World War II the conventional weapons available to tactical and strategic aircraft had changed little. General-purpose bombs, the Mark 80 series, were more streamlined than they had been in World War II and coated with a fire retardant, but mechanically and chemically they were essentially the same. Tactical aircraft delivered bombs in a dive, aiming them by means of the optical-mechanical bomb-sight that sat on the top of the instrument panel in front of the pilot. The pilot's skill in doping the wind, flying his plane, and pickling the bombs at just precisely the right moment determined whether the bombs hit the target. This method was perfectly adequate in decent weather for something as large as a railway yard or shipyard, when an impact error of a few hundred feet in any direction was acceptable for government work, but when the target was a pinpoint target, for example, an enemy ship, or the center concrete pier of a steel-truss bridge, bull's-eyes under heavy antiaircraft fire or while dodging SAMs and midair collisions with your friends became few and far between.

And the window for aiming had shrunk as the aircrafts' speed increased. Most jet dive bombers planned to release the weapons at 500 knots true airspeed, or as close to it as they could get, so as to minimize their exposure to enemy weapons, which fired a greater volume of shells than the antiaircraft artillery (AAA) of World War II. Due to the speed of the aircraft, the angle of approach to the target had to be shallower. Gone was the 70-degree dive of the venerable SBD Dauntless of Battle of Midway fame; now a 40- to 50-degree dive was about all that could be attempted if the aircraft would be able to pull out of the dive without ripping the wings off before it went below thirty-five hundred feet, the approximate ceiling that small-arms fire could reach. In a 70-degree dive, retarded by dive brakes, the piston-engine Dauntless released its single weapon at about 250 knots—about two thousand feet above the target—and pulled out at two hundred feet over the ocean. Now, in a 40-degree dive, with a six-thousand-foot release altitude, Vietnam-era jet pilots found that the slant range to the target at weapons' release was ninety-three hundred feet, which is one-and-a-half nautical miles.

Another major problem was the fusing of the bombs. The mechanical nose fuse was a tried-and-true design from the 1930s. Upon the release of the weapon from its bomb rack, a copper safety wire affixed to the rack was withdrawn from a propeller in the nose of the fuse, freeing it to turn in the wind. After a preset number of seconds, usually about six, the firing train in the fuse was properly lined up and the weapon would detonate when it struck something. The fuse could be set to give a few milliseconds delay to allow the bomb to penetrate if the target material would allow penetration. A solid concrete bridge pier reinforced with steel was not going to be penetrated by a thousand-pound bomb, assuming the delivery pilot was an ice-water-for-blood pro who could score a perfect hit. If the bomb didn't bounce off, it was going to detonate on the surface and take off a few chips of concrete.

Both the Navy and Air Force were attempting to move beyond the mechanical nose fuse. Electric fuses seemed to hold much promise, yet during the mid-1960s they were a work in progress. Several aircraft were destroyed by their own weapons when the electrical fuse on one of the bombs malfunctioned and detonated the weapon at the end of the six-second arming time or even before if the bombs bumped against one another. Mechanical nose fuses were still in widespread use for free-fall bombs until the very end of the Vietnam War.*

★

Hanoi knew that American aircraft could penetrate its airspace almost at will. The Communists' goal was to make the effort as costly as

*The Vietnam experience and the frustration of attempting to take down the Dragon's Jaw Bridge and the Paul Doumer Bridge in Hanoi eventually convinced American military leadership that guided weapons were needed. We will explore the early use of guided weapons later in this book.

possible. Ho Chi Minh and his colleagues did everything in their power to get ready. North Vietnam's first class of fighter pilot candidates was sent to China in 1960 to learn to fly the MiG-15. In 1962 another group finished training in the MiG-17 in Russia. In 1964 the Soviets provided three dozen MiG-17 jet fighters to equip North Vietnam's first fighter unit, the 921st Fighter Regiment, which was roughly equivalent to an American Air Force wing. The airplanes were a gift: apparently the Soviets could also read the writing on the wall and thought the North Vietnamese might just give the Americans a bloody nose. The second unit, the 923rd Fighter Regiment, equipped with MiG-17s, became operational in 1965.[8]

By any measure the North Vietnamese fighter pilots were novices, and they would be up against American pilots who were well experienced, often combat veterans, and masters of their machines. Many Americans arrived in Southeast Asia with a thousand or more hours of flight time. However, except in the US Navy's F-8 Crusader community, dogfighting skills had been institutionally ignored since the Korean conflict.

Conversely, the Vietnamese pilot candidates received only about two hundred hours of flight training in Russia, which was made even more difficult by the language barrier. The first generation of North Vietnamese pilots tended to come from the ranks of the 1950s Viet Minh who had fought the French. The Vietnamese People's Air Force's (VPAF) first ace, Nguyen Van Bay, completed pilot training at the age of twenty-nine. It was said, "He went from the bicycle to the airplane with no stop in between." Without US aviators' education requirements, some applicants began flight training at eighteen or nineteen, winning their wings as soon as four years later.

First flown in 1950, the MiG-17 (NATO code name Fresco) was a subsonic swept-wing fighter-interceptor with an afterburning engine pushing it up to seven hundred miles per hour. Like the MiG-15, the 17 was a bare-bones, short-range defensive fighter. It carried a limited fuel supply, could not be refueled in the air, and, as originally designed, had no radar. In 1951 the Soviets obtained a captured American F-86 Sabre from Korea and copied the optical gunsight and gun-ranging radar. They installed the clones in the MiG-17, which became operational in 1952 yet never served in Korea.

The 17 was smooth where it needed to be smooth—mainly on the leading edges—and less refined elsewhere. Its boundary-layer fences atop the wing were a concession to expedience over engineering elegance, physically keeping a wing's airflow from flowing outward and stalling along its swept span. It lacked refinement by Western standards, but it was cheap, easy to maintain, easy to service, and got the job done. Workmanship was just adequate, in keeping with the Soviet emphasis on quantity—after all, Lenin had famously noted, "Quantity has a quality all its own."

The MiG-17 had a fatal design defect that would have been corrected had it been manufactured in the United States or Western Europe. Like the MiG-15, if more than half the fuel was used, an under-pressure condition could develop in the fuel tanks that could lead to tank implosions, crushing the main fuselage of the aircraft in midair. Apparently never corrected, the design defect led to roughly 30 percent of the 17's accidents, and most of the implosions killed the pilot. The airplane was a flying death trap.[9]

The Vietnamese pilots must have known about the problem and flew the plane anyway. No doubt some of them died when their winged steeds imploded. Their patriotism and courage inspires awe, although it is awe tempered with a large dash of cold reality. North Vietnam was an absolute dictatorship locked in total war. Fighter pilots lived and ate better than the draftees sent south to battle the Americans on the ground or the AAA crews surrounding hard targets like the Thanh Hoa Bridge. Their chances of surviving combat and accidents were probably marginally better than the common grunt. Still, there were few cowards in MiG-17 cockpits.

Hanoi's air defense system was dictated by its fighters' capabilities and constructed on the Soviet model. Due to their limited fuel supply, MiGs rarely launched until an American raid was inbound. Radar controllers on the ground directed interceptors by radio to a favorable position against incoming Yankee air pirates while climbing for altitude, even telling MiG pilots when to arm their weapons. Most engagements were slashing attacks, with the Vietnamese making high-speed passes against US formations, preferably from a height advantage. If things degenerated into a dogfight—the type of air combat the Americans had declared obsolete—most MiG pilots were poorly trained in cut-and-thrust maneuvering against an opponent, though the MiG-17's light wing loading—barely half that of an F-4 Phantom—was a tactical advantage.

Despite his 360-degree view from his canopy, the MiG-17 pilot coped with poor visibility. His ejection seat was nonadjustable, and the canopy fit close to the pilot's head, partly hemming him in. Therefore, he wore a tight-fitting leather helmet and goggles of World War II vintage rather than the bulkier reinforced-plastic helmets of most of the world's fighter pilots. The large lead-computing gunsight and thick windscreen glass also partially obscured the pilot's view forward.

What's more, at 450 knots (515 mph) the MiG's unboosted controls stiffened up, becoming extremely difficult to move at higher airspeeds. The wise MiG pilot also tried to avoid the uncontrolled nose "tip-up" that occurred as the plane flirted with Mach 1. Furthermore, it could enter an uncoordinated "Dutch roll" at 375 knots that spoiled maneuverability. To offset the "energy" of their US opponents' tactics, MiG-17 pilots sought an "angles" fight: come in as fast as possible, preferably in a slight dive, shoot at one plane, and dive on out of the fight.

The MiG-17 had deadly fangs: a 37-millimeter cannon with forty rounds and two 23-millimeters that could fire eighty rounds each. That was enough ammo for five seconds of shooting. A typical two-second burst delivered seventy pounds of metal downrange—a prodigious quantity, enough to shatter any airplane in the American inventory.[10]

★

By April 1965 the North Vietnamese fielded a dozen antiaircraft artillery regiments and fourteen independent battalions with about one thousand guns of all calibers. Twenty-two early-warning radars and four fire-control radars supported them.

That same month Hanoi's electronics capabilities expanded as the Americans detected Russian-made SA-2 surface-to-air missiles (SAMs), with one SAM site growing to about a dozen by the end of the year.[11]

At the time of the bombing pause at the end of 1965 American aircrews reported flak on only 8 percent of their missions "up north." Two months later they discovered that the Vietnamese had used the interval to boost their AAA capability threefold—with more increases to come.[12]

In 1967 US intelligence reckoned the Communist ammunition consumption in North Vietnam at twenty-five thousand tons per month. When the bombing ended in late 1968 the air-defense network had blossomed to more than eight thousand guns, four hundred radar stations, and forty SAM sites.[13]

Amid all this, the Thanh Hoa Bridge became the most heavily defended target in North Vietnam, which is to say, at that time in human history, the most heavily defended target on earth. In fact, more than a target, it became a symbol. American engineer-historian Gary Wayne Foster explained, "Destruction of the bridge became an intense obsession of American military planners. The Vietnamese, obsessing no less, fought to preserve the bridge, which for them had become the supreme symbol of their resistance to American air power. It's not without plausibility then that the destruction of this sacred symbol by the Americans may have been more important than the destruction of the structure itself."[14]

For much of the war, primary responsibility for defending the Thanh Hoa Bridge fell to the 228th Air Defense Artillery Regiment. In 1960 it had turned in its 90-millimeter heavy guns for smaller, faster-firing 57-millimeter weapons. Re-equipped by the end of June, the 228th deployed forty guns and five SON-9A radars, plus generators, spare parts, and ammunition.[15]

In May 1965, after the initial US attacks on the bridge, the 228th deployed to Thanh Hoa, relieving the 234th Regiment. The move was accomplished quickly, with the 228th established by the dawn of May 8. The regimental commander Nguyen Dang Tang and political commissar Tran Chau Kinh deployed 23-, 37-, and 57-millimeter guns around the town and the bridge.

At first the newcomers moved into the 234th's positions, but the disposition was judged inadequate. Some crews set to work building roads and leveling hills to improve visibility and fields of fire, allowing better integration of the 228th's five batteries. The third battery even built a floating firing position in a stretch of sunken paddy fields.

Meanwhile the 228th was augmented by the provincial defense force's Third AAA Battalion, with three 37-millimeter batteries under Comrade Cao Xieu. He sited his guns atop the Dragon's Eye and Jade Mountain Karsts, affording a relatively clear field of fire.

Reportedly, Nguyen Can Coi, commanding North Vietnam's air defenses, personally supervised the installation of AAA weapons atop the Dragon's Jaw. Disassembled guns were hauled up the steep slopes of Rong Mountain on the west bank and Ngoc Hill on the east, while other weapons were placed along likely aerial approaches. Putting guns on both ends of the bridge gave the gunners up-the-throat shots at any American plane diving on the bridge. It also was a very dangerous place to be, as, inevitably, bombs were going to be falling close to or on the guns.[16]

It is too bad that Lyndon B. Johnson and Robert S. McNamara couldn't have been present that day to watch Nguyen Can Coi site the guns. The men manning these weapons were likely to die, probably when the next American strike rolled in on the bridge. Nguyen Can Coi knew it, the gunners knew it, and anyone watching couldn't help but understand it. Here was visual, visceral proof that North Vietnam was going to be a damned tough nut to crack.

Gun crews and support teams worked around the clock, typically in twenty-four-hour shifts, whether in drenching rain or in the cloying Annam Province humidity and heat. Crews changed at midnight so they would be unlikely to be caught in transit by US aircraft. Similarly, small powered craft delivered ammunition to the river banks, sometimes fighting the current twice a night from distribution points downstream. Thus, the Dragon's Jaw area was nearly always in flux, with gun crews going on and off duty, ammunition and supplies being delivered, cooking fires being tended under cover, and people trying to snatch a little sleep.[17]

The most common AAA weapon in North Vietnam was probably the Soviet-designed S-60 57-millimeter antiaircraft gun, which radical American actress Jane Fonda introduced to the American public by posing for the cameras on one in 1972. Of Korean War origin, the S-60 was produced in China as the Type 59. It was a five-ton towed weapon with a crew of seven. It was fed by four-round clips weighing nearly sixty-three pounds each. The mount could swivel 360 degrees, with 90 degrees of vertical elevation, an option seldom employed for obvious reasons. Rate of fire was continuous—typically seventy rounds per minute—as long as ammo clips were inserted in the feed tray.

The 228th also employed the ZU-23, a twin-barreled 23-millimeter automatic weapon. Usually mounted on a trailer, it was served by six men. The ZU was fed linked ammo from fifty-round boxes on either side. The two barrels could spit out a combined two thousand rounds per minute, but disciplined gunners usually maintained a rate of about four hundred rounds a minute of aimed fire. Maximum range against aircraft was rated at a mile and a quarter; on fast crossing targets the Soviets calculated a .023 percent hit probability. However, multiple weapons firing in the same cube of airspace offset the low single-mount success rate.[18]

Two other antiaircraft guns in Vietnam's inventory were pre–World War II Soviet designs. The 37-millimeter automatic defense gun, M1939, was also produced in China as the Type 55. The weapon had a crew of seven or eight. Fed by five-round clips, the gun was rated effective to about fifty-five hundred feet.

Another 1939 design was the 85mm KS-12, firing a cartridge weighing 20.25 pounds. It shot a far larger projectile than the lighter weapons and had a greater reach. The 85-millimeter slant range was nearly twenty-five thousand feet, although the typical engagement range was up to eighteen thousand feet. Each shell contained 1.4 pounds of TNT that could inflict fatal damage on a jet with a proximity-fused air burst. Served by seven men, it sat on a wheeled carriage like the other AAA weapons.[19]

For optimum coverage of a given area, most North Vietnamese antiaircraft installations were laid out in geometric patterns, typically triangular or pentagonal shapes. This disposition had the advantage of creating overlapping fields of fire from multiple weapons, increasing hit probability beyond that of a single weapon.[20] In 1965 all these weapons, with the possible exception of a few 85-millimeter guns, were optically aimed.

The Dragon was ready for the storm.

★

Suppressing Vietnamese antiaircraft fire became an occupational specialty for tactical airmen. *Bonnie Dick* A-4 pilot Lieutenant Steve Gray said, "Flak suppression was the most hazardous mission we flew. Once you began your attack on the gun site, the gun director knew immediately what you were up to and shifted the fire of his battery toward you. It became a 'you or them' situation. The easiest shot for the gunner was up-the-throat, firing directly at the diving airplane with no deflection or lead required. It was very common to see antiaircraft shells passing through the 100 mil ring of the gunsight [100 mils subtended to 100 lateral feet at 1,000 feet range]. But if they were firing at you they weren't shooting at the bombers and you were accomplishing your mission."[21]

Attacking an AAA site reduced modern war to its most basic element. The attack pilot was trying to kill the gunners, and they were trying to kill him. It was raw, visceral violence—to the death.

And it would last more than seven years.

CHAPTER 3

THE FIRST HAMMER BLOW

In November 1964 Lyndon Johnson had been reelected to his first full term as president. At the time his victory was the fourth-largest presidential landslide in American history. Johnson's first priority was his domestic political agenda, the Great Society Program. With his aides and advisers, he also tried to determine what to do with this war in Southeast Asia that he had wanted a big piece of. The American politicians certainly didn't appreciate the advantage that an absolute dictatorship bestowed upon the North Vietnamese leadership. What they did appreciate, though, was that North Vietnam and the People's Republic of China shared a border, and if the war wasn't handled right, they feared that China might send an army to prevent a military defeat of its Communist ally, as it did in October 1950 in Korea.

Being a tough anti-Communist was one thing, but embroiling the United States in another war in Asia against Red China would be an absolute disaster. The Johnson administration set out to walk a tightrope: fight the war in such a way that China would never feel that North Vietnam was threatened with national obliteration, yet apply enough military and diplomatic pressure to force Hanoi to stop trying to conquer the South.

Many have argued that the Johnson administration grossly misread the Vietnamese Communists, who had absolutely no intention of inviting the Chinese into their country under any circumstances. The Chinese were ancient enemies, and having gotten rid of the French, the Vietnamese didn't want to risk becoming a satellite state or province of China either. And Beijing had its own problems, including the Great Leap Forward from 1958 to 1962, which caused widespread famine and starvation, followed by the Cultural Revolution in 1966. Nor were conditions stable in the Soviet Union. In fact, the Soviets and Chinese feuded over territorial, political, and ideological differences throughout the Vietnam War. They even exchanged gunfire along disputed border areas, notably Demansky Island for six months in 1969, with fatalities on both sides.

The feuding and instability in both Communist giants was evident to the Washington elite and anyone who read newspapers during the first four years of the Vietnam War. Still, Lyndon Johnson and his advisers took counsel of their fears, not the true situation of potential enemies. That Johnson and his advisers permitted the thin, nearly nonexistent threat of a wider war with Beijing or Moscow to restrict US efforts and goals in Vietnam—at unnecessary risk to American personnel—was unforgivable. Baldly, the Johnson administration had no intention of trying to win the war but intended to use "limited" force to induce the other side to bow to America's political will.

★

Be that as it may, in 1965 America had a war to fight. As the Viet Cong, supplied by the North Vietnamese, continued to wreak havoc on South Vietnam, the Johnson administration decided to unleash the tactical bombers upon North Vietnam. The air campaign was to be limited to the area south of the 20th parallel, about two hundred statute miles above the 17th parallel's Demilitarized Zone, or DMZ, that the Geneva Convention of 1954 had established to separate North from South Vietnam. The operation was called Rolling Thunder—and the Dragon's Jaw was one of its targets.

The operation was fatally flawed from the start. The objective was to make it difficult or impossible for Hanoi to keep supplying the Viet Cong in South Vietnam. It could not have possibly succeeded, as any second lieutenant or sergeant could have told the arrogant secretary of defense when Rolling Thunder was in the planning stages. The Johnson administration allowed North Vietnam to continue receiving supplies via the port of Haiphong while forbidding bombing within thirty miles of the Chinese border, thus preserving most of the Northeast Railway to China, which ran largely uninterrupted. The North's fighter bases were also situated mostly around Hanoi and were off-limits to American fighter-bombers for years. MiGs could only be shot down if they attacked American aircraft, which of course they were going to do as often as they could. And there was the little matter of the porous, nonexistent western borders of both Vietnams, with roads and trails in Laos and Cambodia that allowed troops and trucks to move south mostly free of American harassment. Be that as it may, and lacking any other options, Lyndon Johnson and Robert McNamara decided to give limited bombing south of the 20th parallel of latitude a try.

The storm of steel and high explosives that Ho Chi Minh and his colleagues knew was inevitable had arrived.

★

Rolling Thunder began in March 1965. In April three important bridges were targeted: Dong Phuong Thuong, Hong Hoi, and Thanh Hoa—the Dragon's Jaw. As a sop to the professional airmen, for the first time the politicians allowed the pilots to drop unexpended ordnance on locomotives and vehicles in designated areas.

The sustained air campaign targeting the bridges began when Air Force fighter-bombers struck ordnance depots about thirty miles south of Thanh Hoa and forty miles north of Vinh on the coast. The defending gunners claimed they downed five American planes but, apparently, got none.[1]

Mission Nine Alpha was the name given to the first assault against the Dragon's Jaw. The 67th Fighter Squadron at Korat, Thailand, did most of its planning. The squadron CO was Lieutenant Colonel Robinson Risner, a forty-year-old fighter pilot at the peak of his profession. He had earned his wings in the final days of World War II, gunned eight MiGs in Korea, and enjoyed a superior reputation as a pilot and leader.

Robbie Risner thrived on combat. He had been shot down on March 22 while attacking a coastal radar site when he violated a basic rule: never make a second pass at an alerted target. His Thud rolled out of control, and he ejected while inverted and landed in the water. Rescued by an amphibian aircraft, he was back flying a few days later. His survival and rescue were sufficiently dramatic to cause *Time* magazine to place him on the cover a few weeks later.

Risner believed in thorough planning and assigned the ordnance portion of the mission to his assistant weapons officer, Captain Wesley Schierman. Because the squadron's senior weaponeer was on Okinawa, Schierman worked up a plan for the Korat strikers while those at Takhli with the 355th Fighter Wing did their own. Schierman was concerned about the lightweight Bullpup missile. He recalled, "The first thing I found was that we had been directed to use sixteen aircraft (I think it was eight from Korat and eight from Takhli) firing two Bullpup air-to-ground missiles each. The rest would carry eight 750-pound bombs. I advised Colonel Risner that the Bullpup with its 250-pound warhead was totally inappropriate for such a heavy target . . . and ours only had instant fusing available. I also suggested that multiple passes over a heavily defended area would be unnecessarily hazardous."[2]

The AGM-12 Bullpup was America's first mass-produced, air-to-surface command-guided missile. It was the tentative first step on the road to guided weapons. Almost fourteen feet long and eighteen inches in diameter, the missile weighed 1,785 pounds, was powered by a rocket engine, and had a range of ten miles. After firing it, the pilot or weapons officer of the attacking aircraft had to watch the Bullpup, which had a flare on the back to make it easier to track visually, and to use a control joystick to send radio signals to steer it toward the target. Stooging around after shooting the missile while trying to guide it to the target kept the attacking aircraft in the defenders' cone of antiaircraft fire—not a situation conducive to long life. The best way to get a hit was to superimpose the missile upon the target and keep it there, which meant the pilot of the shooting aircraft had to follow the missile down, surrendering his ability to jink and evade enemy antiaircraft fire. Certainly, given the tiny 250-pound warhead and instantaneous fusing, choosing the Bullpup against a well-built, heavily defended bridge seemed not only ridiculous but something that foolishly endangered the launching aircraft . . . and, incidentally, the man in the cockpit.

Risner knew all about the Bullpup and kicked the subject up the ladder. Apparently it went all the way to the Joint Chiefs in Washington—an early indication of the micromanagement that would plague the entire nine-year Vietnam debacle. When he got his answer, Risner told Schierman that the pilots were required to "stick with the plan."

That was not all. Fusing for the 750-pound bombs was a concern. Schierman recalled, "We only had old World War II–style bomb fuses, which only gave the option of instant or .25 second delay." The instant setting would cause the bombs to go off in the superstructure over the bridge, and the quarter-second delay would allow the bombs to pass through the bridge deck and go off in the water. "What we needed was a .025 setting, but the newer fuses were not available because they wanted us to use up the old ones first! In essence, we were going on a mission in which sixteen aircraft, each exposed twice, had no chance of destroying the target, and the other thirty or thirty-two had a very low probability, due to using the wrong fusing."[3]

The US Air Force generals appeared to have completely forgotten the lessons learned in World War II and Korea. Welcome to the Vietnam War, a wholly owned subsidiary of the US government.

Wes Schierman proceeded as best he could. He chose a 45-degree dive angle, descending from about twenty-two thousand feet and firing each Bullpup at around twelve thousand feet—giving a twenty-second time of flight to impact. A strong pull after impact would bring the jet level at eight thousand feet or more, well above light-caliber antiaircraft fire. Because the pilots needed a good view of the target to steer the missiles, the Bullpup shooters would attack first, before the free-fall bombs were dropped: smoke from bomb bursts and spray from hits in the river would obscure the target.

Risner briefed his men on all aspects of the mission, using reconnaissance photos of the bridge, defenses, and the surrounding area. He also addressed the onerous subject of rules of engagement (ROE) that would handicap American airmen throughout the war. Schierman added, "The ROE prohibited us from hitting any target, other than the bridge, for any reason!"[4]

Like most Air Force strikes, the overall plan was huge, involving nearly eighty aircraft coordinated over a large area, merging in time and space. Originally the strike was slated for April 2, but not enough aerial tankers were available. However, tankers and weather cooperated the next day, so the mission was a go. The Thailand-based aircraft were forty-six F-105s and ten KC-135 Stratotankers. The tankers—developed from the Boeing 707 airliner airframe—were positioned to support the Thuds in flight along four refueling tracks over Thailand. The attack element from Korat and Takhli approached Thanh Hoa from the southwest, overflying Laos into North Vietnam.

Thirty F-105s carried eight 750-pound bombs, but only half of them were targeted against the bridge; the other half were flak suppressors, assigned to hit enemy antiaircraft guns. If the suppressors could time their dives correctly, they would allow the attackers to do their work over the bridge relatively unhindered.

And there was more. From bases in South Vietnam came twenty-one F-100 Super Sabres, including two weather scouts, seven more flak suppressors, four on combat air patrol, and two flights (eight aircraft total), as a contingency to cover any rescue operations. Additionally, two RF-101 Voodoo reconnaissance jets would provide pre- and post-strike damage assessment photos.

Although it was showing its age, the transonic, single-engine-with-afterburner Super Sabre was a capable second-generation fighter. An outgrowth of North America's fabled F-86 Sabre, it had entered service in 1954, a contemporary of the MiG-17 flown by North Vietnam. On the first Thanh Hoa mission the "Huns," as they were called—short for "Hundreds"—were armed with their standard four 20-millimeter cannon plus Sidewinder air-to-air missiles or bombs and Zuni rocket pods.

The F-105s plugged into their Boeing tankers before entering Laotian airspace so they would have ample fuel for the attack phase of the mission. Once topped off, the four-plane flights proceeded to the initial point (IP) three minutes south of the bridge. Timing was critical so as to avoid an aerial traffic jam in the target area—precise navigation and airspeed management were the mark of professional airmen.

"Time on target" was 2:00 P.M.—1400 hours military time. The sky was clear, but ground haze reflected some of the early afternoon sun, obscuring the target for some of the pilots.

The Super Sabres were precisely on time, diving on identified AAA positions, dropping bombs, and firing Zuni rockets. The five-inch Zunis had a rocket motor that boosted their speed to sixteen hundred miles per hour and burned for 1.5 seconds. For antiaircraft suppression the warhead's proximity fuse was set to detonate above the ground, spraying shrapnel across the enemy gun positions like a giant shotgun blast. After the Huns attacked, the Thud suppressors rolled in, adding their ordnance to keep the gunners ducking, even if they missed the antiaircraft sites.

Despite the flak-suppression flights, the Vietnamese gunners scored. In the explosive-speckled sky, First Lieutenant George C. Smith from St. Louis disappeared in his F-100D. His squadron mates thought he'd been hit by a 57-millimeter shell, but they could not make radio contact. He had just turned twenty-five.[5]

Among the attackers the four Bullpup flights rolled in first, one airplane at a time, as they needed a clear view of the bridge to guide their radio-controlled ordnance. Each Thud launched its first missile from about twelve thousand feet altitude; then after guiding in the weapon, the pilot added power, pulled up, and wheeled around to position himself for his second pass in the aerial daisy chain. It was an unavoidable requirement of having to shoot two missiles. Some pilots thought the process resembled an exercise in the Nevada desert more than a genuine combat mission. Flak filled the sky.

Air Force doctrine was to blame: the gunners on the ground had only one attacking airplane at a time to shoot at. Although antiaircraft artillery had improved tremendously since World War II and Korea due to the nearly universal adoption of the proximity fuse, and there was a lot more of it, Air Force doctrine hadn't changed. We'll fight this war like the last one, boys.

Robbie Risner's Thud was tagged by flak. Just as his second Bullpup scored on the bridge, a 57-millimeter shell exploded nearby. Losing fuel and with smoke wafting into the cockpit, he was forced to divert southward to DaNang, 220 nautical miles away in South Vietnam.

Other missile shooters had grave doubts about their ordnance. Flying in the third Bullpup flight, Captain William H. Meyerholt waited for the smoke to dissipate before firing his first missile. As he wheeled around for his second pass, the West Pointer, class of 1957, could see no damage to the structure—merely blackened steel from previous hits.

Flying north from the IP at seventeen thousand feet, the F-105 bombers could see the bridge's east-west span across the Song Ma. From there they rolled into a right-hand "wagon wheel" descending circular approach, winding up on a northeasterly attack heading, outbound for the gulf. They were angled about 45 degrees from the bridge's axis—tactical wisdom dating from as long ago as 1918.

In dive-bombing deflection errors nearly always exceed range errors. Deflection errors are caused by the wind, unperceived or not properly accounted for, or aircraft skid, which meant the aircraft's rudder was not properly trimmed for the release speed or properly positioned by the pilot. A straight approach to an exceedingly narrow target, only fifty-six feet wide, meant that, absent a perfect run, the entire bomb string would go into the water on one side of the bridge or the other. Diving across the span at an angle gave less chance of a left-right error and raised the probability that at least one bomb in the string would hit the bridge.

One of the strikers was Captain Ivy McCoy of the 67th Fighter Squadron, and he had a grandstand view of the strike. The Louisianan recalled, "When I rolled in the bridge was still standing and I felt, 'Here is your chance.' I put a perfect stick of eight 750s across the bridge. As I circled around, climbing out, all I could see was water and smoke. But as it cleared, the damn bridge was still standing."[6]

Elsewhere that day American and Vietnamese fighters tangled for the first time. While attacking Dong Phong Thuong Bridge ten miles north of Thanh Hoa (seventy miles south of Hanoi), a USS *Hancock* F-8 Crusader was damaged by MiG-17 cannon fire. Though the Viets joyously announced a kill, Lieutenant Commander Spence J. Thomas landed his damaged fighter at DaNang in South Vietnam. The People's Air Force would come to know the Crusader as their worst enemy in the next two years. However, a *Hancock* A-4C Skyhawk did fall to antiaircraft fire, and Lieutenant Commander Raymond A. Vohden became the third US Navy prisoner of war (POW).

Over the Dragon's Jaw AAA flashed and spewed smoke as shells tore at the sky. Amid it all the missile shooters and bombers dove at the bridge *one at a time* and laid in their ordnance. Billowing clouds of smoke and water raised by bombs in the river obscured the bridge; the attackers were long gone by the time the smoke and mist cleared. Now it was time for the reconnaissance planes to photograph the damage so specialists could assess it. The North Vietnamese knew the drill, of course, and they reloaded their antiaircraft weapons and waited. When they appeared, the photo jocks would be welcomed appropriately.

Two RF-101 Voodoos flew out of Tan Son Nhut Air Base in Saigon. One was piloted by Captain Hershel S. Morgan, who had flown more than ninety sorties in the previous six months. After his pass over the bridge through the flak storm, he proceeded south to his second photo objective, a radar site near the coast. There he ran flat out of luck. Antiaircraft fire crippled his jet, and he limped away, running out of altitude. Scotty Morgan ejected near Vinh, a provincial capital seventy-five miles south of Thanh Hoa, and spent the next seven years as a prisoner of the North Vietnamese.

When the reconnaissance photos from the surviving Voodoo were developed hours later, it was found that 32 Bullpups and 120 750-pound bombs had barely dented the Dragon's Jaw.

The other two bridges targeted that day were down, but the Dragon's Jaw was a much tougher target. In the military, which is apt to keep repeating a failed experiment, the saying goes, "If the first hammer blow fails, hit it again, and again and again . . ."

More hammer blows were coming. A second mission led by Robbie Risner was immediately laid on for the following day.

CHAPTER 4

"HE DID NOT WANT ANY MORE MIGS SHOT DOWN"

The next day's attack had a few new twists. Forty-eight F-105 bombers supported by twenty combat air patrol fighters and weather report F-100s arrived at the Dragon's Jaw shortly before 11 A.M. on April 4. No flak suppressors accompanied the bombers. One possible reason was that damage assessment photos showed the previous day's efforts had caused minimal damage to the flak sites guarding the bridge. A more likely reason was that the decision was made to use every available plane to attack the bridge. In any event, this day there would be no flak suppressors.

The weather was worse than the day before, with low clouds and more haze, providing perhaps a maximum of five miles visibility. Visibility was so bad that the attack force was forced to run into the target from the east, away from the potential sanctuary of the sea, although few Air Force pilots thought of the ocean in those terms.

Rather than participating in the strike, Risner remained overhead as strike coordinator, "directing traffic" and evaluating the effectiveness of each flight's bomb run. He also noted disposition of flak sites from their muzzle flashes, though it was unlikely any had been moved during the night.

Because surface winds were unknown, the wingmen in each four-plane flight watched their leader's bomb hits, then compensated accordingly. The technique was called "chasing the wind" or "going to school on Lead." Unfortunately one had to wait until the Lead's bombs struck the ground to see where they hit, so the deliveries were inevitably delayed. Every second of delay increased the attack force's time over the target and gave the antiaircraft gunners more time to shoot at and connect with each individual airplane.

First to roll in was the leader of Steel Flight, Captain Carlyle "Smitty" Harris, a Marylander one week short of his thirty-fifth birthday. He had flown the previous day's mission in the last bombing flight and knew the problems erratic winds posed. In a steep, fast dive he placed the bridge in his bombsight, let the pipper track, and pressed the bomb release button on the stick. But he had waited too long.

His eight 750-pound bombs came off the plane at only four thousand feet, and the Thud lifted perceptibly, three tons lighter.

Harris bottomed out a thousand feet above the ground, pulling hard to avoid Mother Earth. As the G's pressed him into the seat, he felt the impact of an AAA shell.

It was probably a 37-millimeter round, but it could have been anything because the low pullout put the Thud within the range of everything the defenders had except pistol bullets. Whatever it was, the shell struck the fuselage well aft. The aircraft yawed violently, the left drop tank was wrenched off, and the single jet engine quit.

With fire and system warning lights vying for his attention, Harris was riveted on job one—flying the airplane. He was only ten miles inland, but it might as well have been fifty. His jet, now a crippled glider, was shuddering and decelerating.

Harris' wingmen had a good view of their Lead's stricken Thud. The plane was streaming flames and shedding parts, threatening to disintegrate. Harris descended into the low cloud deck and didn't hear his friends screaming on the radio, "Get out!" because his radio was dead.

Smitty Harris braced himself in the ejection seat, blew the canopy, and pulled the handle. He was rocketed from the dying Thud and tumbled through the air only a few hundred feet above the ground. The small drogue chute on his seat stabilized his descent, the parachute opened, and he was dragged out of the ejection seat.

Captain Harris splashed down in a rice paddy within earshot of the bridge—he could hear bombs exploding nearby. Then he became the focus of fifty or more Vietnamese running toward him, thrilled at the opportunity to capture a Yankee air pirate and take private revenge. Harris was fortunate he didn't die at their hands.

Last in the Thud daisy chain was a flight of four from the 355th Wing out of Takhli, Zinc Flight. The four pilots were reasonably experienced, with as many as three thousand total hours of flight time and from four hundred to six hundred in F-105s. However, they were new to the war, and none had flown more than five combat missions; not only that, Air Force combat training was often skipped or shortened. Zinc Four, Captain Richard D. Pearson, possessed limited gunnery training and had only fired two Sidewinder missiles while in training. One survivor of a later MiG engagement that year confided he had not flown an air-to-air training mission since 1954.

The problem was not the fault of the pilots. After all, Air Force pilot applicants signed up to fly—the more, the better. The problem was institutional. In the late 1950s and early 1960s the US Air Force was focused on fighting a nuclear Armageddon in which aircraft like the F-105 were expected to strike Communist targets around the world. Old-fashioned dogfighting had gone out with MiG Alley in 1953. Everybody knew that.

Everybody except MiG pilots.

The Vietnamese fliers were aware of their shortcomings and very conscious of their adversaries' capabilities, but some of them exuded confidence nonetheless. One recalled, "We were quietly confident at the time and did not have any fear of the Americans, although we respected their experience and more modern equipment."[1]

Zinc Lead was Major Frank E. Bennett, a Rhode Island athlete from a family of athletes. Frank was a standout baseball and football player, and his older brother Robert had medaled as a hammer thrower in the 1948 London Olympics. At the age of thirty-two, Bennett had logged 470 hours in Thuds since 1962.[2]

Bennett's wingman was another major, James A. Magnuson Jr. He had also been flying F-105s since 1962 and accumulated nearly 475 hours in type. These totals are deceiving, as these pilots were averaging merely fifteen hours or so a month, barely enough to maintain proficiency.

Zinc Flight was late, delayed by refueling problems en route. Thus, Bennett was about fifteen minutes behind schedule when he checked in with Risner, the on-scene commander. Risner directed Bennett and company to orbit about ten miles south of the bridge at fifteen thousand feet.

Completing a left-hand orbit, Zinc Three, Major Vernon M. Kulla, and Zinc Four, Captain Pearson, flew about eight hundred feet above and on the outside of the turn. Kulla glimpsed the flight ahead of them about two thousand feet lower through some haze, which was thick. Zinc Lead was maintaining 325 knots airspeed, or about 375 miles per hour, lugging eight 750-pound bombs on the wing-racks.

The pilots knew that MiGs had been airborne the day before but posed no threat to the Dragon's Jaw attackers. The Viets had flown about thirty miles south of Thanh Hoa, reversed course, and disappeared northward. Today at the brief, intelligence had advised that MiGs would probably be airborne again, stalking them.

In his turn Vern Kulla, leading the second section, glanced northward and spotted two bogies—unidentified aircraft—approaching from astern. Kulla noted that the intruders were approaching in a 20-degree dive from nearly a mile back. A few heartbeats later he identified them as MiGs. They were tracking the lead section.

Vern Kulla keyed his radio mike: "Zinc Lead, break! You have MiGs behind you! Lead, break! Zinc Lead, we're being attacked."

Neither Bennett nor Magnusson responded, although other pilots in the area heard the transmission. Richard Pearson, Zinc Four, repeated the warning.

The MiG-17 interceptors belonged to the 921st "Red Star" Fighter Regiment, North Vietnam's first fighter unit. The regiment's executive officer, Nguyen Van Tien, led eight MiGs from the Noi Bai airfield northeast of Hanoi. Their radar controller on the ground, Dao Ngo Ngu, had had a decent picture of the developing situation since the Americans began concentrating around Thanh Hoa. Dao deployed one flight as a decoy to draw off the American CAP and another to attack the bombers.

The first two MiGs were well positioned—their controller had done his job. They dived in from the lead Thuds' five and six o'clock position while a second section of MiG-17s closed on Zinc Three and Four.

Zinc Three, Vern Kulla, called for a section break, taking his wingman Richard Pearson to the left. The two Thuds hit the emergency jettison button, shedding their six-thousand pounds of ordnance, and put their noses down to unload the aircraft and accelerate to fighting speed, then they rolled into near-vertical banks and began pulling big Gs. Their opponents sped past them, above and behind, continuing southward and making an estimated Mach .85, roughly 640 miles per hour at that altitude. The Americans got a good look at them—light gray overall with Communist star and bar markings. Three and Four crammed their throttles forward and lit their burners, but acceleration from 325 knots was far too slow to gain an offensive position.

Leading the four attacking Viet fighter pilots was the commander of the regiment's first company, or squadron, Tran Huy Han, a thirty-two-year-old former political commissar. Descending through the clouds in a high-speed dive, Tran sighted Zinc Flight. His momentum took him past the F-100 MiG CAP, and, covered by his wingman Senior Lieutenant Pham Giay, Tran selected the lead American.

Now aware of their peril, Bennett and Magnusson jettisoned their bombs—far too late.

As Tran closed to four hundred meters range, Bennett tried breaking into an evasive turn, but the heavy Thud with supersonic wings could not hope to turn with a MiG. In fighter pilot jargon, Frank Bennett was meat on the table.

Tran flipped up the cover atop his control stick and placed his thumb on the firing button for the 37-millimeter cannon and his finger on the trigger for the two 23-millimeter cannon. He opened fire, and heavy shells raked the Thunderchief's airframe.

Through his G-blurred vision, Vern Kulla saw pieces hacked off Zinc Lead's airframe. Bennett's wingman, Magnusson, called, "Lead, you have a MiG behind you."

Tran saw flames gush from the enemy aircraft. Pulling out of his attack, he thought he glimpsed Bennett's plane dive into the water. What he may have seen was the splash of a bomb rack with weapons attached as it hit a rice paddy.[3]

Then Tran's second element, flying almost wingtip to wingtip, attacked Zinc Two. Lieutenant Le Minh Huan began shooting at Frank Magnusson. Le saw hits flashing across the American jet. Fuel-fed fire spewed from Zinc Two's tail, and Magnusson radioed, "I've been hit."

Between seven hundred and eight hundred feet ahead of Magnusson the two Vietnamese pilots rolled into level flight and sped ahead, exiting the fight. Not that it had really been a fight. It had been an ambush in the finest tradition of aerial warfare—sneak up on an unaware opponent, shoot him in the back, and escape before the victim's friends could retaliate. These two Communist fighters were last seen in a gentle right bank when they disappeared into the haze.

By the time Pearson could look "out the window" again the MiGs were gone. Taking no chances, Pearson wracked his bird into a descending spiral and checked his tail. He was clear, but Kulla was gone. Nonetheless, Richard Pearson busted past Mach 1, climbing to join the lead section. He wanted to join Jim Magnusson's crippled jet and left Vern Kulla to escort Frank Bennett.

Yet Magnusson wasn't up high. Pearson backed off the throttle, decelerating rapidly. Magnusson was limping along at merely two hundred knots about five hundred feet above the ground. Still descending and decelerating, Pearson quickly overshot Magnusson and lost him in the haze. As he reversed course, hoping to join up, he heard Magnusson call that he was ejecting.

Magnusson had headed for the ocean. Steel Flight told him to shift to the emergency channel for easier monitoring, and Magnusson had complied. He nursed his dying jet about twenty-six miles southeast of the Dragon's Jaw and seven miles offshore before his final call: his controls were dead and he was ejecting.

Meanwhile Kulla had his hands full. Expecting to escort Bennett from the area, Zinc Three glimpsed gun flashes behind him. Though making Mach .84 at ten thousand feet, he pulled harder, loading more G on the plane, then he slightly bunted the nose and rolled inverted through the turn, reversed his heading, and started climbing.

In his climb Kulla kept turning to keep his assailants in sight. He saw the two MiGs closing again, so he rolled left as if to begin a split-S. The Viets followed.

The squadron had just been briefed on the best way for a 105 to "hit the brakes" and force an enemy to overshoot. The officer from Nellis Air Force Base, Captain John Boyd, had irritated some of the Thud drivers with his self-confident attitude, but he knew his business. His passion was energy management in three dimensions. An abrupt pitch-up into a snap roll induced considerable drag on the Thud's large airframe, and although Kulla had not practiced the maneuver in his four hundred hours in Thuds, he had been flying fighters for eight years. Now on the naked edge, he was desperate enough to give anything a try.

The maneuver worked. With his nose perhaps 30 degrees above the horizon, the snap roll killed about two hundred knots of airspeed. The MiG section skidded outside the turn, winding up ahead of the lone Thud. Kulla gawked as one MiG dove past him in a near-vertical dive, the other at a shallower angle. He wondered whether MiG One could pull out in time and hoped he couldn't.

Then Kulla wondered about himself. He crammed on full throttle, lowered his nose, and saw a windscreen full of North Vietnam. He pulled the nose up and leveled off less than a thousand feet above the dirt. The MiGs disappeared into the haze.

Once free of the stalkers, Kulla could again think about his friends. He asked Bennett to transmit a homing signal on the radio and advised him to gain as much altitude as possible. Miraculously, he found Bennett in the haze and joined up. Heading south, the pair topped at about twenty-one thousand feet, and Kulla made a visual inspection of Zinc One. There was a large hole beneath the fuselage near the speed brake, some damage to the afterburner pedals, and a one-foot hole in the left flap. The speed brakes were partly open, evidence of a damaged hydraulic system. Kulla also noticed hydraulic fluid leaking around the tailpipe.

Back near Thanh Hoa, Richard Pearson, Zinc Four, searched frantically for Jim Magnusson in his parachute. Clouds obscured swatches of ocean. Pearson thought he glimpsed the impact site of Magnusson's Thud just offshore, but he might have just seen drop tanks jettisoned by F-100s impacting the water.

An Air Force HU-16 amphibian arrived to search the area until darkness, but the Albatross came up empty.

Lacking options, Pearson decided to join Kulla and Bennett as they tried to gain the safety of South Vietnam. He rendezvoused with his two friends headed for DaNang.

About twelve miles from the field at fifteen thousand feet still over the ocean, Frank Bennett began his descent and was cleared for an emergency landing. Then his engine lost all oil pressure and quit. In the big silence that followed, Bennett leveled off, slowing from about three hundred knots, and radioed his friends that he was going to eject.

Kulla and Pearson were close enough to see Bennett lose his helmet during the ejection. They watched for the blossom of the parachute but did not see it. Still in his ejection seat, Frank Bennett fell through the clouds and was lost to sight.

Pearson, critically low on fuel, remained high to conserve JP-4 while Kulla dumped a wing and spiraled down through the clouds toward the water pulling Gs, seeking a glimpse of a chute in five-mile visibility. Kulla saw nothing. He stayed as long as he possibly could, only leaving when an Air Force helicopter from DaNang came in sight.

Inbound, Pearson overflew the cruiser USS *Canberra*, wagging his wings to attract attention. The ship got the message and turned toward the HH-43 chopper from DaNang. Meanwhile, though at an emergency low-fuel state, Kulla confirmed the likely "splash" location with the helo before heading for DaNang. He and Pearson landed with fumes remaining.

The *Canberra*'s crew found Frank Bennett's body. His parachute had deployed but apparently not in time to slow his fall into the Tonkin Gulf.

The Air Force looked for two days yet found no trace of Jim Magnusson. He was first listed as missing in action and eventually changed to KIA.[4]

★

After Jack Graber's flight passed Zinc Flight following the MiG attack, they rolled in to attack the bridge. Graber recalled,

> I had just released my bombs, retracted the speed brakes, gone full throttle, selected afterburner, pulled hard (I think we all pulled more than four Gs on average, more like five or six). Then as the nose came up through the horizon, unload, stomp on the rudder, and roll into a serious jinking maneuver and score your bombs at the same time. If Lead went left, then we went right, reversed, and finished with a quick join-up.
>
> Well, that was the plan. But as I was jinking and pulling all those Gs, I accidentally pulled the throttle out of burner. I had never done that before. I think it was my guardian angel that did it. While I was trying to get a relight, the airspeed was bleeding off something

serious. I was down to 350 knots and had to force myself to push the stick forward and ease off the G-load, waiting for a burner relight.

Meanwhile, at my twelve o'clock was more flak and tracers than I had ever seen. It reminded me of those military weddings where everyone holds a sword up to form a tunnel for the bridal party to walk through. I had a tunnel of tracers coming up in front of me, which I was flying through. I think the gunners had decided to concentrate their fire on the next guy down, which was me. But they had never seen an F-105 fly that slow. All the fire went out front, and I never got a scratch.

My guardian angel must have been busy with me because I never received any battle damage in any of my 116 missions.[5]

*

Although three Thuds were fatally damaged, one unknown to the Vietnamese, the air action continued over the Dragon's Jaw.

Escorting the strike were F-100 Super Sabres of the 416th Tactical Fighter Squadron from DaNang. The unit had flown the first Rolling Thunder mission on March 2, and on April 4 the nearest MiG CAP flight was led by the CO, Lieutenant Colonel Emmett L. Hayes, with two wingmen, one having aborted.

The F-100 and MiG-17 were contemporaries, both going operational in the early 1950s. The lighter MiG enjoyed better performance, both in turning and climbing, but the American pilots were more experienced and better trained.

When the MiGs jumped the Thuds, the Super Sabres responded yet were unable to intervene immediately. Engaging offshore, beyond the range of their 20-millimeter cannon, Hayes selected a Sidewinder heat-seeking missile. The geometry was wrong. With the MiGs between the Thunderchiefs and the Huns, it was impossible to know precisely which heat source a missile was tracking. Hayes waited until he got a clear view of a MiG and heard the AIM-9Bs "growl" in his earphones. He pressed the trigger, and the Sidewinder streaked forward off the rail, homing on its target. Hayes saw the missile pass close over the MiG without detonating—likely a fuse failure.

Hayes' partners included Captain Keith B. Connolly, who selected guns and tackled the MiGs *mano a mano*. He got a quick front-quarter shot at a second MiG, but the Vietnamese pilot evaded into the haze.

The rescue CAP flight also tangled with Vietnamese fighters. Led by Captain Wayne Lanphear, the four Huns faced two MiGs nose to nose at nineteen thousand feet. The F-100s tried to jettison their auxiliary drop tanks to decrease weight and drag, yet only Lanphear's and Captain Donald Kilgus' tanks were successfully jettisoned.

The MiG-17's superior maneuverability showed immediately. The bandits gained a firing position after one circuit, and each of them targeted a two-plane Super Sabre flight. The third and fourth Huns, although still burdened by drop tanks, were able to evade the assailants, although barely. Robin Three, Captain Ronald R. Green, resorted to an unusual technique. With 23- and 37-millimeter cannon shells zipping by inches from his wing, "I decided the best thing to do was to deliberately depart the aircraft to the right and enter a spin. I slammed in full aileron and opposite rudder, and as advertised, the Hun departed to the right and entered a right spin."[6]

The violent maneuver cleaned off Green's stuck drop tanks, but one smashed into a rocket pod, twisting his right wing's leading-edge slat nearly upright. Nonetheless, he coolly reduced throttle to idle, placed his hands in his lap—and waited. Watching the ocean getting closer as he spun through ten thousand feet, Green still waited. In seconds it was all-or-nothing time. Green jammed in rudder to stop the spin and fed in forward stick. Out of the spin and flying again, he pulled back on the stick and crammed on full power. "Looking at a windscreen full of ocean," he recalled, "I prayed that the airplane would pull out in time. Miraculously, it did—at an altitude I estimated to be fifty feet."[7] One wonders how many G's Green pulled.

★

Meanwhile the dogfight swirled onward. With the lead MiG still a threat to the Huns who had shed tanks, Lanphear called for a split, which would force the Communist pilot to pursue one F-100 or the other and thereby become vulnerable to the one he didn't pursue.

Don Kilgus was a twenty-seven-year-old ROTC product from Detroit with three years of experience flying the Hun. He related, "We saw something coming up from the haze, and one thousandth of a second later . . . it's a MiG. I turned into him, jettisoned my aux fuel tanks, and in that instant he turned ninety degrees to me."[8]

The lead MiG overshot Kilgus, leaving his wingman to attack. But Kilgus outmaneuvered the enemy wingman and concentrated on the leader, hosing a short burst from his four 20-millimeter cannon. "Knowing I was in an advantageous position because I was above him, I allowed him to get a little separation from me. I went on afterburner and saw 450 knots on my airspeed indicator."

When the MiG dropped its blunt nose into a near-vertical dive, Kilgus hung on. He knew the Vietnamese fighter could pull out of his dive more steeply than his fighter could, so he intended to destroy it before reaching critical altitude: "I fired a burst. Now training came into play. I tried to remember everything I'd learned, and began shooting seriously at him at [an altitude of] 7,100 feet." Kilgus was not worried about expending his thousand rounds of ammunition: a MiG in a fighter pilot's gunsight was an absolute gift.

"I saw puffs and sparks on the vertical tail of the MiG, and very shortly thereafter I didn't see anything. I could have been at 580 knots. I won't embroider the story by saying I got spray from the Gulf of Tonkin on my windshield, but I pulled out at the last minute."[9]

When Kilgus got his last glimpse of the MiG, it was shedding parts at extremely low altitude. He rejoined some of his friends and returned to DaNang.

Although the Air Force credited Don Kilgus with only a "probable," years later the North Vietnamese acknowledged losing three planes and pilots that day. Two were probably shot down by friendly fire, flak from North Vietnamese batteries, but the third almost certainly was Kilgus' victim, Senior Lieutenant Pham Giay. Don Kilgus scored the F-100's only air-to-air kill of the war and was the first American pilot to down a Vietnamese MiG.

★

The air combat was over, but the action was not.

Two A-1H Skyraiders of South Vietnam's 516th Fighter Squadron were assigned to the Rescue CAP, call sign "Sandy," orbiting offshore as top cover in case a pickup was needed.[10]

When Jim Magnusson's Thud splashed seven miles offshore, the A-1s were first to respond. However, the leader, Captain Vu Khac Hue of the South Vietnamese Air Force, was shot down by shore-based batteries. His American adviser, flying as a wingman, was thirty-two-year-old Captain Walter Draeger of Wisconsin, who saw Sandy Lead parachute into the water perilously close to land.

Walt Draeger had an unusual career path. Winged in 1957, he was originally an interceptor pilot who transitioned to transports in Panama. Subsequently he was accepted for A-1 training with a Navy squadron at Corpus Christi, Texas, and joined the Vietnamese program in November 1964.

The Douglas A-1 Skyraider was an anomaly, a World War II design from Edward H. Heinemann, the aeronautical engineering genius who produced the war-winning SBD Dauntless dive bomber, two record-setting experimental airplanes, and two Navy attack aircraft—the twin-engine A-3 Skywarrior and the indispensable A-4 Skyhawk. Originally designated the AD-1 (Attack by Douglas, first model), it became the A-1 in Robert McNamara's 1962 redesignation scheme for military aircraft but was popularly called the "Spad," allegedly for single place AD or, because in the jet age it was an anachronism, a throwback to a French World War I ancestor. It was flown by the US Navy and Air Force as well as the South Vietnamese Air Force. Big, potent, and long legged, with a huge turbo-charged eighteen-cylinder radial piston engine developing twenty-two hundred horsepower—and even more in later models of the engine—the Skyraider carried lots of ordnance on wing stations and was ideal for close air support and interdiction. The main problem with the airplane was that it was just too damn slow.

After Vu went down, Walt Draeger spent about an hour scouring the area looking for his partner in the water. It was a gutsy move, as the splash site was only a mile and a half offshore, and Draeger's Spad was a slow target. Yet airmen lived by a tacit pact: we take care of our own. They expected it not only of each other but of themselves as well.

While circling the area, Draeger coached in the rescue team, a Grumman HU-16 amphibian and two Hiller HH-43 Husky helicopters from Quang Tri.

Working around an oil slick at the crash site, the Albatross and Huskies searched back and forth at low level, often drawing gunfire from shore batteries. Draeger was the only one armed, and his efforts to suppress some of the AAA drew a heavy response. Rescue pilots saw his Skyraider streaming smoke, veering erratically, then diving into the water from five hundred feet. No parachute was found.

★

After two days of intense air strikes against the Dragon's Jaw, the results were disappointing. The Air Force had expended 384 bombs and missiles, cratering both approaches, blowing out slabs of concrete, and causing one of the two spans to sag visibly. Traffic was interrupted briefly, and in the interim the industrious Vietnamese forged crossings at shallow fords up and downstream and set up pontoon bridges. Seeing how quickly the Vietnamese could recover from the loss of use of the bridge should have been a wake-up call for American military planners, but it was not. One reason was because targeting was being done in Washington by McNamara's staff—all civilians.

During the two days of combat over the Dragon's Jaw the North Vietnamese claimed forty-seven Yankee air pirates shot down by AAA guns and MiGs. Because they could undoubtedly count wrecks, the North Vietnamese must have known that figure absurd but lied to bolster national morale and international propaganda. In fact, American losses in the two days of strikes were three F-105s, an F-100, an F-101, and an A-1 Skyraider, plus a South Vietnamese A-1. Regardless of the real totals, the gun crews of the 228th Air Defense Artillery Regiment were decorated for their actions in "the Great Spring Victory." They received the Victory Order (one of four gongs established in 1965) and the Military Exploit Order.

★

Fifty-plus years after these April attacks on the Dragon's Jaw one may reasonably ask: What the hell happened there? Ignoring the political reasons the United States was in Vietnam, why did all these aircraft achieve so little in their attacks on an admittedly difficult target? Two aircraft had been lost the first day, with one pilot dead and another captured by the North Vietnamese. Several more aircraft were damaged. On the second day five aircraft were lost, with four pilots killed and one captured. What was wrong?

In the years after the Korean War America prepared to fight a nuclear war with the Soviet Union. Little money or thought had been devoted to improving conventional ordnance, which this day proved was not up to the job of dropping an overbuilt steel and concrete bridge. That fact had been obvious to the professionals charged with planning the strike. Yet the attackers were sent anyway.

Civilians may not appreciate how different a military organization is from a civilian enterprise. In the military everyone obeys orders. There are no boards of directors, no committees, no searches for consensus. The president is the constitutionally appointed commander-in-chief, and he gives orders to the generals and admirals, who are expected to salute and carry them out. They give orders to their subordinates, and the orders go down the line through the various chains of command to the actual war fighters, in this case the men in the cockpits, who also salute and do as they are told, even if it costs them their lives. The system works because of the valor of the war fighters, who have only each other and their individual concepts of duty, honor, and manhood to sustain them. Military organizations have always worked this way, from the Roman legions to the present day.

And yet it is the duty of the senior commanders on the scene, those who directly supervise the war fighters, to ensure they have the weapons and tactics suited to the job at hand. Failure accomplishes nothing and squanders expensive military assets and human lives. Perhaps it is inevitable that in this system senior officers are under intense pressure to do as they are told even if, in their professional judgment, the war fighters are being sent on fool's errands. There were a great many fool's errands in Vietnam—arguably the entire war was one—and the pressure from the top was excruciating.

Part of the problem was that in much of the military, peacetime bureaucratic routine prevailed. Giant bureaucracies, which the American armed forces certainly are, are not ships whose course can be changed by turning the helm. In a bureaucracy inertia is the dominant force. Throughout the war the Air Force often ordered pilots into combat who had minimal training and were not combat ready—getting a body into a slot was the priority. The Colonel Blimps who demanded that the old bomb fuses be expended before issuing new ones were merely symptoms of larger problems.[11]

Another piece of the equation was that the strategy and tactics being used in Vietnam were not intended to win the war but to force a recalcitrant opponent to the bargaining table. That being the case, those who made waves and defied their superiors did so at the cost of their careers.[12]

Finally, the politicians, with their rules of engagement and obsessive, paranoid fear of Chinese intervention, forced the Air Force and Navy to ignore rule number one of aerial warfare: *First win aerial supremacy over the battlefield.* Throughout much of the war the North Vietnamese had safe-haven airfields in the Hanoi area from which to operate their MiGs. Some of McNamara's bright young men thought the Air Force and Navy's obsession with MiG bases was ridiculous, since Vietnam could base MiGs across the border in China if their own bases were knocked out. That would have been a major political move by Hanoi, one it didn't want to make, and the greater distances involved would have put the short-ranged MiGs at a serious tactical disadvantage.

Failure to win aerial supremacy would cost American airmen their lives and contribute to the POW population, which Hanoi used for propaganda and political advantage, until the very end of the conflict. Lyndon B. Johnson, Robert S. McNamara, and the ineffectual Secretary of State Dean Rusk were directly responsible for those lost lives and the suffering of the POWs, who were forced to endure more than any human should be required to bear.

★

Captain Smitty Harris, the lone survivor of the first Thanh Hoa shootdowns, continued fighting his war from a prison cell in the Hanoi Hilton. With three others—Lieutenant Phillip Butler, Lieutenant Robert Peel, and Lieutenant Commander Robert Shumaker—he implemented the tap code that POWs used to communicate with each other. Morse code, which needed two sounds, dit and dah, wouldn't work. But tapping would. The code was a five-by-five grid containing every letter of the alphabet except K, which doubled for C. Thus, A was signified by one-one; M by three-two; Z by five-five, and so on. Aggressive communicators could tap, cough, or sweep with a broom at remarkable speeds. They developed their own shorthand, such as *GBU* for "God bless you."

Captain Walt Draeger received a posthumous Air Force Cross for his effort to protect rescue aircraft from gun batteries ashore.

The victorious F-100 pilot, Captain Don Kilgus, never received acknowledgment for downing the first MiG of the war. He returned to combat repeatedly throughout the Southeast Asian "conflict." Although four other nations flew the Hun, Kilgus was the only F-100 pilot to ever score an air-to-air kill.

An Air Force historian described a political element to this MiG encounter: "One PACAF pilot believed he scored a hit. As the air-to-air incident appeared to be unduly inflammatory, President Johnson informed the service chiefs that *he did not want any more MiGs shot down,* although circumstances would soon dictate otherwise."[13]

LBJ's priority was his Great Society program, which he hoped would be his political monument. In order to win the 1964 election, he dragged the nation into a direct conflict with North Vietnam that would cost fifty-eight thousand American lives, at least a million Vietnamese lives, and untold billions of dollars, a conflict he had no intention of fighting hard enough to win, a conflict that would poisonously influence American politics for at least two generations and ultimately help shatter the base that had supported the Democratic Party since the Great Depression. Lyndon B. Johnson had sold his soul to the Devil.

As a harbinger of things to come, on April 5, the day after the second strike on the Dragon's Jaw bridge, a reconnaissance flight over North Vietnam returned with photos of a SAM site. The air war was entering a chilling new dimension, and the Dragon's Jaw defenders were about to get a powerful new weapon.

CHAPTER 5

A GRIM BUSINESS

Facing increased pressure by US airpower, the Communist regime in Hanoi asked Moscow for surface-to-air missiles—SAMs. After some initial reluctance, the Soviets began sending SA-2s, launchers, radars, and the necessary control gear to Vietnam along with the technical experts to make the system work and teach the North Vietnamese how to use it.

The SA-2 was a two-stage radar-guided missile. After radar found an airborne target within range, the missile would be fired from its launcher. The solid-fuel first stage would burn for six seconds, boosting the missile past Mach 1, then drop off. Only then would the receivers on the back of the missile be exposed to the firing radar, which began to send guidance signals to the missile as the second stage rocket engines accelerated it to terminal velocity, about Mach 2 in the early versions of the missile, or twice the speed of sound. Later versions of the missiles had a terminal velocity of as much as Mach 3.5. With the missile now under his control, the technician in the radar van manually steered it toward its target. Later the control mechanisms would be automated to some degree, but in the early stages of the war control was manual.

US Air Force and Navy commanders sought permission to destroy SAM sites under construction, but the politicians intervened again. Self-assured, condescending Secretary of Defense Robert S. McNamara denied permission to attack launch sites because he thought killing Russian technicians would lead to a wider war.

John T. McNaughton, assistant secretary of defense for international security affairs, also dismissed the request to bomb SAM sites. The former Harvard Law professor sniffed, "You don't think the North Vietnamese are going to use them? Putting them in is just a political ploy by the Russians to appease Hanoi."[1] How the United States ended up with smug, arrogant college professors and automobile company executives running a war is one of the conundrums of our age. In an amazing twist of fate, Professor McNaughton died in a plane crash in 1967, depriving McNamara of his preferred choice as a compliant secretary of the Navy.

The pragmatic Vietnamese Communists harbored no such delusions. They began building more launch sites, easily identifiable by the characteristic star configuration for the six launchers with the radar dish on a van in the middle.

And they began shooting their new toys. On July 24, 1965, an SA-2 battery shot down an Air Force F-4. Washington then finally took note and authorized strikes against missile sites outside the Hanoi-Haiphong sanctuary zones. However, the Vietnamese foxed the Yankee air pirates by placing dummy SAMs on the sixth and seventh sites identified. When the raiders rolled in on July 27, concentrated AAA guns opened fire. Four Thuds went down, with three pilots killed and one captured.

Meanwhile fighter-bomber pilots were left to their own devices. Missions seldom went north if there was cloud cover above eight thousand feet because pilots needed vertical separation to evade airborne SAMs. The hard reality was that pilots who were targeted by one or more SAMs had to see them—the missiles were making Mach 2, and if they were in front of you, the closure rate was the total of your airspeed and the missile's—and maneuver to avoid them. The missiles were relatively easy to see at night, a little less so in daylight, because of the exhaust plume, which appeared as bright as a spot of the sun. Except, of course, in thick haze. Or if the missile were obscured by a cloud. The evasive maneuver had to be exquisitely timed: if the pilot of the target aircraft tried to evade too soon, the missile would track him; if he tried too late, he was meat on the table. Every maneuver bled off energy, which was airspeed and altitude. If the enemy launched enough missiles, inevitably one would catch the low, slow, writhing victim in its blast envelope.

Then-Major James R. Bassett of the 388th Wing put it this way: "We were taught to avoid a SAM by putting it in your two o'clock position in order to judge the closure rate, then dive toward it. Hold your trajectory until you couldn't stand it any longer, wait just a bit more, then abruptly roll over the top. The missile couldn't turn with you and would continue ballistically. It worked quite well with one missile, but the gomers got smart and started sending up clusters. SAMs were everywhere it seemed. . . . Soon they were coming in bunches like bananas. I recall one time . . . at debriefing we totaled twenty-two sent against my flight alone (but I guess there were multiple counts of same SAMs—it's hard to accurately count when you're twisting and rolling). . . . You just wriggle pathetically knowing that the 'ten and two' counter could run you right into one of a bunch coming your way."[2]

Both Air Force and Navy brass understood they had a problem that needed to be solved. The Air Force response was the "Wild Weasel"—modifying a two-seat fighter with radar detection equipment and arming it with a specifically designed missile to destroy SA-2 batteries. Yet until the missiles were available, planes targeted against SAM sites tackled them with cluster bombs and 20-millimeter cannon shells. With far less room aboard aircraft carriers, the Navy could not afford squadrons dedicated to SAM suppression; instead, they modified some existing attack planes in deploying squadrons—first some A-4s, then A-7s and A-6Bs—to perform the "Iron Hand" mission of detecting and attacking SAM radars, NATO code name "Fansong."

The AGM-45 Shrike was a Navy anti-radiation missile developed in 1963 and available to carrier and Air Force squadrons two years later. Throughout the war Shrike and the AGM-78 Standard Anti-Radiation Missiles (Standard ARM), also developed by the Navy and deployed in 1968, were used by Navy Iron Hand and Air Force Wild Weasels to deter SAM launches and destroy the batteries if they did launch. A seesaw battle of electronic wizards ensued, with the advantage shifting occasionally much as the British and Germans had dueled with measure and countermeasure during World War II. Eventually the Americans gained the upper hand in Vietnam, but the knowledge acquired was paid for in blood and torn metal.

Shrike allegedly had a fifteen-mile range; tactical aviators preferred to shoot inside ten. Standard ARM could hit at fifty miles with a more lethal warhead, yet it was a larger missile with a computer inside that allowed it to memorize the location of the target radar and fly to that location even if the radar went off the air. Shrike had no such capability, and the North Vietnamese learned to defend themselves from Shrike by turning off their radar as soon as a Shrike launch was detected. If they didn't, they risked eating a missile. Shutting down, of course, caused any SA-2s in the air being guided by that radar to go "stupid," or ballistic.

Shutting down the controlling radar might or might not work with the Standard ARM, depending on the launch distance and at what intervals during the missile's flight the target radar was emitting. If either missile scored a hit on the target radar, it didn't just knock out the radar; the shrapnel from the warhead destroyed the control van on which the radar was positioned and usually killed everyone in the van regardless of their nationality. The shrapnel might even cook off a SAM or two if the launchers were close enough to the control van.

Anti-radiation missiles were expensive. Rumor at the time had it that a Shrike cost Uncle Sam $7,000 to acquire, and a Standard ARM $100,000. Regardless of the actual cost, the price of war was escalating drastically. If anyone cared to notice, the United States had taken another tentative step away from free-fall weapons on a path that would ultimately revolutionize war in the air.

The first Wild Weasels flew two-seat F-100F Super Sabres with a "bear" handling the electronics in the backseat. The bear appellation began as pilot humor, referring to the weapons system operators as "trained bears." Yet very quickly *bear* became a term of heartfelt respect as the WSOs mastered the electronic gear that was the heart of the mission.

Weasels arrived in Thailand in November 1965, with F-105Fs replacing the Huns in July 1966.

Wild Weasels wrote a blazing record in the Southeast Asian skies. At war's end Captain Merlyn Dethlefsen and Major Leo Thorsness received Medals of Honor, while fifteen other weasels received the Air Force Cross. A Navy Iron Hand, Lieutenant Commander Mike Estocin, was awarded a posthumous Medal of Honor for 1967 combat.

A senior Thud pilot, Colonel Jack Broughton, described the pulse-pounding experience of witnessing a SAM launch. "The first stage booster that launches the SAM creates a good-sized dust storm on the ground, so if you happen to be looking in the right direction when it blasts off, you know that SAM is airborne and on the prowl. After the booster has done its job, it drops off and falls back to earth, leaving the propulsion to SAM's internal rocket power. If you can see SAM, you can usually escape. It has little stubby wings and is going like hell, so it can't turn very well. You can take it on just like another aircraft, and if you force it into a commit position and outturn it, it will stall out and auger in."[3]

Navy Commander John Nichols, a three Vietnam-tour carrier pilot, wrote of the SAM threat: "Surviving a SAM launch became an exercise in sweaty-palm patience and pulse-pounding judgment. Articulate aviators have spoken of the soul-searing experience of dueling with an inanimate object that pursued its prey with almost human intelligence."[4]

Weasels and Iron Hands made their presence known. Combined with Air Force EB-66 Destroyers and Navy EA-3 Skywarriors jamming enemy radar and communications, the Shrike shooters put a dent in

Vietnamese SAM effectiveness. The best measure was evident in the SA-2's declining success ratio: from a high in 1965, with eleven Yankee air pirates downed by nearly two hundred missiles, the 5.7 percent effectiveness rate dropped dramatically. Though more than three times as many American planes fell to SAMs in 1966, the kill percentage was cut in half among more than a thousand SAMs fired.

At the time of Johnson's bombing halt in 1968, SAM effectiveness was miniscule: less than 1 percent, with just three shoot-downs. When the air war ended in early 1973 the overall figures showed sixty SA-2s were required to knock down a targeted aircraft.

However, SAMs continued affecting US air tactics. Inevitably a maneuver to defeat a missile forced a pilot to shove his nose down to gain the additional airspeed required when he pulled hard into the threat, forcing the missile to overshoot. Yet the altitude loss often placed the fighter-bomber pilots within the range of Vietnamese antiaircraft guns, which posed by far the greatest peril throughout the war.

★

By May 1965 five Thunderchief squadrons were based at Takhli and Korat, Thailand. Representing three wings, they were an eclectic bunch, typifying the increasingly helter-skelter Air Force pilot assignments on an as-needed basis. The orderly peacetime wing organization began falling apart under the growing press of operations, as always occurred in aerial combat.

Additionally, some F-105 squadrons briefly flew from DaNang, alternating between Thai and Okinawa bases. For example, the 23rd Tactical Fighter Wing—home-based at McConnell Air Force Base in Wichita, Kansas—rotated squadrons between Yokota, Japan, and Takhli between April and December 1965. The 563rd Squadron flew from Thailand from early April to mid-August.[5]

With more planes available, strikes against the Thanh Hoa Bridge continued, lasting through May. And the strike aircraft incurred losses.

On May 7 the 355th Tactical Fighter Wing contributed heavily to a strike against the bridge. Major Charles Watry of the wing's 354th

Squadron led the base element—twenty-eight Thuds supported by three dozen other aircraft. The Thuds were loaded for the Dragon with some 350 750-pound bombs and more than 300 2.75-inch rockets.

While the bombers hammered the bridge, the flak gunners returned fire—and they scored. Watry's plane took hits that began siphoning fuel, but he remained overhead, directing each flight in turn. His dedication to the mission earned him a Silver Star.[6]

The gun crews also hit Major Robert A. Lambert's right wing, so he turned eastward for the relative safety of the ocean. Lambert's Thud carried him ten miles, where he made a "feet wet" ejection.[7]

The timing could not have been better. Approaching the splash coordinates, HU-16 Albatross pilot Captain Richard Reichardt spotted Lambert's descending parachute. But as usual, Vietnamese coastal traffic was dense, with dozens of fishing and commercial junks in sight. Any one of them could scoop up the American and deliver him into years of torturous captivity.

Reichardt told his radioman to contact the circling fighters and direct them to clear a path to Lambert's splashdown position. The Thud pilot hit the water just as the HU-16 turned upwind to land in the water amid a flotilla of Vietnamese small craft.

F-105s used their 20-millimeter cannon to herd junks out of the way or to shred the closest to Lambert. Other jets, out of ammo, screeched overhead in what a later generation would term "nonkinetic measures" to dissuade would-be captors.

Meanwhile Reichardt maneuvered his ungainly amphibian around or through the junk fleet, applying throttle when necessary, to beat the Communists to the downed flier. Once alongside Lambert, the Albatross lurched to a stop; the crew opened the side hatch and hauled an immensely relieved Thud pilot inside.

Fighters with remaining ammunition shot a path for the Albatross to accelerate onto the "step" of the hull and, after a long run, take off. Bob Lambert was delivered from captivity, only slightly injured from his adventure.

Thailand-based Thuds hammered the bridge twice more during the day, with little to show for their efforts. Ordnance experts determined that the standard M117 750-pound bombs could not penetrate the Dragon's Jaw sufficiently to destroy it, although more damage might be inflicted with better fusing. Pending the arrival of modern fuses that permitted bomb detonation inside the bridge structure, operational planners also anticipated receiving the new AGM-12C Bullpup missiles.

The C-model Bullpup was a serious weapon, far more potent than the B-models used in early bridge attacks. Weighing almost 1,800 pounds, its 970-pound warhead packed nearly four times the explosives of the earlier version. Its rocket engine boosted speed to nearly Mach 1.8, with an advertised range of ten miles. But, the drill still required the shooting airplane to follow the missile down, and the requirement for a clear view of the target meant that the pilots had to attack one by one. Clearly, they needed something better than Bullpup.[8]

However, three days earlier Lyndon B. Johnson ordered a five-day halt in Rolling Thunder, the campaign against North Vietnam south of the 20th parallel. McNamara proposed the halt, naively hoping it would somehow induce the Communists to negotiate. Predictably, the military opposed it, worried that any progress toward interdicting supplies into South Vietnam would be frittered away. Yet Johnson bought McNamara's recommendation. McNamara states, "Criticism of Johnson's Vietnam policy among liberal intellectuals and members of Congress had grown markedly in recent weeks, and, irked, Johnson sought to answer and still it if possible. It was this—rather than any personal faith that a pause at this stage would spark negotiations—that led him to accept my proposal."[9]

During the halt Washington directed that F-105s drop leaflets over North Vietnam on the theory that the leaflets might help convince the North Vietnamese population to end the struggle. Plainly, the big pooh-bahs in Washington were living in la-la land. North Vietnam was an absolute dictatorship—the Communists in the Politburo gave not a damn what the peasants thought. The Air Force swallowed its objections and the leaflets were dropped.

Because the Dragon's Jaw was the northernmost significant span in the permitted operating area, less than ten miles south of the 20th parallel, it remained on the hit list when the bombing resumed. A postwar survey concluded, "It was the final bridge to safety in the bomb-free upper latitudes, and despite the fact that its strategic importance had seriously diminished with the effective interdiction of the rail line to Vinh, it remained a valuable target."[10]

Despite the Americans' inability to destroy the bridge, its temporary closure yielded military benefits. In combination with other bridges they had dropped, Vietnamese supplies often were stranded north of the 20th parallel, where Johnson had prohibited bombing. South of the bomb line, locomotives and truck convoys became rare sights during daytime, as the Vietnamese avoided air attacks by moving at night. Often trucks exposed during the day were parked in towns or obviously populated areas to render them immune to attack. Those Americans . . . they didn't want to hurt anybody.

For a few days that spring the Communists could not move all the stalled southern rail traffic to safety north of the 20th parallel. Caught in the open, three locomotives and 144 railcars were claimed destroyed by fighter-bombers trolling permitted areas. Yet the Dragon's Jaw, with a full-time repair crew, always returned to business.[11]

★

When Washington finally realized that the bombing halt hadn't moved Hanoi's determination to resist one solitary inch and granted approval once more, F-105s launched against the Thanh Hoa Bridge for the fourth time on May 30—but with a difference.

During the bombing pause operations officers and strike leaders had taken stock, examining the first three Thanh Hoa Bridge missions and seeking better ways to conduct future strikes. One of the problems, they thought, was that there had been too many strike aircraft over the bridge. Although counterintuitive—especially considering the

Clausewitzian concept of Mass—large numbers of attackers complicate the tactical problem enormously. Heavy smoke and dust from the first bombs and rockets obscured the target, forcing following flights to attack partially blind or circle until visibility improved and they could once again see the target. That requirement burned more fuel, allowed the Vietnamese antiaircraft crews to reload, and left following attackers more exposed to increasingly capable defenses.

Therefore, instead of four dozen Thuds "fragged" in the first two missions and twenty-eight on the third, only four bombers were slated for the next Thanh Hoa attack.

The fourth strike on the Dragon's Jaw was flown out of Takhli on May 31. The 563rd Tactical Fighter Squadron sent four Thuds of Buick Flight with thirty-two 750-pounders. They were in and out fast and got some hits on the bridge.

One Buick Flight pilot was First Lieutenant Robert D. Peel, a twenty-six-year-old second-generation flier from Memphis, Tennessee. Aviation was in his genes: his father flew with the British during the Great War, and his brothers were Fred, a bomber pilot in Korea, and Dudley, an Air Force security officer.

Peel had graduated from Castle Heights Military Academy, where he had been a regional swimming champion. He attended the University of the Old South in Sewanee, Tennessee, but transferred to Ole Miss to pursue an engineering degree. He left in his junior year to become an Air Force flying cadet. Upon completion of pilot training at Vance Air Force Base in Wichita Falls, Texas, he received the Outstanding Flying Award for his class.

His first assignment was flying the F-102 Delta Dagger at Clark Air Force Base in the Philippines. Upon completing that tour in 1964, he transitioned to the F-105 at Seymour Johnson Air Force Base in North Carolina and then did a deployment to Incirik, Turkey. Following that NATO tour, Peel went to the 333rd Tactical Fighter Squadron and deployed on temporary duty to Takhli.

"I was assigned to the command post at Takhli, but I volunteered to fly missions," Peel said. "I had a good relationship with Major Hank

Buttelman, who ran the CP, and with Lieutenant Colonel Peters of the 563rd, so I flew with them." All of which proves that if you want it bad enough, there is always a way. Buttelman was on his second war: he had been one of the youngest aces in Korea.

On his fifteenth combat mission—his sixth over North Vietnam—Peel flew a rarity, a 105 with a name painted on the side of its nose: *Give 'Em 'L.*[12]

During the May 31 attack Peel's jet was hit hard just south of the bridge, forcing him to eject into captivity. He was the eighteenth F-105 pilot downed in Southeast Asia and the twelfth to survive.[13]

A poststrike bomb damage assessment (BDA) showed that the Dragon's Jaw had sustained "only moderate damage, although the bridge was briefly closed to road and rail traffic." The Vietnamese were nothing if not persistent, and their increasingly expert repair crews reopened the vital artery in a few days.[14]

The first four missions against the bridge had expended nearly eight hundred bombs and missiles, totaling more than three hundred tons of high explosive, to no significant effect.

★

The need for heavy ordnance against hard targets like the Thanh Hoa Bridge led to requests for M118 bombs in Thailand. Of early 1950s vintage, the M118 was three thousand pounds of smashing potential. The typical bomb actually weighed 3,049 pounds and contained nearly two thousand pounds of Tritonal, an amalgam of 80 percent TNT and 20 percent aluminum powder. Ordnance engineers rated Tritonal as 18 percent more powerful than unboosted TNT due to the aluminum's greater heat production. What the weapon lacked was a casing sufficiently rigid to allow it to penetrate deeply into a target before exploding.[15]

The 18th Wing's 12th Tactical Fighter Squadron introduced the M118 to Vietnam combat. The 12th was an old-line outfit with combat in World War II and Korea, flying almost every fighter in the inventory in those years. Its emblem was a stylized eagle bearing a sword above the motto, *In omnia paratus*—Ready for Anything.

On July 28 Teak Flight blasted off Korat's active runway bound for Thanh Hoa. Leading four bombers was the CO, Lieutenant Colonel Charles W. Reed, with a major and two captains. Teak Five was armed with camera pods to record the M118's debut in North Vietnam.

As ever, the gunners were ready. Traversing and elevating their weapons toward the now-familiar screech of inbound jets, they put up a barrage of 37- and 57-millimeter flak that the Americans considered moderate to heavy. The bridge took some damage from the M118s that hit it, yet it remained intact.

Undeterred, the 18th Fighter Wing crews returned five days later, on August 2, 1965. Colonel Reed led Oak Flight with three captains as wingmen, packing M118s.

Conditions were adequate for an attack: ceiling ten thousand feet with five miles of visibility. As the Thuds plunged through five thousand feet on their pullout, Captain Robert N. Daughtrey's plane took some flak, probably 37-millimeter. Whatever the caliber, it started a fire in the fuselage. Recognizing he had had the stroke, Daughtrey fired his ejection seat and was hurled into the sky over North Vietnam.

Daughtrey was a thirty-one-year-old pilot from Del Rio, Texas, with a wife and three children aged four to seven years. He had left Texas A&M in his sophomore year for an Air Force commission and silver wings. His post-Vietnam plans included a mathematics degree. All that work and hope for the future vanished in a twinkling as his crippled F-105 plunged toward Thanh Hoa province.

The force of the ejection broke both of Daughtrey's arms. When he hit the ground he was scooped up almost immediately. Less than two months later he appeared in propaganda photos released by the North Vietnamese to the international press.[16]

★

Nearly six months after the first bridge strike, Robbie Risner was still at it. His leadership of the first two missions had earned him the first Air Force Cross of the Vietnam War. He was undeterred after being shot down in late March and landing a shot-up Thud in early April. He continued flying and leading the 67th Tactical Fighter Squadron from the cockpit.

Increasingly sophisticated anti-SAM tactics had evolved over the previous months. By late summer the Thailand-based Thuds were operating in hunter-killer teams: a four-plane flight to locate a site and mark it with napalm and cluster bombs, which could destroy the radar van, with the killer flight following with heavy bombs.

On September 16 Risner found the SAM site at Tuong Loc—the fifth identified in Vietnam, Site NV-05—five miles north of the Dragon's Jaw. He took his leading Pepper Flight inbound to the target at treetop level, making five hundred knots, when he barely cleared a rise. The gunners were waiting. "As I topped it, the first thing I saw were tracers," he recalled. "I was hit immediately."

As the cockpit filled with smoke, Risner's wingman called, "Get out, Lead! You're burning! You're burning all over."*

The three-war warrior was not giving up yet. Selecting afterburner, he accelerated straight ahead and punched the jettison button that cleaned the external stores off his plane in the small hope of doing some damage to the site and, incidentally, making his plane fly faster. Merely three miles from the coast, Risner turned east, hoping to reach the sanctuary of the ocean. At 550 knots, he thought he could make it.

Then his Thud died: the airplane no longer responded to control inputs. The nose dropped, leaving him no choice. He blew off the canopy and squeezed the handles on the ejection seat, ending his fifty-fifth Vietnam mission. As he wrote in 1973, "I made my reservation for seven and a half years in the Hanoi Hilton." He was well known there—the North Vietnamese read *Time* magazine too.[17]

Oak Flight was also targeted against Site VN-05. Major Raymond J. Merritt was flying with Oak Flight. Born in Oregon and raised in California, he enlisted in the Navy but wrangled a transfer to the Air Force.

*In his memoir Risner identified himself as "Oak Lead," but there is no doubt he was leading Pepper Flight.

Upon completing flight training in 1953 he went to Korea, where he flew one hundred missions in Republic F-84 Thunderjets, the predecessor to the F-105.

Afterward he spent a glorious three years of uninterrupted flying as a gunnery instructor at Luke Air Force Base in Phoenix, Arizona. He earned a bachelor's degree at Texas Tech in 1961 and did a tour at the ballistic missile division of the Air Research and Development Command.

Merritt transitioned to F-105s, joining the 67th Tactical Fighter Squadron on Okinawa in 1964. At age thirty-five, he was a seasoned professional fighter pilot and career officer.

Attacking Site NV-05, Merritt shunned evasive maneuvers to concentrate on accurate bombing. His decision to "press" rather than jink gave the gunners a good shot. They hit him hard. With his bird on fire, Merritt ejected fourteen miles northwest of the Thanh Hoa Bridge. Armed peasants seized him immediately.

The site, which may have been a decoy, cost the US Air Force a superb squadron commander and a highly experienced flight leader, plus two irreplaceable aircraft, each valued at $2.1 million. There would be no more F-105s—the production line was now closed, with the last one delivered to the Air Force in January.

So it went. The 67th Squadron lost eight planes and six pilots in three weeks of August and September. Nor was that all. Throughout 1965 the two Thailand wings lost sixty-eight planes to all causes, well over one a week, with eleven in September alone. The odds of escaping death or capture if you were shot down were less than fifty-fifty. Thirty-one F-105 pilots were rescued, fifteen killed or missing, and twenty-two captured. It was a grim business.

★

By July 1965 US air operations against Communist North Vietnam had been underway for eleven months. The JCS in Washington formed a study group to assess the overall effect of the campaign, with a dolorous conclusion.

The data miners in the Pentagon gave Secretary McNamara what he favored—numerical quantification of results. After all, number crunching had pulled him up the ladder at Ford.

By July 1 some 10,000 sorties had been launched against 122 North Vietnamese targets, an increase beyond the original 94 that McNamara approved, with 240 on the tentative list as of July.

Although the combined air effort in June 1965 was one-third more than May's, results remained disappointing. There had been eighty-six strikes "up north," eight of which included South Vietnamese aircraft, while nearly seventy US armed reconnaissance missions trolled enemy lines of communication and targets of opportunity, including coastal traffic.

The best the Joint Chiefs' analysts could claim was that bombing increased the transit time for supplies from North Vietnam to South Vietnam and complicated logistics for the Pathet Lao. Still, the monsoon season, with drenching rains and swollen rivers and streams, likely contributed more to Communist problems than aerial action.

The air campaign's effects on North Vietnam's economy were marginal, affecting the GDP of North Vietnam by "only a few percentage points." Although some air power strategists still clung to World War I Italian general Giulio Douhet's theory that aerial bombing could break the enemy's will to resist, the JCS working group concluded, "From analysis of available evidence there is nothing to indicate definitely that the bombings have caused either physical damage or lowered morale to the extent that would compel the DRV [Democratic Republic of Vietnam] to negotiate."

The document, signed by the chairman of the JCS, Army General Earl Wheeler, ended, "In summary, the DRV still seems ready to endure further air strikes . . . the strikes have not yet reduced DRV overall military capabilities to train and support covert infiltration to South Vietnam."[18]

In short, American air efforts to the end of June were a flat failure.

At least two of the service chiefs were very pessimistic and vocal. Air Force Chief of Staff Curtis LeMay, who had fire-bombed most of the major Japanese cities and launched both atomic bombings during World War II, and Marine Corps Commandant Wallace M. Greene felt that if a war was worth fighting, it was worth winning. They urged Johnson "to get in or get out"—advice Johnson didn't want to hear.

Despite this assessment from the military professionals, Johnson and McNamara continued with the same policy as before. Because they weren't clinically insane, it is doubtful they really expected different results. One would think that any normal man reading every week the totals of American youth killed, wounded, maimed, missing, and captured in desperate combat in Vietnam and of the increasingly strident protests against the war that were sweeping American college campuses would have swallowed hard and chosen between one of two options: win the war or get out. But Johnson didn't. Both options were too dangerous. He damned the torpedoes, kept steaming as before, and vowed to fight this war to a stalemate. In public he continued to lie to the American people and insist that the nation was on the road to victory.

★

On the other side of the world the Dragon's Jaw had weathered its first year of the war rather well. Repeatedly damaged and repaired, the structure seemed sound. Guns and gun crewmen that had succumbed under American bombs had been replaced. The Dragon was very much alive.

CHAPTER 6

ENTER THE NAVY

By the time the Dragon's Jaw bridge was dedicated in May 1964, the US Navy had more than four decades of experience operating aircraft from ships and nearly twenty years with jets. The transition to jets immediately after the glory days of World War II, which had been fought with piston-engine carrier planes, meant the Navy had to start almost from scratch learning how to take these new-fangled aircraft to sea. The problem was multidimensional: jet engines rev up slowly, whereas piston engines give power almost as soon as the throttle is advanced, and the wings of jets were designed to allow the planes to go faster to take advantage of the new power source, which meant that takeoff and landing speeds were much higher than their predecessors. Borrowing heavily from the Royal Navy, the Americans incorporated three critical developments in their existing aircraft carriers and the new ones under construction: the angled flight deck, the mirror landing system, and steam catapults.

In the straight-deck era the portion of a flight deck forward of the arresting wires was guarded by woven-steel barriers raised and lowered as needed. Usually a landing aircraft snagged one of several wires with its lowered tailhook and was dragged to a stop. But not always. In the event of a botched landing or a "hook skip," the errant aircraft crunched into the barrier, usually sustaining serious damage. In the worst case, the plane went over the barrier and smashed down on planes parked in front of it. Postwar aviator Wally Schirra, later a three-flight astronaut, summarized, "In those days you either had an arrested landing or a major accident."[1]

The axial deck solved the landing problem. By canting the landing area 8 to 11 degrees to port and realigning the arresting wires, the parking and taxiing area forward was safe from planes that failed to catch a wire. In every landing, whether he was arrested or not, the pilot upon touchdown retracted his speed brakes and went to full power on his engine or engines. The arresting gear was strong enough to catch the aircraft despite it being at maximum power. And if the tailhook failed to snag a wire, the aircraft "boltered," a British term meaning that it continued straight ahead and ran off the angled deck, rotated to the proper angle of attack, and climbed away to rejoin the landing pattern. Never once during a landing did the plane surrender its flying speed unless it was arrested. The days of the full-stall landing aboard ship were over—the angled deck saved naval aviation.

Almost concurrent with the angled deck was introduction of the mirror landing system. Ironically, the Japanese Navy had used a similar arrangement on its carriers, employing two lights that, when properly aligned, gave the landing pilot the optimum glide path. Today the concept is used at most American civilian airports: the visual approach slope indicator (VASI).

However, until the late 1950s the British and Americans used landing signal officers—"batsmen" in the Royal Navy and LSOs in the American—wielding handheld paddles to tell a landing aviator if he was properly aligned, on speed, and on glide slope. The manual system worked well for slower piston-engined aircraft, but jets required faster response time because they approached faster, and with speed came the need for greater precision. The window to catch the third wire was only eighteen inches thick when the landing aircraft came across the ramp, the aft end of the flight deck. The pilot needed a direct visual cue to fly his airplane this precisely, especially when the deck was moving in response to waves and swells.

A British aviator and engineer devised the mirror landing aid, allegedly using his secretary's compact and lipstick as an example. With it, a strong light was shown onto a concave mirror and reflected up the glide slope. Mounted almost halfway up the deck, portside, the mirror showed a landing pilot a "meatball," which he compared with green datum lights mounted on each side. If the ball was centered between the datum lights, the pilot was on glideslope. If it was high, above the datum lights, he was high, and if it was below the datum lights, he was low too. The feedback was automatic and instant. LSOs remained a vital part of the equation, however, monitoring each approach with the ability to issue terse radio comments, such as "Keep it coming . . . little power . . . watch your line-up," or to initiate a wave-off vocally or by flashing the datum lights.

Between these two improvements, the angled deck and the mirror landing system, carrier accident rates were cut in half, and refinements in equipment and technique resulted in further savings.

Still, an arrested carrier landing remained the ultimate aviation challenge, requiring more precision than any other aspect of the aviator's art. It was especially so at night or in foul weather. During the Vietnam War a Navy physiological survey found that pilots often experienced more stress attempting a night landing than they felt in combat. One F-4 pilot wired his intercom system to his tape recorder and played back the tape that night after he trapped. He found that he had stopped breathing during the last thirty seconds of the approach.

LSOs graded every approach, whether a trap or not, and grades were assessed regardless of rank or seniority. It is instructive of the carrier culture that an excellent pass merely received a grade of "OK." For instance, "OK-3" meant a good approach and landing that caught the target wire, which was the third of the four stretched across the deck. Pilots sought to make a "rails pass," smack-on lineup and glide-slope with perfect airspeed control and no deviations. A nocturnal underlined "OK-3" was the *non plus ultra* and could not be topped.

A carrier pilot's skill at landing was on display for all to see with every approach, but it was also recorded on posters in his ready room. An OK pass was colored green, fair or "fleet average" could be orange or yellow, and a substandard pass could be blue for a bolter or red for a wave-off due to pilot error rather than deck conditions. Thus, anyone familiar with the system could read a greenie board with a glance and instantly determine who were the best "sticks" in the squadron.

Finally, steam catapults permitted progressively bigger and heavier aircraft. World War II catapults were hydraulically powered, with physical limits and a harsh kick in the back. The kick occurred because hydraulics imparted their full impetus immediately, whereas the British innovation of steam catapults not only had greater kinetic energy but also continued to accelerate uniformly through the entire length of the stroke. One aviator noted, "Hydraulic was Boom, steam was Varoom."

The acceleration the catapult delivered could also be immediately tailored to the launch weight of the aircraft, from a nine-ton loaded A-4 to a thirty-ton A-3 full of fuel. The goal was to give each aircraft—taking type, weight, wind over the deck, and ambient air temperature into consideration—stall speed plus fifteen knots. Too much oomph would overstress the airframe; not enough would put the plane into the drink.

Daytime steam catapult launches of fully loaded aircraft were the ultimate aviation thrill. Even veteran naval aviators were known to emit an orgiastic whoop when riding the cat . . . during the day—nighttime shots were a wholly different animal. The catapult would throw a fully loaded aircraft—for example, a fifty-four-thousand-pound A-6—from a standing start to fifteen knots above the stall in about two and a half to three seconds. At the end of the catapult stroke the pilot would find himself in total darkness, on instruments, sixty feet over the ocean in an airplane that was barely flying. Any emergency at that moment, such as an engine flaming out on the shot, dumping a generator, or any one of more than a hundred things, could instantly overload the pilot. For most carrier aviators night shots, especially in filthy weather, were exercises in terror, a ride on the rabid pig. If a pilot were ever going to accidentally fly into the ocean, this was probably when it would happen.

In addition, on rare occasions a steam catapult would malfunction, resulting in a "cold" catapult shot that left the launching aircraft sixty feet over the water without enough airspeed to fly. If a pilot got a cold shot, immediate ejection was the only way to save his own life. The possibility of ejecting right in front of a large ship churning through the dark ocean was the stuff of pilot nightmares on hot, sweaty nights in his bunk. Or as he taxied to the cat for a night shot.

Unlike the Air Force, the Navy had divided up the fighter and attack missions in the 1950s and optimized airframes for each, with the exception of the F-4 Phantom. In 1964 the US Navy carrier air wing organization was well established. In fact, it varied little from the Korean War formula more than a decade before, with obvious technological differences due to operating more advanced aircraft. The Navy operated two types of air wings from carriers: attack wings and antisubmarine wings. The antisubmarine warfare (ASW) platforms were converted World War II *Essex*-class carriers; although they deployed to the Tonkin Gulf, the water there was too shallow for effective submarine operations.

An attack carrier air wing (designated CVW, for carrier, fixed-wing) was a small, fully integrated air force whose airport could travel the oceans of the earth at speeds of up to thirty-five knots. At the heart of the wing was its attack component, usually two A-4 Skyhawk squadrons, although some carriers embarked a third. In the coming years large carriers exchanged an A-4 squadron for an A-6 Intruder squadron, which provided a dedicated night and all-weather strike capability.

Each attack carrier also embarked two fighter squadrons, F-8 Crusaders for the converted World War II *Essex*-class and usually two F-4 Phantom outfits for the "big deck" *Midway*- and *Forrestal*-class ships. Occasionally an air wing had a squadron of F-8s and one of F-4s.

The Vought F-8 Crusaders were marginally useful for bombing—each plane could carry precisely two bombs. Crusaders were single-seat, single-engine, thousand-knot fighters, pure and simple. The single engine was equipped with an afterburner that gave the light airframe a tremendous acceleration or dash capability. F-8s were armed with four 20-millimeter cannon and could shoot heat-seeking Sidewinder air-to-air missiles.

As the North Vietnamese were about to find out, F-8 Crusaders were excellent MiG killers. Without a radar or computer to help with the interception problem or the necessity to learn the craft of dropping bombs, F-8 pilots practiced dogfighting in the old style: find your enemy with your eyes, maneuver to get behind him, and hammer him with your guns or put a missile up his ass. They were good at it. In the air war over the north, Crusaders shot down nineteen North Vietnamese fighters—sixteen MiG-17s and three MiG-21s—while only three Crusaders fell to MiG-17s. Partly due to problems with the cannon shells jamming in the feed trays to the four 20-millimeter cannon during high-G maneuvers, only four of the F-8 kills were made with guns, the rest with Sidewinders.

The F-8 was difficult to land aboard ships because of the tendency of the wings to lose lift rapidly if optimum airspeed were lost. The small carriers, with their pitching decks and plumes of opaque stack gas, made getting the supersonic fighter aboard even more interesting.

The Crusader set records from its inception—only two years from initial flight to the fleet. More remarkably, as the Navy's first supersonic fighter, it broke Mach 1 on its maiden test flight in 1955. The long, lean Vought just kept going faster, as the classic F-8E was rated at Mach 1.8, or about twelve hundred miles per hour.

It became a cult machine, flown by aviators with a perverse pride in its astronomical accident rate: the 1,219 Crusaders were involved in 1,106 incidents and accidents. With its speed and range, the F-8 inevitably became a reconnaissance aircraft. Cameras replaced guns in the RF-8A, and in 1957 a Marine major named John Glenn set a transcontinental speed record in one. Navy and Marine F-8s were instrumental in giving President Kennedy vital information during the Cuban

Missile Crisis of 1962. Many were remanufactured as the RF-8G and remained operational until 1987.

The photo Crusader's mission profile—low and straight—translated to significant losses. Among naval aircraft it sustained the highest loss rate and by far the highest hit rate by AAA fire. RF-8 pilots also suffered the second-highest killed-or-captured ratio among naval single-seaters, narrowly exceeded by Skyhawks. In fact, the last loss over the Thanh Hoa Bridge was a photo Crusader in 1972.[2]

The French Navy flew F-8s from 1964 until 1999, ending a remarkable forty-two-year career for this classic carrier jet.

★

Essex-class carriers also had several attack squadrons embarked, flying either A-1 Skyraiders, a piston-engined, straight-wing, single-seat attack bird that carried guns, bombs, and rockets, or A-4 Skyhawks. Although slow, the A-1 could remain airborne for up to ten hours and deliver a terrific punch. A-1s were used extensively in Korea. The South Vietnamese Air Force would use them throughout the Vietnam War for close air support and the US Air Force for search and rescue in low-threat environments. The Navy was quick to discover that the Skyraider was too low, slow, and vulnerable to survive in the high-threat inferno that North Vietnam was soon to become and removed them from aircraft carriers.

The venerable Douglas A-4 Skyhawk, a single-engine, single-seat jet, was designed to deliver a nuclear weapon carried on a center-line belly station. But if it wasn't tossing a nuke, the Skyhawk still did a great job with conventional ordnance and rockets, if the load was light enough. The highly maneuverable delta-winged A-4, or Scooter, was small, with a wingspan of only 26.5 feet. It also lacked an afterburner, so with a full load of external weapons aboard, it was slow, often struggling to indicate 250 knots at fifteen thousand feet. Weapons delivery was by visual bombsight, which could double as a gunsight when the two internal 20-millimeter cannon were used for strafing.

The Navy's newest attack plane, the A-6A Intruder, was just arriving on the big decks of the fleet in the mid-sixties—finally, an attack plane with all-weather capability. The A-6A had twin engines without afterburners mounted inside the fuselage; carried two radars, a search and a track; plus a computer, inertial navigation system (INS), and a Doppler radar that enabled it to fly at tree-top level at night in any weather to find and attack its target. The plane was subsonic because the wing was optimized to carry an enormous load of bombs, up to fifteen thousand pounds of them, plus an ample supply of fuel. A pilot flew the two-seater while a bombardier navigator (BN) operated the electronic suite. The crew sat side by side because the radars in the nose demanded a large nose cross-section. The pilot could also deliver the bombs visually. The Intruder lacked guns, thanks again to the admirals who blithely assumed the day of the gun was over, and although it could carry Sidewinder missiles for self-defense or gun pods on wing racks for strafing, to the best of the authors' knowledge it never did so during the Vietnam War. With only five hard points—two on each wing and one on the belly—the Intruder's ability to carry bombs, its raison d'être, would have been drastically reduced with gun pods or Sidewinders.

The Intruder was cutting-edge technology when it was designed in the late 1950s, yet the A-model flown in Vietnam was a severe maintenance hog. Keeping the delicate radars and computer working were tasks that required the patience of Job and a fully stocked maintenance pipeline, which the Navy never had. The computer was so rudimentary that it didn't even use software—Bill Gates was still in diapers and software hadn't yet been invented when the computer was designed. The entire program was contained on a rotary drum, much like an antique piano roll, which revolved once every .52 seconds. If the drum froze for any reason, the recommended fix was for the BN to kick the computer, which resided in a pedestal between his legs, in the hope that the impacts would set the drum revolving again. Sometimes it worked; sometimes it didn't.

Nevertheless, the Grumman-built A-6A was a formidable dive-bomber during the daytime, with up to twenty-two five-hundred-pounders under its wings, or fifteen one-thousand pound bombs, or five two-thousand pounders, and, when the system worked, a terrific all-weather day-or-night bomber. In Vietnam the belly station was usually used for a two-thousand-pound drop tank, giving the plane eighteen thousand pounds of fuel for its mission, leaving the two external stations on each wing for ordnance. A better digital suite for the A-6 was on the way, with one solid-state phased-array radar and a state-of-the-art digital computer that rarely failed. This version would be called the A-6E and made its debut in 1971, but because the technology was absolutely cutting edge, A-6Es were never used in Vietnam, a strategic decision to ensure that none were lost for the Soviets to examine and clone. The technology was constantly updated through the years and so tightly held that the A-6 was never exported to American allies. Intruders were finally retired in 1997.

The A-6B model of the airframe was set up to shoot anti-radiation missiles, Shrike, and Standard ARM. Another version, the KA-6D, had the radars and computer completely removed and was used as a carrier-based aerial tanker for fuel-thirsty fighters, usually F-4s. The KA-6D was routinely configured with five two-thousand-pound drop tanks so that it could carry and pump twenty-six thousand pounds of fuel.

Navy Intruder crews called their aircraft BUFs—big ugly fuckers. Resembling a flying drumstick with the fat end going first, the appearance of the plane took some getting used to, but its performance and all-weather capabilities endeared it to its crews and naval strike planners.

The Ling-Temco-Vought A-7 Corsair II made its appearance on Navy flight decks in 1967 and was first used in Vietnam in December of that year. Designed as a replacement for the A-4 Skyhawk, it was a single-seat, single-engine attack plane without an afterburner. The Corsair carried two 20-millimeter guns to strafe with and a reasonable load of bombs that could be delivered visually with the aid of a radar and computer. The pilot pointed the nose of the plane directly at the target and pushed a button designating it for the computer, which began calculating an attack solution and presenting heading and pull-up information to the pilot. The computer released the free-fall weapons automatically. By using the computer, much of the guesswork and Kentucky windage was taken out of the visual dive delivery, so accuracy improved markedly, *if* the pilot could visually acquire the target.

The Air Force was reluctant to adopt another Navy design, but the Army was pushing them to develop a genuine close-air support aircraft. Although the A-7 Corsair II wasn't a supersonic hot rod, Secretary of Defense Robert McNamara decreed that the Air Force was going to use it anyway as a replacement for the A-1 Skyraider, the F-100 Super Sabre, and the F-105 Thunderchief. Navy Corsair pilots like to refer to their bird as a SLUF, or short little ugly fucker. One pilot wit noted that the A-7 "is not fast, but it sure is slow." The Air Force version, the A-7D, had a more powerful engine that the Navy adopted for the A-7E. The Air Force's A-7Ds became operational in Vietnam in September 1972.

The A-7A entered service with Pratt & Whitney's TF-30 engine, originally rated at 11,300 pounds of thrust, increasing to 13,400 in the Charlie model, and finally to 15,000 pounds with the Allison TF-41 in the ultimate A-7E variant. The SLUF never fully replaced the Scooter on Tonkin Gulf flight decks, but from 1968 onward it bore an increasingly greater share of the load.

In Southeast Asia the Navy lost a hundred A-7s from 1967 to 1972; the Air Force lost six during 1972–1973. Corsair IIs also fought in Grenada (1983), Lebanon (1983), and Libya (1986). US Navy use ended with Operation Desert Storm in 1991, with Air Force retirement coming two years later. Additionally, A-7s flew for Portugal and Greece, with the last one retiring from the Hellenic Air Force in 2014, a forty-seven-year service life.[3]

★

The Navy-inspired F-4 Phantom that equipped the larger carriers was intended as an interceptor that would shoot down its victims with missiles. Its radar and computer were optimized for the interception role, so it had no ability to find land-based targets. Navy F-4s were often used as dumb bombers, being given an A-4's bomb load of six five-hundred-pounders, which they delivered like an A-4 with an optical-mechanical bombsight. The Phantom could carry more ordnance, but fuel usage rose dramatically when it did. The Phantom's thirst for fuel when used as a bomber bothered the Air Force not at all—the Air Force used KC-135s, the size of Boeing 707s, as tankers. Unfortunately, however, the big tankers couldn't be shoehorned onto a ship, so getting gas aloft for the fighters was always a problem for the Navy, which used converted A-3s as tankers, then A-4s with a buddy store, A-7s with a buddy store after they replaced the A-4s, then KA-6Ds. The "buddy store" was a drop tank configured with a hose and reel from which a plane needing fuel could get a drink: "Hey, buddy, can you spare a dime?"

Arguably the Phantom was the deadliest-looking plane in the American military during the Vietnam War, a distinction it reluctantly surrendered when the F-14 Tomcat came along in 1974, after the Vietnam War ended. With its upturned wingtips, downward-turned horizontal stabilators and massive intakes, the F-4 looked fast and mean even on the ground. Sitting on a catapult, with the nose gear extended eighteen inches for the shot as both afterburners shot white-hot flames ten feet out the tailpipes, the bird reminded one of a Top Fuel dragster ready to pop the clutch.

The F-4 was also a tricky plane to handle off the catapult. Just a slight over-rotation put the plane into a fully stalled condition in which each increment of power, if the pilot had any to add, only deepened the stall. The region was called "the back side of the power curve," and any pilot inadvertently entering this flight regime found his afterburner exhaust creating a rooster-tail in the ocean with no way to increase his speed unless he jettisoned his ordnance. Over-rotating off the catapult at night in an F-4 was a good way to find out how you stood with Jesus.

Rounding out the air wing were the "cats and dogs" from fleet support units that provided detachments of special-mission aircraft. They included reconnaissance, electronic warfare, early warning, and aerial tanker duties, although the huge A-3 Skywarrior was still deployed in squadron strength aboard some ships. Increasingly, however, the Douglas "Whale" became the KA-3 dedicated tanker.

Finally, a helicopter detachment was available for rescuing downed fliers and transporting personnel and supplies from ship to ship.

Commanding the air wing was a veteran aviator, an attack or fighter pilot who usually was qualified in at least two of his three or four primary aircraft. He was a commander, equivalent to Air Force lieutenant colonel. The squadron COs were also commanders, as were their executive officers, whereas special-mission detachments were led by lieutenant commanders (equal to an Air Force major). Carrier air-wing commanders were called "CAG"—rhymes with "rag"—after the World War II term for commander air group, although McNamara's Department of Defense changed naval air groups to wings in 1962. But CAG remains even today, partly from tradition but largely because no one wants to be called CAW.

Carrier skippers were captains—equivalent to Air Force colonels. They were former CAGs who had done well enough in their "deep draft" ship assignments to earn a flattop. After successfully conning a fleet oiler or replenishment ship, a carrier became a possibility. Though few aviators enjoyed "driving boats" as much as flying airplanes, carrier command was the final step to an admiral's stars. One extremely accomplished pilot reflected, "I could fly formation at five hundred knots. How hard could it be keeping station on a carrier at twelve knots? Well, I learned!"[4]

The Vietnam generation of aviators came up through a succession of increasingly capable aircraft. Two of the most significant carrier planes of the nine-year Vietnam War were a subsonic attack aircraft, the A-4, and a supersonic fighter, the F-8. Between them they accounted for a large portion of the first two years' operations against the Dragon's Jaw.

★

The Douglas A-4 Skyhawk—also called the "Scooter," "Tinker Toy," or "Bantam Bomber"—began life as a carrier-based attack airplane to keep the Navy in the Armageddon nuclear-bombing business when the Air Force seemed intent on gaining a monopoly. Instead, the A-4 had a forty-year career. When delivered to the fleet in 1956 the plane was already obsolete. The Navy's original nuclear bomb that the A-4 was designed to carry was huge, so the plane sat on long, spindly legs and was taxied without nose-wheel steering, just differential braking. (As you would imagine, this created problems on wet, greasy flight decks, so a tow bar was installed on the nose wheel that a sailor maneuvered to get the plane positioned on the catapult.) By the time squadrons began flying the jet, much smaller nukes were available, but the landing gear design was set and there was no going back. Single-seat attack pilots trained rigorously to deliver nuclear weapons, quipping that the A-4 was "one man, one bomb, one way." And the cockpit was so tight that pilots said, "You don't get in an A-4—you put it on."

Simply designed with a delta wing, the Scooter was subsonic—typical max speed was about 650 miles per hour—but it was incredibly rugged. A-4s returned shot full of holes that could have destroyed a lesser airframe. Nonetheless, more A-4s were lost in Southeast Asia than any other naval aircraft: 271 Navy and 91 Marine.

This was because Scooters logged nearly twice as many sorties over North Vietnam as the A-6 and A-7 combined, and thus over twice the combined losses. A-4s had the third-highest loss rate of tailhook aircraft, behind reconnaissance Crusaders and RA-5C Vigilantes.

Two-seat TA-4s were produced as advanced jet trainers and also served as Marine Corps forward air controllers, or FACs. Skyhawks left the fleet in 1975, but the last Navy A-4s, flown as adversary trainers, remained until 2003.

For an interim design, the A-4 proved remarkably popular. Skyhawks were purchased by ten nations and logged combat time for the militaries of Israel, Argentina, Indonesia, and Kuwait. Perhaps one of the most remarkable aspects of the A-4's long Vietnam service is that none of them were lost while directly attacking the Thanh Hoa Bridge.

★

Beginning in May 1964 Seventh Fleet carriers launched covert "Yankee Team" reconnaissance missions over northeastern Laos, providing the nominally neutral Vientiane government with information on Communist rebels' movements. One of the first aircraft lost in Laos was an RF-8 Crusader off USS *Kitty Hawk*, shot down on June 7. Secretary of Defense Robert S. NcNamara, a self-made bastard, callously thwarted a rescue effort, and by the time President Lyndon Johnson approved a rescue attempt, the pilot, Lieutenant (Junior Grade) Charles F. Klusmann, was captured. Amazingly, Klusmann managed to escape in late August, one of the few successful escapes from Communist captivity during the Vietnam War.[5]

Carrier aircraft featured prominently in the controversial Tonkin Gulf incident that the Johnson administration had willingly accepted, despite the confused and contradictory reports, for a perceived political advantage over the hawkish Republicans.

From August 1964 the "Tonkin Gulf Yacht Club" flew support and recon missions in South Vietnam from "Dixie" Station as well as increasingly "Up North" from "Yankee" Station. Naval aviators had heard about the Dragon's Jaw before they began flying against the bridge. A fighter pilot recalled, "The first story I heard about the bridge after arriving on Yankee Station was that MiG-17s had gotten behind a long chain of F-105s rolling in on the target and shot down the tail-end Charlies. Also heard the rumor that Air Force guys actually spoke with the French engineers that built the thing."[6] Of course, the bridge that existed in 1965 was designed and built by the Vietnamese, but the rumor illustrated the notoriety and soon-to-become-legendary status of the toughest target of the war.

Early Navy missions against the Thanh Hoa Bridge were conducted under the aegis of Task Force 77, the naval organization that owned all the ships in the Gulf of Tonkin. The Navy launched its first strike against the bridge on June 17, 1965.

Naval aviation tactical doctrine was partly dictated by the aerial assets available aboard the carriers as well as the physical problems of operating them from a ship. It also took the shape it did because of the Navy's experience attacking heavily defended land and sea targets during World War II. One or more carriers would launch as powerful a strike force as they could assemble along with the fighters to protect the strikers, flak suppressors, tankers, and electronic warfare planes, all of which would assemble at their appointed places and head for the target. The objective was to overwhelm the defenders with lethal force, destroy the target with minimum exposure to defenders' fire, and then "haul ass"—or egress. These maximum-effort strikes were called "Alpha" strikes, named for Annex Alpha, an early Joint Chiefs authorization for significant targets in North Vietnam. The term eventually became generic in carrier aviation, referring to as big an organized strike as could be assembled. Large-deck ships could launch as many as forty-five airplanes on Alphas, one-third of which would be bombers and as many as one-fourth of them fighters on combat air patrol (CAP) against Vietnamese MiGs.[7]

Air Wing Fifteen's 1967–1968 Alpha strike mix from USS *Coral Sea* was representative of that stage of the war:

- Twelve to sixteen A-4 bombers
- Four F-4 Phantoms on MiG CAP at the target
- Four to six F-4s for flak suppression
- Two to four A-4s anti-SAM "Iron Hands"
- Four to eight F-4s on barrier and MiG CAP over the ship
- An RF-8 photo-recon plane with F-4 escort
- Three KA-3 Skywarrior airborne tankers
- Two E-2A Hawkeyes for early warning and strike control
- Two to four A-1 Skyraiders for Rescue CAP

An Alpha strike involved a diverse cast of professionals weaving three-dimensional arabesques perfected through dress rehearsals long before an air wing arrived on Yankee Station in the Tonkin Gulf. When attacking North Vietnam, the strikers would "coast in" from the gulf at fifteen thousand to eighteen thousand feet while making 300 knots (about 350 miles per hour), and they would then descend to twelve thousand feet at 350 to 400 knots upon entering the SAM threat envelope.

The bombers might split into two groups, attacking from different directions, with time over the target varying by no more than ninety seconds. The goal was to get the entire strike onto and off target in the minimum amount of time, usually defined as less than a minute for each strike group.

Each bombing group was made up of flights of four. Typically a flight leader would move his three wingmen into right or left echelon and approach the desired run-in heading at an angle of about forty-five degrees. The desired dive angle—that is, the vertical angle the bombers hoped to achieve as they dove at their targets—had already been briefed and the appropriate mil setting for the bombsights computed from ordnance delivery tables. Each pilot had dialed in the setting—now it was up to Lead to get as close as possible to the desired dive angle, which was usually 40 to 45 degrees. Once in the dive, the pilot would compare his dive angle to the briefed angle and place his bombsight aiming pipper accordingly—there was not enough time in the dive to diddle with the bombsight.

Lead took his echelon in toward the planned run-in heading, and when experience told him he was there, he would "kiss-off" his wingmen and roll his plane about 135 degrees, then pull the nose down below the target and roll upright. If he did the maneuver correctly, he was on the proper dive angle, on the preselected run-in heading, and the pipper was tracking toward the target as he accelerated downward toward his release altitude. The track of his pipper, a dot of light in the sight, would be affected by the wind, which would cause the airplane to drift right or left or make it steep or shallow. The attack pilot had to correct for the wind and watch his altitude, and if he did everything perfectly, he would arrive at his desired weapons-release altitude at the desired airspeed, usually about five hundred knots true airspeed, with the pipper offset just so for the perceived wind.

Upon weapons release, the pilot would now pull four or five Gs to raise the nose above the horizon, bottoming out above the maximum range of small-arms fire, and then he would keep the nose rising so he could turn excess airspeed into altitude while jinking wildly to throw off the aim of any enemy gunners tracking him. Behind him his wingmen had waited only one or two seconds before they rolled in, which gave them a slightly different run-in heading, and down they came, one after another, each offset slightly from Lead so someone shooting at Lead wouldn't hit the guy behind him by mistake. If you were fated to get zapped, you prayed it wouldn't be by mistake—you wanted the bad guys to have to work to do it.

The only pilots to get a clear view of the target were the strike leader and perhaps his wingman—everyone who rolled in after them was going to put the pipper in their bombsight in the boiling smoke where the target *ought* to be, pickle their ordnance, and pull out, trying not to have a midair collision with their fellow strikers or someone who screwed up the run-in heading or a flak suppressor who did it backward. Meanwhile the bad guys were shooting everything they had while someone was shouting into his lip mike about SAMs, as if a dive bomber had some spare time to look for them.

It was common for the number-four man in a flight to see two planes diving ahead of him slightly to the left or right in the bombsight, with Lead's bombs exploding on the target. If he did, everyone in the flight was going in expeditiously and not wasting seconds, which gave the gomers more time to shoot. Yet while this flight was diving, other flights were also, so that everyone was diving in the minimum amount of time and reducing each plane's time of exposure to enemy AAA fire.

The choreography rarely worked out perfectly, of course, and clouds in the target area could affect the strikers profoundly, but the goal remained the same: maximum ordnance on the target in the minimum amount of time.

Alpha strikes were the orgiastic climax of naval aviation, the supreme moment when the billions spent on ships and planes, the years of training, the excruciating family separations, and the long months at sea for everyone from seaman to admiral finally bore fruit. At that critical instant the trigger was pulled and bombs fell. Ships died under strikes like these during World War II. During that war, the Korean War, and in North Vietnam shipyards were flattened, railyards obliterated, supply dumps pulverized, power plants smashed, and bridges felled.

Except the Dragon's Jaw Bridge at Thanh Hoa. That sucker just wouldn't fall.

CHAPTER 7

"UNLIMITED LOSSES IN PURSUIT OF LIMITED GOALS"

Early Navy missions against the Dragon's Jaw were much smaller, more informal affairs than the Air Force strikes. The Navy launched its first strike against the bridge on June 17, 1965, from the USS *Midway* and the USS *Bon Homme Richard*. The bombers were A-4s from the *Bonnie Dick*, and the MiG CAP was composed of six F-4 Phantoms belonging to VF-21 aboard the *Midway*. The six fighters flew in two-plane sections.

One of the CAP sections was led by Fighter Squadron 21's (VF-21) executive officer, Commander Lou Page. With some four thousand hours in tailhook aircraft, including Korean combat, Page was highly regarded in the fighter community at NAS Miramar in San Diego. One of his troops said, "Those silver-gray eyes, they burn right through you."[1]

Page's radar intercept officer (RIO) was the vastly experienced Lieutenant John C. Smith. A former A-4 pilot, "J. C." lost his wings after a youthful aerial indiscretion but refused to stay grounded. He applied for the new RIO program and graduated near the top of its first class. A master of the F-4's systems, he helped write the first RIO instructor's manual while he served for two years as an instructor at VF-121, the West Coast F-4 training squadron. He considered Page "the best in the business."[2]

Page's wingman was Lieutenant J. E. D. Batson Jr., with Lieutenant Commander Robert Doremus in the backseat. Batson and Doremus were a tight team, having flown together through much of the training syllabus at VF-121, the West Coast F-4 Replacement Air Group (RAG).

Today the six VF-21 Phantoms carried four missiles each: two AIM-9B heat-seeking Sidewinders and two AIM-7E Sparrows, the latest version of this radar-guided missile. Aircrews dubbed the Sparrow "the great white hope" because of its color and the optimistic pronouncements of the Bureau of Naval Weapons for it.

The manual on the Sparrow said it could hit an aircraft target head-on from twenty nautical miles away—yet only if the target was illuminated by the shooter's radar from launch to impact. Lacking an emitting radar of its own, the missile merely homed in on the energy reflecting from the target by the shooting aircraft's radar. If the shooter's radar lost the target for any reason, Sparrow ceased to guide. This limitation had a profound effect on the tactics that the launching aircraft could use, since it had to keep the target in front of it for the missile's entire flight, which, fortunately, wasn't long, yet enemy fighters rarely flew straight and level while waiting to get zapped. Dogfights are often swirling hairballs, but the Sparrow was designed for shooting down bombers on the way to attack a carrier battle group, not shoot down maneuvering fighters.

Conversely, Sidewinder was a "fire and forget" missile that would track the enemy's heat signature once it was locked on, regardless of what the shooter did. However, due to the speeds involved, a highly maneuverable fighter like the MiG-17 could avoid the missile if it were properly flown by a pilot who had the oncoming Sidewinder in sight and was willing and able to pull lots of Gs.

To get a lock-on with Vietnam-era Sidewinders, the shooter had to be in the enemy's rear quarter. The missile was very fond of the sun: if given a chance, it would zip off after our star until it ran out of fuel. Finally, there was no way for the pilot shooting a Sidewinder to know exactly which heat source the missile had locked onto—one had to be careful to not shoot down one's friends. Later versions of Sidewinder had better, more sensitive seeker-heads and were more maneuverable, so eventually, in future wars, the missile became an excellent dogfighting weapon that could be fired head-on or from an amazing angle once the seeker locked on its target's heat signature.

Additionally, as we previously stated, F-4 Phantoms were designed without guns, the weapon of choice for a Vietnam War dogfighter.

While VF-21 had trained for set-piece interceptions on relatively slow, nonmaneuvering targets, Lou Page was unconvinced. He and a few other aggressive aviators had explored the Phantom's exceptional vertical performance, using the tremendous climb rate to pull up and over the top of a lighter, more agile opponent. Thus, the VF-21 Freelancers entered combat confident of their ability to handle either long-range or "knife fight" encounters.

Page and Batson established their CAP station northwest of the bridge, circling at eleven thousand feet. Monitoring the strike frequency, they heard the *Bonnie Dick*'s A-4s hit the bridge—without much effect—and an affiliated barracks nearby. While the attackers exited and headed for the safety of the ocean, Page in Sundown 101 called for one more sweep. Upon turning north, Smith saw a telltale blip on his scope: bogeys at thirty miles.

Seconds later Doremus in Sundown 102 also had the contact. His pilot, Ed Batson, shifted from an abeam search position to a three-mile trail behind Page, his lead. It was standard procedure: in a head-on intercept the lead fighter would identify the two bogeys and, if necessary, call for the trailer to shoot.

As the Freelancers climbed at full power, J. C. Smith ran the intercept, well aware that almost every aircraft over North Vietnam had white stars on its wings. The iron-clad rules of engagement (ROE) required that American fighters obtain a positive visual ID before firing. Still, both RIOs armed their Sparrows in anticipation of a long-range engagement, checking their "ready lights." Smith controlled the "sort," taking the trailing bogey and assigning Doremus the leader. With good radar locks, the RIOs exchanged confirming calls.

The Phantoms maneuvered for more horizontal separation, forcing the bogeys to show their type and intent. If the bogeys turned in toward the Phantoms, the fight would be on.

Smith kept calling distances as the range closed—twelve miles, ten. . . . Finally, the targets became visible. The location was about thirty-five miles north of Thanh Hoa.

At five miles the lead bogey rolled into a banked turn toward the Americans, revealing the distinctive bat-winged shape of a MiG-17. Lou Page yelled, "MiGs, MiGs, MiGs! Shoot, shoot, shoot!"[3]

With his eyes still in the radar hood, Smith pushed the launch button. So did Doremus in Sundown 102. On each plane a four-hundred-pound missile was ejected from the recesses beneath the fuselages and the solid-fuel rockets ignited.

When Smith looked up from his scope, he got the surprise of his life—he realized that his target was not one MiG but two. They had been flying so close together in "parade formation" that the two planes had merged into one blip on his screen. The North Vietnamese had launched a flight of four led by Lieutenant Lam Van Lic, who turned in toward the Americans when he acquired them visually.

Both Sparrows rode their invisible rails to their destinations. The sixty-pound warheads blasted the MiGs apart. Batson and Doremus' victim disintegrated almost directly over Sundown 101, while Page and Smith's lost its tail to the Sparrow's continuous-rod warhead.

Comrades Cao Thanh Tinh and Nguyen Nhat Chieu ejected and parachuted safely to earth.

Unknown to the Americans, another of the MiGs also went down. Perhaps wounded by shrapnel from the warhead that shredded his wingman or trying to avoid being a target for another missile, Lieutenant Le Trong Long piled into a hillside and died on impact—instantly. All things considered, it was a good, pain-free way to go.[4]

The last MiG, piloted by Lam Van Lic, nearly collided with Sundown 101. Smith looked down and clearly saw the pilot straining in the cockpit, "pulling for all he was worth."

Page pulled nose-high to avoid the surviving MiG and entered a solid overcast. When he dropped back below the cloud deck he saw a square parachute and drifting smoke from the two explosions that resulted from planes striking the earth. But the last surviving Communist fighter was gone, having successfully escaped.

VF-21 had made history. For the first time in aerial warfare air-to-air missiles had destroyed enemy aircraft nose to nose. It had been a classic NAS Miramar Phantom intercept, with aircrews, radars, and missiles performing flawlessly.

And it hardly ever happened again. In this war a head-to-head shot was going to be a rarity. The Air Force managed a few, but most Sparrow kills were only obtained when American fighters got behind fleeing MiGs. Experience would also prove that Sparrows were delicate instruments easily put out of commission by the inevitable rough handling of repeated loadings onto aircraft, numerous flights, carrier arrestments, and down-loadings before they were eventually fired in combat. Sparrows' "failure to guide" would leave many fighter pilots cursing. The reliability rate fell so low that in any Sparrow engagement the shooting pilot launched multiple missiles in the hope one would guide and get a hit.

That June day the victors came aboard *Midway* amid a raucous celebration already underway. On the flight deck Commander Bill Franke, the squadron skipper, was waving his arms while the maintenance chief petty officer jumped for joy. Even the steely-eyed F-8 Crusader gunfighters of VF-111 hollered and hooted.

Anticipating more action to come, as the crew of Sundown 102 deplaned, Bob Doremus quipped to his pilot, "Four more to go!" As it developed, the Navy had to wait seven more years to crown its first

Vietnam ace, Lieutenant Randy Cunningham, and his RIO, Lieutenant (Junior Grade) Willy Driscoll. Meanwhile, aboard *Midway*, the social amenities were observed. When Batson hefted a coffee cup, he found it filled with Scotch.[5]

Much later the Americans learned that the North Vietnamese claimed that two F-4s were shot down in that encounter. Because none of the MiGs had managed to obtain a firing position, the claim was obviously bogus—obvious to the Americans, that is, who recovered all their fighters back aboard ship. No doubt the propaganda claim bucked up the morale of the North Vietnamese home folks, and that is probably what it was intended to do.

★

The Thanh Hoa Bridge was one of many targets in North Vietnam that Pentagon planners routinely designated for attention. The target list for the next day's strikes arrived at various commands as a classified message, encrypted as all messages were.

In the Tonkin Gulf Task Force 77 staff "fragmented" the target list by assigning various targets to the air wings aboard the ships on Yankee Station, and aboard each ship CAG staff divided the targets further into missions assigned to individual squadrons, which assigned pilots and crews to each mission on a document called the Air Plan. The missions might be anything from an Alpha strike using every plane that could be launched to a single-plane night mission. Road recce, two or four planes against a supply dump, aerial tanker duty, barrier combat air patrol (BarCAP), reconnaissance, Iron Hand—all appeared on the Air Plan and had flight crews and planes assigned. Meanwhile the various maintenance departments were working around the clock to provide airplanes ready to fly. As the time for a launch approached, the ordnance required by the Air Plan was raised from the ships' magazines below the water line, and the go planes and perhaps some spares were spotted on the flight deck, fueled, and loaded with ordnance.

Meanwhile pilots and crews visited the air intelligence spaces to look at aerial photography, radar photography if available, and whatever intelligence existed on each individual target. Then in individual ready rooms around the ship the crews assigned to each mission received a weather brief, briefed the mission, read the maintenance logs on their assigned aircraft, donned their flight gear, and climbed a steep set of stairs—a "ladder"—or rode an escalator to the flight deck to man their planes.

Flight decks always appeared to be orchestrated bedlam. Actually, a better simile was a very large football team in action. Men performing various functions wore different colored jerseys: purple was for fueling personnel, red was ordnance, yellow for plane handlers, white for safety supervisors, and green for catapult and arresting gear personnel. Blue was for the heaviest labor—the guys who carried, installed, and broke down tie-down chains. Any plane without a pilot in the cockpit and engines running had to be secured to the deck with chains. The supervisors of each group communicated via short-range radios that doubled as sound suppressors.

Carriers on Yankee Station routinely flew for twelve hours a day, from noon to midnight or midnight to noon. Because there were usually at least two carriers on station, they alternated shifts, with occasionally some overlap during the day so they could launch a coordinated Alpha strike. Typical cyclic operations called for eight launches—or "events"—an hour and a half apart, with the final recovery taking place an hour and a half after the last launch. The Navy standard work week at sea was nominally twelve hours a day, seven days a week. During cyclic flight operations some sailors worked as many as twenty hours a day, every day. The pace was hectic and brutal.

From the time when ancient mariners first went to sea, sailors have had to not only sail their ships but also maintain and repair them. No differently, in addition to the flight deck operations and the squadrons with their maintenance departments, the ship's company had to sail, maintain, and repair the carrier. Bakers, shipfitters, pipefitters, electricians, engineers (aboard nuclear-powered ships nukes who ran the reactors), supply clerks, medical personnel, signalmen, communications techs, radar technicians—the list goes on and on. USS *Enterprise*, the largest American carrier to serve in Vietnam and the only one nuclear powered, carried five thousand men.

Lower-ranking enlisted lived in large berthing areas with the bunks stacked three deep. Each man had a small locker for his personal gear and perhaps a drawer. Petty officers (E-4 through E-6) lived in compartments with fewer roommates and more personal space. These men ate on the mess deck, a large space barely above the waterline that was also used for bomb or missile assembly when not being used for meals.

Chief petty officers (E-7 through E-9) had their own berthing spaces and their own mess. Junior officers had six- or eight-man bunkrooms, a locker, and a personal desk with a safe for classified documents, personal weapons, and, often, illegal booze. Depending on the spaces the ship had, lieutenants and above usually ended up in two-man staterooms, and commanders had staterooms of their own.

Commissioned and warrant officers had two wardrooms to choose from: the formal wardroom below the hangar deck, with white tablecloths and stewards and real china, or the "dirty shirt" wardroom up forward between the bow catapults where the food was served cafeteria style on plastic trays and you bused your own table. Because one had to be in uniform to eat in the formal wardroom, at sea ship's company officers usually ate there while aircrews in flight suits and officers in jerseys who worked the flight deck ate in the dirty-shirt wardroom amid the cacophony of catapults throwing planes off the pointy end just over their heads.

Ship's systems never ran at 100 percent capacity, especially on older vessels, where much maintenance had been deferred to meet operational schedules. Regardless of its age, every Vietnam-era carrier had to ration water for bathing. Seawater had to be desalinated by evaporators. The priority for fresh water went to the boilers that made steam to run the engines and catapults, then for drinking and cooking, and finally, for the crew to bathe in. The ship's engineering department controlled the valves in the water system, and on older ships they often secured the fresh water to the showers for as much as twenty-two hours a day. The hours when water was going to be available in showers were published in the ship's plan of the day and were known as "water hours." Some Vietnam-era carriers went on water hours when they unplugged from the NAS North Island or Alameda water supply at the pier when they got underway and didn't come off them until they docked upon their return nine months or so later. When the water was flowing, all sailors, from the admiral to the lowest swabbie, took "Navy showers," which involved turning the shower head on to get wet, then turning if off, soaping up and scrubbing, and turning it back on just long enough to rinse off. If the engineers secured the water before a man rinsed off, they got a royal cussing, although there are no recorded incidents of foul language ever causing more water to flow from the showerhead.

Salt water taken from the sea was used to flush commodes and urinals, which led to pipes becoming encrusted with salt, causing urine and sewage to overflow onto the floors of the heads.

And finally, there was air conditioning—or, rather, the lack thereof. Steel ships operating in the tropics are floating ovens. Circulating outside air inside the ship can only lower the internal temperature to the ambient temperature outside, if that. *Enterprise* reputedly had the best air-conditioning system in the fleet during the Vietnam years, yet the system was designed to lower the air temperature inside the ship just *ten* degrees below the ambient temperature outside. Further, the spaces where test equipment and computers had to be cooled had first priority for cool air. These spaces often had limited access, partly because some of the test and repair equipment was classified but also to keep sweaty riff-raff from crowding in to cool off. Both the air circulation and conditioning systems had to be secured during general quarters, when the compartments were made water- and airtight. In the US Navy GQ, or battle stations, drills are run at least once a day.

The social tensions rocking America during the Vietnam War were also present aboard Navy ships. During the 1960s the Navy had no trouble filling enlistment quotas with young men who didn't want to get drafted into the Army but who scored high on the qualification test. Black youth, relegated to poorer educations throughout most of America, were few in the Navy's enlisted ranks, and young men with the lowest test scores got the most menial jobs. In the early 1970s, as the nation backed away from the draft, high-quality enlistees became harder for Navy recruiters to find. More young black men without any more education than their predecessors came into the Navy, and racial tensions aboard ships escalated. *Kitty Hawk* suffered race riots in 1972, and the violence spread to *Constellation* and the fleet oiler *Hassayampa*, among others.

Then there was the antiwar movement, with radicals attempting to inspire sailors to commit sabotage aboard their ships. At least two carriers, *Forrestal* and *Ranger*, had far too much of it, including fires and damaged machinery. A few guilty sailors were court-martialed, but most weren't caught.

Drug use was epidemic outside the Subic Bay Naval Base in the Philippines, and inevitably some of it went to sea.

Despite all that, a management expert would have been amazed at how well these hot, filthy, overworked young sailors performed. Young men only six months to a year out of high school became valuable members of highly specialized teams led by a chief or senior petty officer. These men worked together, ate together, berthed together, and went ashore on liberty together. Slackers, malcontents, and those who lacked the emotional maturity to do a man's work or be away from home and mama were usually quickly weeded out. Solid friendships were often formed. Ask any former sailor of whatever age or length of service what ships he served aboard, and you will hear genuine pride in his voice as he answers. Some of these young sailors found the Navy so congenial that they decided to stay for a career. These "lifers" were and are the backbone of every military service.

★

The first-fleet A-6 squadron was Attack Squadron 75 (VA-75), the "Sunday Punchers," and they went to Vietnam aboard the USS *Independence*—"*Indy*." In mid-1965 the VA-75 commanding officer, Puncher

One, was Commander Jeremiah A. Denton Jr., a naval aviation professional from the Annapolis class of 1947, the same year Jim Stockdale graduated.

A former test pilot and flight instructor, Denton helped develop fleet tactics, having graduated from the Armed Forces Staff College and the Naval War College, where he received the President's Award for the most outstanding thesis in the senior course. In 1964 he earned a master's degree in international affairs from George Washington University. Then he returned to the cockpit to conduct international affairs in an A-6 Intruder.

On July 18, 1965, Denton briefed an Alpha strike against a supply complex adjacent to the Thanh Hoa Bridge. It was his thirteenth combat mission, three days past his forty-first birthday. Denton's BN was thirty-year-old Lieutenant (Junior Grade) William M. Tschudy, a former Marine who enlisted because his father served in World War II and a brother served in Korea.

The target was the Ham Rong port facility, a cluster of warehouses on the south side of the Ma River just a mile east of the Dragon's Jaw Bridge. Denton led Indy's twenty-eight plane strike inland, bypassing the target and descending before turning eastward so the jets would be pointed toward the Gulf of Tonkin when egressing.

The weather was unusually clear, so the aircrews had no trouble seeing the target—warehouses with barges tied up alongside in the river.

Denton keyed his mike, telling the strike group, "Rainbow Leader rolling in," and dove for the target. He tracked the target in his bombsight, and passing six thousand feet at 500 knots true airspeed, about 440 knots on the airspeed indicator, pushed the pickle button on his stick, and felt the jolts as the bombs ejected from the racks.

He began his pullout . . . and his Intruder rocked from the impact of a major detonation. Denton's plane suffered massive damage. The generators failed, both hydraulic systems failed, the throttles were unresponsive. With a total electrical failure, neither crewman could talk to the other or transmit on the radio.

Then the jet began an uncommanded roll that couldn't be corrected with stick or rudder. The plane was dying—the crew had to get out.

Jerry Denton, the cool test pilot, waited for the wings to come level with the horizon before pulling the face curtain on his ejection seat and blasting upward through the canopy. Bill Tschudy's seat on the right side of the plane went through the canopy an instant before Denton's.

Then, as Denton recalled, "We were falling from one world into another."[6]

Tschudy descended into a village, where an officer shouted, "Hands up, Yank!"

Denton splashed into the water. Not the Gulf of Tonkin but the middle of the Ma River. His left leg was injured, so he couldn't swim very well. Two Vietnamese civilians overtook him in a canoe, one visibly enraged and wielding a machete. The man swung the blade several times, hitting Denton on the back and neck and drawing blood.

Soldiers on the riverbank forced the civilians away and dragged Denton ashore. "Dazed and bleeding as I was, my principal emotion was fury," he said. "I was mad as hell at being shot down and even angrier at being captured."

Denton and Tschudy had not been shot down. The A-6 had been a victim of its own ordnance. There had actually been an A-6 lost in June to the same cause when a five-hundred-pound Mark 82 bomb exploded shortly after release over Laos. That crew ejected and narrowly escaped capture on the ground in the dark jungle; they were rescued by an Air America helicopter the next day. The cause of the loss was not immediately known, so flight operations continued.

An *Independence* A-4 Skyhawk pilot recalled, "We were an 'all-electric fusing air wing' with a standard whirly-gig nose fuse with a wire as the back-up second fuse. We didn't manage to shoot down any Scoots, but I distinctly remember being in a 60-degree dive in a crowd and a b'jesus HUGE explosion amongst us. What kind of flak was *that?*

"As I recall, when the bomb left the rack, it pulled out a cord with a connector to the bomb, which initiated the electric fuse on separation.

I think that was when the bombs blew off the Intruder's wings. Until they officially quit using electric fusing until a remedy was found, a whole lot of us not-so-dumb boys would only arm the mechanical fuse. Sometimes it doesn't pay to be on the bleeding edge of technology."[7]

Then, on July 24, another Sunday Puncher crew ejected over Laos after another premature detonation. The fliers were rescued, but clearly the Intruders could not continue using the suspect fuses. Corrections to solve the problem included fusing and wiring changes and adding ejector racks that pushed bombs away from each other to prevent collisions after they were pickled off.

During July 1965 the carriers lost six planes, including *Independence* Intruders to their own ordnance. But Navy casualties doubled in August. That month three of the five WestPac carriers lost thirteen planes on combat missions—three a week. Six of those came from *Midway*. The war was becoming even more expensive.

★

The first Navy aircraft loss over the Thanh Hoa Bridge came on August 24, 1965, before the Seventh Fleet assumed larger responsibilities for the Thanh Hoa region.

Commander Fred A. "Bill" Franke was the thirty-eight-year-old Brooklyn-born CO of VF-21 aboard USS *Midway*. Crews from his squadron had scored the first Navy MiG kills of the war on June 17. Franke came into the Navy as an apprentice seaman in 1944 in the aviation cadet program and was discharged in 1946. He attended Louisiana Polytech and the University of Oklahoma, then was awarded a direct commission in the Naval Reserve in 1948. He logged about two thousand hours flying F4U Corsairs before transitioning to F9F Panthers and Cougars, then to F3H Demons. His commission was upgraded to regular Navy. Finally, Franke transitioned to F-4 Phantoms. In the summer of 1965 he had about a thousand hours of experience in Phantoms.

Franke was an extremely accomplished aviator, having gone through the Naval Test Pilot School at NAS Patuxent River, then, after gaining some operational test and evaluation experience, returning to the Test Pilot School for a tour as an instructor. By that day in August 1965 he had logged about fifty combat missions. He and his wife, Jackie Louise, had a son and two daughters.[8]

Recalling the campaign to destroy the Dragon's Jaw, Franke said, "We'd go up there on a regular basis to knock it down or at least try to put it out of commission. The poor Spad [Douglas A-1 Skyraider] pilots carried a load of old World War II dumb bombs and used fixed sights to aim with while flying through heavy ground fire . . . that was quite a feat. My hat was off to those pilots. The A-4 teams had a little advantage with speed and altitude, but not much of one.

"There wasn't a pilot in the air wing with World War II experience, too long ago, and just a few holdovers from Korea. All those strikes on the bridge were led by CAG Bob Moore or one of the attack skippers."[9]

On the afternoon of August 24 Franke and his RIO, today Lieutenant Commander Robert Doremus, escorted a bridge strike, their second mission of the day. A reserve naval flight officer (NFO) since 1956, Doremus was a New Jersey native who first flew aboard early-warning aircraft in Hawaii. He left active duty in 1958 but was recalled three years later and put to work training antisubmarine crews. Then the Navy sent him to NAS Miramar to become an F-4 radar intercept officer. Doremus joined VF-21 in April 1963 and frequently flew with Bill Franke, who became the squadron CO. As mentioned earlier in this chapter, Bob Doremus had been in the backseat and helped pilot Ed Batson score a MiG kill on June 17.

Inbound to Thanh Hoa on August 24, Franke and Doremus in Sundown 112 and their wingman were the target of multiple SAM launches. Making about 350 knots at eleven thousand feet, Franke was unable to evade a SAM, which detonated close to the Phantom.

The effect of the four-hundred-pound fragmentation warhead was devastating to Franke's fighter. The shrapnel blew off much of the port wing. Warhead fragments riddled the left side of the aircraft, severed fuel lines, and snuffed out both engines. With a fire blazing aft of the cockpit, no electrical power, and dead engines, the crew ejected.[10]

In F-4s, upon ejection the backseat fires first so that the rocket blast from the pilot's seat doesn't fry the RIO. So out they went, Doremus first and Franke a fraction of a second later. They landed in a rice paddy near Phu Banh, north of the target, where the Vietnamese immediately captured them. As Franke recalled, "My wingman reported seeing no parachutes, so we were officially listed as killed in action shortly thereafter." In any case, no rescue attempt could have been made with darkness descending. Some shot-down aviators were simply beyond help.

★

While aircrews were flying and bleeding, the summer of 1965 was a weird, wiggy period in the United States. President Johnson opted for a wider war and ordered more American troops to South Vietnam.

The Department of Defense, with McNamara at the helm, ordered unit reports to omit the phrase "shot down" in favor of "lost in combat." Connoisseurs of bureaucratic obfuscation will appreciate this effort: "shot down" sounds violent and final, like the slamming of a coffin lid, whereas "lost in combat" seems much less final, as if someone made a wrong turn somewhere and the errant soul might, in the fullness of time, come wandering back. About the time this nonsense was flying around, headquarters of the Naval Air Forces, Pacific, advised squadron skippers to meet their unit quotas for United Fund donations.[11]

During a Tonkin Gulf visitation McNamara told USS *Oriskany* aviators that they should expect to endure "unlimited losses in pursuit of limited goals." McNamara's declaration had a predictable effect on *O-Boat* morale, but the air wing commander, Commander James B. Stockdale, had other ideas. A tough-minded intellectual Naval Academy grad, he recognized that with real flak in the air, politics became irrelevant. Two decades later he told a Tailhook Convention audience, "Even in a limited war there's nothing limited about your efforts over the target."[12]

The point McNamara apparently failed to grasp was that the war wasn't a limited one for the North Vietnamese Communists, who were engaged in total war. The gunners defending the Dragon's Jaw also had no illusions: they would fight until they died at their guns or American planes stopped coming.

CHAPTER 8

THEY NEEDED A BIGGER BANG

If any naval aviation leader was loved by his men, it was Commander James "Jim" Stockdale. A stocky, wavy-haired, forty-one-year-old Midwesterner with bright blue eyes, he was equal parts philosopher and warrior. He had graduated from Annapolis in 1946, a year early, in the top one-sixth of his class. A former test pilot, Stockdale got a master's degree in international relations from Stanford, with a concentration in Marxist thought. A more thorough education for a leader in the Vietnam War is difficult to imagine.

Oriskany's CAG Stockdale led from the front. Sailors said that occasionally he stalked the flight deck before a launch, looking for an airplane with an ordnance load-out that appealed to him. He might jerk a thumb at the pilot in a "get out" gesture and take his place. True or not, the story fits his reputation.

That attitude—part personal, part professional—became evident in gallows humor typical of combat airmen since the Great War. Adding an addendum to the growing JCS list of restrictions on where and how bombing could be performed, an irreverent *Oriskany* junior officer posted the following: "Rule: Buy your way into the squadron duty officer watch and stay aboard ship. Money is no object!"[1]

Whatever the Dragon's Jaw contributed to ready-room guffaws, it nonetheless remained all too real. Commander Wynn Foster of VA-163 aboard *Oriskany* recalled, "The degree of antiaircraft protection given the Thanh Hoa Bridge reflected both its strategic value and North Vietnam's pride of accomplishment. Air Wing Sixteen [aboard *Oriskany*] flew Alpha strikes against the bridge in July and August [1965] but neither was successful. Other air wings were pounding the bridge and failed as well. The Thanh Hoa Bridge thus became a challenge to us as periodic reports of its destruction proved false. Its alleged indestructibility gave birth to tongue-in-cheek theories. The bridge was the hinge holding the world together, and God would not allow its destruction. Or less theistically, the bridge was simply an illusion, done with mirrors."[2]

One of Stockdale's senior attack pilots was then-Lieutenant Commander Thomas F. Brown, who recalled, "I flew with him [CAG] quite a bit, and often he would show up as my number four, having swapped with the original guy. We had some fun! One day in 1965 I was briefing for a road-recce, and in came CAG Stockdale with an idea. He said, 'Let's put together a mini-Alpha strike and go bomb the Thanh Hoa Bridge during the next cycle. I have directed them to put bombs on my two F-8s.' And so we did it—six A-4s and two F-8s . . . no flak suppressors.

"The weather was good, and we gave it a good shot. My wingman and I had a great run at the bridge, but there was a tad more wind than I planned for, and our bombs missed by about 100 to 150 feet. We really got hosed down with AAA but sustained no damage to any of our aircraft. That was the only time I went against the bridge, but our air wing often used it as a bad weather alternate target."[3]

The *Oriskany* CVW-16 team was a guild of tailhook warriors determined to accomplish the mission, and screw the rules. One of the squadrons aboard was VMF(AW)-212 flying F-8s, one of few Marine units deployed to carriers off Vietnam. After the air wing had been losing a plane a week in the Thanh Hoa area, the Marines' executive officer, Lieutenant Colonel Edward Rutty, suggested that the bridge might be destroyed with heavier ordnance. The F-8E Crusader could carry two one-ton bombs on hard points under the wings, and Rutty thought that the extra explosive weight might do the trick. Although the A-4s could carry one one-ton bomb, that load sacrificed their combat potential.

Rutty did his homework. When he raised the prospect with Stockdale, the Marine presented his plan for loading, arming, and dropping Mark 84s from Crusaders. It was part innovation, part heresy because F-8 pilots prided themselves on their air combat skills as "the last of the gunfighters."

But Stockdale was receptive to the suggestion, an idea that had never before been attempted. It was easy to see why: with full fuel and two tons of external ordnance aboard, F-8s could not reliably get airborne from the O-Boat's catapults. The solution: launch the fighters with partial fuel loads and top them off from airborne tankers.[4]

Jim Stockdale liked the idea a lot. He took the proposal to the ship's skipper, Captain Bartholomew J. Connolly. It would have been easy for Connolly to say no. The procedure suggested was experimental, and by rights the naval aviation and weapons bureaucratic fiefdoms should have studied it—a process that could take months or even years to be approved, if it was approved at all. But Bart Connolly was an unconventional officer. An Annapolis man four years senior to Stockdale, he had earned a Navy Cross as a PT boat skipper in World War II and won his gold wings in 1947. The two Annapolis grads talked Rutty's idea over and decided to give it a try after some tests. As Stockdale recalled, "Once we agreed it was practical, he said to go with it. Without mentioning it, we both agreed to let Washington go to hell."[5]

The *O-Boat* was tasked to hit the bridge again on September 9, a maximum-effort Alpha strike. Stockdale had thirty-two A-4E Skyhawks and F-8E Crusaders as bombers, supported by eight escorting Crusaders plus four A-3B aerial tankers and an electronic jamming aircraft. Two RF-8A photo planes were assigned to get pre- and poststrike "imagery"—photographs.

As launch time approached, the aircrews were strapped into their cockpits, awaiting word from the weather scout. The 10:30 launch time came and went. Pilots closed their canopies to escape pelting rain. Finally the weather recce pilot reported that in his opinion conditions were acceptable over the target. The rear admiral commanding the task force gave the "go" signal.

Engines were started and the bomb-laden planes were taxied carefully to the catapults, which began slamming them into the moist Tonkin Gulf sky. The pilots formed into four-plane divisions circling the ship.

At 11:00 Stockdale had his squadrons formed up, ready to head outbound, when the weather pilot called again. The bridge was "zero-zero," with no ceiling or visibility that would permit an attack. Reluctantly Stockdale radioed his division leaders to proceed to their secondary targets, mostly along the coast.

Stockdale's wingman was Commander Wynn Foster, executive officer of VA-163. A Korean War veteran, Foster was as nautically blue-blooded as they came: he traced his lineage to a *Mayflower* ancestor.

The two Skyhawks flew to a point south of the Thanh Hoa Bridge, expecting to hear from Foster's skipper, Commander Harry Jenkins, who was looking for a SAM site. The backup plan was that if "Old Salt One" found the site, he would call Stockdale and Foster to join in the attack. But as the fuel gauge needles dropped toward the "bingo" point, requiring return to the ship or a tanker, no word came. Stockdale and Foster had enough fuel to hit a secondary target if they could find it and then return to the ship with a minimum reserve.

Flying low at three hundred knots, the attack pilots noted an offshore checkpoint and abruptly turned to their run-in heading for the secondary objective—a camouflaged facility next to a railroad track about fifteen miles south of Thanh Hoa.

As the scooters neared the target Foster shot a glance northward. There was the Dragon's Jaw, visible in the thinning fog and mist beneath a four-thousand-foot ceiling. He marked it as yet another lost opportunity in an increasingly lengthy war.

Then it was all business as both pilots double-checked their armament switches. Stockdale turned south, following the railroad. As he approached the target, Foster lagged about a mile behind to avoid the leader's bomb blast. CAG's ordnance rippled across the target area, spewing debris and tree branches.

In his dive Foster glimpsed a row of obscure objects covered by tarpaulins. He put the pipper in his bombsight on the area. "My pipper slid smoothly to the near rear of the row and I pressed the pickle four times in quick succession, walking my bombs two at a time along the length of the target."[6]

Pulling up from his attack, Foster looked for his leader. There he was, three thousand feet high, a delta shape against the overcast—with black-brown splotches erupting around him.

The antiaircraft gunners had the range.

Stockdale keyed his mike: "Uh, Old Salt 353. Mayday!"

His A-4 was mortally wounded. The nose dropped as the little bomber plunged toward Vietnam. Foster's pulse spiked, and he shouted into the mike in his oxygen mask, "Pull up, CAG! Eject! Eject!"

Jim Stockdale pulled the black-and-yellow striped handle, sending his canopy spinning into space and firing the rocket under his seat. He separated from the seat, felt his parachute deploy, and was abruptly jerked upright as the chute opened. As he fell toward the earth he thought, "Four years. At least four years."[7]

Four years was a far-too-optimistic prediction. Stockdale was a prisoner of the North Vietnamese for almost eight years.

A *Ticonderoga* A-4 squadron commander who had gone to Test Pilot School with Stockdale said, "Jim will do all right. He's the toughest guy I know."[8]

★

The North Vietnamese AAA defenses were getting some kills, but not anywhere near enough for the propaganda ministry. So they made some up. Like this one from the *History of the 228th Anti-Aircraft Artillery Regiment*, as translated by Merle Pribbenow:

In December 1965 North Vietnam's 228th Anti-Aircraft Artillery Regiment conducted an integrated radar and artillery engagement against an American electronic warfare aircraft using winter weather to advantage. It was identified as a Douglas AD-5 but the 1965 designation was EA-1E or F.

The 228th's Second Battery reported heavy frequency-band jamming, indicating coverage for an inbound air strike. Since heavy jamming usually precluded firing a Shrike anti-radar missile, the command post directed continued tracking, especially low-altitude ingress routes.

Both radar operators turned their antenna to the designated quadrant. When the jamming abated they were able to break out a target return signal, which came and went. Because they could no longer track the target in automatic mode, the Vietnamese shifted to manual tracking.

The most experienced radar operator, Duong Van Le, reacquired the jamming aircraft. When it drew within effective range, the Second Battery Commander ordered a prolonged burst on the target vector, firing tracers. Other batteries opened barrage fire on that visual cue, producing a claim for a kill. The wreckage reportedly was found on the outskirts of Tu Quang hamlet, entered as the *fifty-third* U.S. aircraft downed over Ham Rong.

The unit history concluded, "This was a model battle fought by the regiment that displayed unique aspects of exploiting our radar fire-control system."[9]

No comparable US loss has been found for December 5 or that time frame.

★

The carrier phase of the war continued. By November *Oriskany* was operating with her sister *Essex*-class ships *Ticonderoga*, the "*Tico*," and *Bon Homme Richard*, the "*Bonnie Dick*," plus the world's first nuclear-powered aircraft carrier, the USS *Enterprise*, the "*Big E*," and the *Forrestal*-class carrier, the USS *Kitty Hawk*, the "*Hawk*."

Thus, Task Force 77's five active carriers owned eleven A-4 squadrons, *Kitty Hawk*'s A-6 squadron, plus four squadrons equipped with A-1s, a total of sixteen attack squadrons. Although each carrier embarked an A-3 Skywarrior detachment, increasingly the large, seventy-six-foot-long "Whale" was devoted to the vital task of airborne tanking. The four prop-driven A-1 Skyraider outfits on the small decks seldom ranged far inland, owing to their slow speed. Moreover, that huge four-bladed propeller made a magnificent radar reflector. "Spads" were best employed on close air support, coastal hunts, and rescue missions.

With a dozen jet attack squadrons available, the carriers launched strikes day after day against targets in North Vietnam. The targeting wizards in Washington wanted everything hit all at once, and even a dozen jet attack squadrons weren't enough.

Missions were scheduled willy-nilly against the bridge when weather allowed. The carriers sent two or four planes on two dozen small daytime missions throughout May of 1966. Often the bridge was a secondary target when the primaries were weather-bound. The total effort—only sixty-five sorties—amounted to merely 128 tons of ordnance and achieved nothing worthwhile. A four-plane division dropping free-fall bombs simply could not put enough ordnance on this hard target to do more than harass the Vietnamese, who were now experts in bridge repair.[10]

★

Meanwhile the Americans were busy dividing up the responsibility for the bombing campaign against North Vietnam among the various services and commands. In November 1965 the Pacific Command commander-in-chief, Admiral US Grant Sharp Jr., divided North Vietnam into "route packages," or areas of responsibility for the Navy and Air Force. Numbered with Roman numerals I through VI, the "route packs" were further subdivided as the war progressed. Tellingly, as dictated by the micromanagers in Washington who were thoroughly frightened of the possibility of Chinese intervention, restricted zones were set in concrete. The area within thirty nautical miles of Hanoi and ten miles from the center of Haiphong were off limits as too politically sensitive to be bombed. Additionally, a twenty-five-mile buffer zone ran along the North Vietnamese/Chinese border. Although we have previously mentioned this restriction, one cannot understand the insanity of the air war over North Vietnam unless one realizes that these off-limits areas were sanctuaries for MiGs, within which and from which they could operate with impunity. Until they flew out of the sanctuary area, MiGs were safe from US fighter attack.

★

At the end of 1965, after seven months of on-again, off-again bombing, the Dragon's Jaw still stood in place across the Ma River near Thanh Hoa. Though now a blackened, warped structure standing in a cratered landscape that resembled the surface of the moon, it remained semifunctional. The concrete roadways on either side of the railroad track were obliterated, leaving an impossibly narrow target, a sixteen-foot-wide railway.

Conventional 500-, 750-, and 1,000-pound bombs clearly were insufficient to drop the bridge. American ordnance analysts examined the recon photos and other evidence and drew the obvious conclusion: they needed a bigger bang. One-ton- to 3,000-pound weapons were needed to slay the dragon, and aviators needed a means of placing those bigger bombs with greater precision. Reports were written, endorsed with comments by admirals and generals, and sent up the chain of command. Back in the States the bureaucratic wheels began to turn.

★

The increased pace of air operations over North and South Vietnam had effects throughout the Navy and Air Force. For instance, the Air Force found itself short of qualified aircraft maintenance technicians. Major Bob Krone at Korat in Thailand mentioned in a letter home, "The flight line is bustling with activity, as it is every night. The maintenance men work all night to reconfigure the planes with the proper loads and make necessary repairs for the next day. The maintenance area is especially critical now."[11]

Experienced noncommissioned officers were in such short supply that some crew chiefs assumed responsibility for two planes simultaneously. In order to meet operational commitments, the men worked seven days a week, which degraded efficiency and morale. Yet the "wrench turners" out on the flight lines and the maintenance shops were as professional as the pilots. The squadrons kept providing "up" jets.

Although aircrew shortages were not yet evident, they would soon become a serious concern. As veterans of the first phase of the air war completed their tours, the training pipeline in the States was usually able to meet the increased demand. Yet, inevitably, more fliers finished a second combat tour, leaving a widening gap of experienced aircrew. The Air Force personnel bureaucracy struggled with the problem and inevitably began looking farther afield. Pilots who had spent most or all of their careers in bombers and transports received orders to fighter-transition training. Although some relished the thrill of converting from B-52s or C-130s to Thuds or Phantoms, others were less than enthusiastic; they were astute enough to recognize that eighty hours in a fighter-bomber did not ensure combat competence when flak and SAMs filled the sky.

★

In a broader context the war expanded dramatically in the second half of 1965. Between June and December of that year the number of US military personnel in South Vietnam increased threefold, from fewer than 60,000 to more than 184,000, in accordance with President Johnson's July 28 address to the nation. Personnel elsewhere in Southeast Asia, including Thailand—and, if you were a cynic, Laos and Cambodia—numbered nearly 43,000, for a grand total of 227,000 at year's end.[12]

The political heat was rising significantly in the United States. That August one-quarter of Americans told pollsters that they opposed sending troops to Vietnam. The figure slowly grew over the next three years, mirroring the rising tide of public disaffection, and it reached a saturation point in 1968, when Lyndon Johnson took himself out of contention for reelection.[13]

Meanwhile US military spending increased $2.4 billion over 1964, reaching almost $191 billion, although the defense share of the gross domestic product declined from 9.5 percent to 8.2 percent.[14]

★

Back in Washington in December 1965 Lyndon Johnson was torturing himself over his efforts to wring "victory" from this war into which he had dragged America. His problem lay in keeping disillusioned voters with him while at the same time coaxing North Vietnam into surrendering its dream of national reunification. Someone in the White House hit upon the idea of a "Christmas peace initiative." Baldly, it was another bombing pause that lasted from Christmas Eve through the end of January 1966.

One of Johnson's problems, although he probably didn't know it, was that there was a serious possibility that the North Vietnamese leadership thought they were doing much better against the Americans than they actually were. Having integrated their air defenses over the previous two years, they had succeeded in achieving a layered air defense system that was increasingly lethal to Yankee air pirates. At the end of 1965 the Hanoi Politburo reckoned and announced that Military Region Four covering the southern two-thirds of the country had shot down 834 American aircraft. The actual number of American planes lost throughout all of Indochina since 1962 was barely 300.[15]

One possible explanation is that the North Vietnamese leaders were lying for domestic and international political reasons. Although we assume they could count wrecks, it is also possible that the cadres manning the guns and missiles were reporting inflated numbers up the line. Bureaucracies are like that: give the boss the numbers he wants. Report a shoot-down and get a medal, some extra food, maybe even a promotion and your picture in a newspaper. There was bound to be a crash somewhere that could plausibly be attributed to the claimant, and everyone knew some of the damaged Yankee planes crashed into the sea.

The AAA gunners and SAM operators were taking serious casualties throughout North Vietnam outside the sanctuary areas—a lot of them, although the actual numbers will probably never be known. US flak suppressors attacked AAA batteries and SAM sites, now valid targets. Navy Iron Hand and Air Force Wild Weasel shooters fired missiles, and scattered bombs, aimed or not, were hitting gun emplacements near important targets. The carnage was real. Reportedly the casualty rate among gunners around the Thanh Hoa Bridge was so high that the North Vietnamese converted a hollow cavern in the limestone formation on the west side of the bridge into a military hospital. Perhaps the fictional victory statistics were part of what it took to keep the defenders shooting.

One suspects that we will never learn the real reason for Hanoi's inflated shoot-down numbers. Victors of a war write its history, and the North Vietnamese won theirs. In Vietnam the victory totals are now historical "fact."

Meanwhile the religious aspect of the Christmas peace initiative was pure propaganda for American and international consumption. South Vietnam was about 80 percent Buddhist, while North Vietnam was not more than 8 percent Christian. Ho Chi Minh and his colleagues were 100 percent Communist: they ignored Lyndon B. Johnson and used the bombing pause to resupply and reload.

And re-arm the Dragon.

CHAPTER 9

PAYING THE PRICE

The aviator who flew the most missions against the legendary Dragon's Jaw was probably then-Lieutenant Commander Samuel L. Sayers, who logged three Alpha strikes, four single-plane night-attack missions, and four other day missions, for a total of eleven against the bridge.

Sam grew up in West Texas and attended the University of Missouri in 1952 on a baseball scholarship. He was on the 1954 NCAA Championship baseball team and somehow wound up in the Missouri Sports Hall of Fame. During the summer he did midshipmen cruises and "learned to cuss like a sailor." He graduated in 1956 with a major in statistics, turned down a pro baseball contract offered by the Detroit Tigers, and went to Pensacola to learn how to fly.

After some years in the fleet Sam was selected for the Navy's Test Pilot School at NAS Patuxent River, Maryland, where his mathematics background was fine preparation for a crash course in aeronautic engineering. Upon graduation he was ordered to A-6 Intruders, which were the newest birds in the fleet. In November 1965 he was in VA-85, the Black Falcons, aboard USS *Kitty Hawk* on her way to Vietnam, the second A-6 squadron to deploy. "The aircraft was not ready," Sam recalled. "The airplane had not completed Op Eval [operational evaluation] and still had some bugs to be worked out. We went anyway."[1]

The electronic countermeasures gear in the A-6s in 1965 was primitive by later standards and only provided an audible warning when a Fansong radar illuminated it. It also flashed red warning lights on the pilot's glare shield and sounded a high warble when it picked up the high PRF signals that indicated a missile was in the air and being guided by the Fansong. What the bombers lacked in 1965 and 1966 was a device that indicated the direction of the threat. The A-6B missile shooters did have this gear, and the squadron had three of those birds.

Kitty Hawk's air wing became heavily involved in the air war over North Vietnam upon its arrival on Yankee Station. On December 22, 1965, Sam and his BN, Charles D. Hawkins Jr., were number three in a four-plane night strike against the Hai Duong Bridge between Hanoi and Haiphong. The A-6s went in low, a few hundred feet above the deck, in trail, each pilot using the terrain avoidance feature of the A-6 navigation system. There was a lot of flak. Tracers arced upward: the gunners shot at the sound of jets running low and fast, and some merely shot upward in the hope that an American plane would run into the steel shell stream. There were SAMs in the air that night, and the squadron skipper, Commander B. J. Cartwright, may have flown into the ground trying to avoid one. He and his BN, Lieutenant Ed Gold, were never heard from again. They were listed as MIA, missing in action, presumed dead, until their remains were identified in November 1994.

On February 18, 1966, VA-85 lost an A-6 during the day over North Vietnam, killing Lieutenant (Junior Grade) J. V. Murray and Lieutenant (Junior Grade) T. A. Schroeffel, who were flying as a wingman in a flight of two. A truck was spotted. No flak was noted, so Murray dove on the target from six thousand feet and dropped two bombs. Lead cautioned him about the target elevation, which was unknown. Buckeye 812 hit the ground in a nose-high attitude. The evaluation was that "target fixation combined with inexperience prevented recognition of an extreme set of circumstances."[2]

Sam flew his first strike against the Dragon's Jaw on March 13, 1966. The target was the Thanh Hoa Barracks. It was a daytime Alpha strike, which meant the *Hawk* launched at least four A-6s and perhaps eight other A-4 bombers, plus F-4s that were usually used as flak suppressors and combat air patrol to defend the strikers, MiG CAP. KA-3 Skywarriors provided aerial tanking, and an RA-5C Vigilante did photo recon.

Navy doctrine was for the bombers to roll into their dives within a second or two of each other, with each flying a slightly different path to their individual release point while the flak suppressors' ordnance exploded upon the guns. Each AAA crew on the ground could pick a plane to shoot at, but the volume of fire aimed at each plane was less. That was the theory, anyway. The goal was to get the bombers to deliver their ordnance within one minute and then exit the area as quickly as possible. But it only worked that way at bombing ranges in the States. In Vietnam, with its typical limited visibility due to haze and clouds, plus flak, SAMs, and MiGs, every Alpha strike was a unique fire drill. The wingmen tried to hang onto their leader no matter what and rolled in when he did, hoping the target would then be visible in the bombsight.

As Sam recalled, no bomb damage assessment (BDA) trickled down to the squadron level from that strike.

On April 17, 1966, Sam and Charlie Hawkins were flying an A-6B Shrike mission southwest of Vinh when a 37-millimeter shell went through a wing, starting a fire. Sam jettisoned his ordnance and headed for the coast as the wing burned fiercely.

As you sit in your easy chair reading this account, try to imagine the emotions of the pilot and BN, who had been sitting in a familiar cockpit, adrenaline pumping, when the airplane shook from the impact of an AAA shell and began to burn. The crew was instantly shoved to the naked edge, staring at death or imprisonment and torture in North Vietnam. They knew intellectually that it might come to this, but they hoped and prayed it wouldn't. Now it was here—death or capture. Their airplane was on fire and wouldn't last long. Perhaps mere seconds.

Navy doctrine dictated that the crew eject at the first visible sign of fire for a very cogent reason—the airplane could explode at any moment. But Sam and Charlie didn't eject. No doubt they had talked about it, as every A-6 crew did. They had made up their minds to stick with the plane for as long as it was flyable, even if it was ablaze.

Sam steered for the water. The beach passed under the plane, so perhaps they were delivered. Fear turned instantly to elation. Yes, yes, yes. Then, seconds later, no more than a mile from the coast, Sam found the flight controls no longer worked. He and Charlie Hawkins had to get out. They pulled their face curtains and ejected through the canopy, which was the preferred method for A-6 crewmen to abandon their airplane—the Grumman designers didn't want to risk the possibility that the canopy would not leave the airplane upon command, so they designed the ejection seats to blast upward through the glass. Hawkins' hand was severely cut by the Plexiglas. When they hit the ocean and got rid of their chutes, both men managed to get into the tiny life rafts contained in the seat pan of their ejection seats.

They floated in the ocean, Hawkins bleeding, looking around for North Vietnamese fishing or patrol boats. Hoping. Praying. Were they delivered or doomed? They sat in their little rafts remembering the shoot-down and the burning plane and the fear, wondering . . .

Between forty-five minutes and an hour later an HU-16 Albatross amphibious plane from DaNang appeared out of the sea haze, landed in the ocean beside Hawkins, and pulled him aboard. Then the plane taxied a few hundred yards to where Sam was huddled in his raft. To the pilot's amazement, a man rose from the water with a knife and began slashing. It was the rescue crewman from the Albatross, slashing at the raft to sink it,* but it gave Sam another big shot of adrenaline.

When the Albatross landed at DaNang, Charlie Hawkins was soon sent off to USS *Repose*, a hospital ship anchored in the bay, to have surgery on his hand. At DaNang the Air Force doctor who examined Sam

*Survival rafts were always sunk when the survivor was rescued so that they would not attract other rescue aircraft.

found only minor scratches. "What can I do for you," he asked Sam, "while you wait on a COD [carrier on-board delivery plane] to take you back to your ship?"

"I can think of three things that would be mighty nice right now," the mellow naval officer replied. "My cigarettes got soaked in my raft, so I'd like a fresh pack. Second, I'd like a bottle of Jack Daniels, and third, I'd like to pick up a phone and find my wife on the other end."

The doctor nodded and said, "I'll see what I can do. You wait here."

Twenty minutes later the doctor returned with a pack of Lucky Strikes and a bottle of Jack Daniels. As Sam flicked his Zippo a few times to see if it still worked, then lit up, the doctor picked up the telephone on his desk and held it out to Sam. Sam's wife, Janet, was on the line.

When the COD finally arrived to take him back to the ship, Sam had finished the bottle of Jack Daniels.

On April 21 the squadron's new skipper, Commander J. E. Keller, and his BN, Lieutenant Commander Ellis Austin, were hit by AAA and killed in action over North Vietnam.

The next day Lieutenant Commander Robert F. Weimorts and Lieutenant (Junior Grade) William B. Nickerson were hit on a bombing run near Vinh. Following the pullout Weimorts headed for the ocean, yet his wingman observed Weimorts' aircraft impact the water about five miles offshore. No chutes were seen, and there were no survivors.

On April 27 Lieutenant (Junior Grade) Brian Westin saved his wounded pilot, Lieutenant William R. Westerman, who had been hit in the lung by a bullet that came through the canopy during a day strike over North Vietnam. Leaning across the side-by-side cockpit, Westin flew the plane out to sea. The BN's side of the airplane had no flight controls, nor was the BN a trained pilot; he was a naval flight officer (NFO). Westin put the plane on autopilot and took the laces from his G-suit to rig a line to the alternate ejection handle between the pilot's legs. Unlike the F-4, the A-6 did not have command ejection. Going by the ship, Westin pulled hard on his jury-rigged cord, ejecting

Westerman, then he ejected. The rescue helicopter picked up Westin first, and he directed the chopper crew to the approximate location of the pilot. When the chopper crew found the wounded Westerman, who had been bleeding into the water, they spotted a shark.

The pilot was unable to get into the horse-collar rescue sling. So Westin jumped back into the ocean to save him. After Westerman was aboard the helicopter, the hoist mechanism malfunctioned. Westin pointed toward the carrier, so the chopper departed to get medical treatment for the now-unconscious Westerman. Five minutes later a second rescue chopper plucked Westin from the sea. Both men survived the adventure, and Brian Westin was awarded a well-deserved Navy Cross.

Sam was back flying two weeks after his shoot-down with a new BN, Mike Anderson. On May 15 he and Mike flew a single-plane night strike against the Dragon's Jaw. On May 20 the two-man crew was part of another Alpha strike on the bridge.

Soon thereafter *Kitty Hawk* headed back to the States. The squadron had lost four crews in combat. Two other planes had been lost due to combat damage, but both crews survived. One plane was lost in an accident, and that crew also survived.

For the air wing aboard *Kitty Hawk* the toll was equally grim. Twenty-two airplanes had been lost, one of which was an A-3 Skywarrior shot down by a MiG over the South China Sea. All three men aboard were killed. In total at least thirteen airmen had been killed in action, and the North Vietnamese had taken five prisoner. Three of the POWs would die in captivity: Lieutenant Robert Taft Hanson Jr., Lieutenant (Junior Grade) W. L. Tromp, and Commander Greg Abbott.

The *Hawk* had pounded North Vietnam, and the Dragon's Jaw still stood.

★

Sam Sayers returned to Vietnam with VA-85 on the *Hawk* after a turnaround in the States. He flew another Alpha strike and seven more single-plane strikes against the Dragon's Jaw.

The A-6 Intruder was designed for all-weather attack, the only Navy airplane capable of this mission. At night the crew would go in low, under five hundred feet and, if terrain would permit, as low as two hundred feet, trying to stay under enemy radar surveillance. The BN had to find the target with radar, then the crew would attack it, hopefully carrying bombs that had been modified with "Snake-eye" retarding fins. When dropped from an airplane, a bomb travels in a parabola that steepens as the weapon loses speed. Dropped from a low altitude in level flight, a "slick" bomb impacts the target just a few hundred feet behind the bomber, and the shrapnel from the blast can catch up with and severely damage the delivery airplane. With snake-eyes, however, four clam-shell fins replaced the general-purpose bomb's tail fins. The clam-shells opened when the weapon was released from the rack and retarded it, slowing it rapidly, and causing it to fall on a much steeper trajectory that allowed the delivery airplane to be farther away when the bombs detonated. Unfortunately the snake-eye fins were not available in the quantity needed, so A-6s often took to the night skies with "slick" bombs that forced the plane to climb to a safe altitude, at least fifteen hundred feet, when on the bomb run. This pop-up maneuver made the plane visible on radar and put it precisely into the heart of the AAA envelope surrounding the target.

The coastal plain of North Vietnam was remarkably flat, with few hills rising above a few hundred feet except in the northern part of the country. The terrain avoidance presentation on the pilot's multifunction display required fierce concentration. The A-6 didn't have an autopilot that could be coupled to the terrain avoidance feature, so at night the pilot flew the plane manually while watching vigilantly for rising flak that had to be avoided while keeping a wary eye on his radar altimeter.

The North Vietnamese used tracers, about one for every six or seven shells, so vivid streaks marked the rising flak columns. The guns were usually fired when the first sound of the plane's engines reached the gun crews. Hiding in the darkness, the bombers were invisible to the gunners. Old-pro pilots tried to fly at 420 knots true airspeed so they would have more control of the airplane, but inevitably when the flak started to rise, the throttles went forward until they were against the stops and the two engines were giving everything they had, which worked out to about 480 knots with a typical bomb load. Speed was life. The North Viets often sited guns in rows along a road, the only dry surface in a country cut up by rice paddies, and the guns put up a steel curtain. The pilot had to pick his way through, praying that the gap he selected was not about to be filled by a gun that had delayed its barrage for just that purpose. It was the guns ahead of him the pilot had to worry about. The ones to either side were usually fired late, and the tracers appeared to curve and go behind the plane.

A pilot had to concentrate so as to not get distracted and accidently fly into the ground, a collision that would instantly send both men into eternity. Over the course of the war many A-6s were lost on night low-level missions for unknown causes. They crossed the coast inbound and never returned. The most experienced crews in A-6 squadrons usually were assigned the toughest night missions, yet inevitably, as junior crews gained experience and a squadron absorbed casualties, junior crews found themselves over North Vietnam at night flying as low as they dared and dodging flak as they sought out their assigned targets.

The low-altitude approach at night made targets with a low radar signature extremely difficult for the BN to find. The all-steel Thanh Hoa Bridge, however, was easy to pick out of return on the search radar screen, even at very low grazing angles. Still, to give the system the best chance of hitting it, the BN would try to get the track radar to lock on the bridge and feed gimbal angles to the computer. Unfortunately, keeping the delicate track radar functioning despite repeated catapult shots and arrested landings was almost impossible for most A-6 avionics shops, so A-6 crews routinely launched on night missions with a "down" track radar.

The navigation-attack system in the A-6A was primitive in relation to the giant strides then being made in solid-state radars and computers. The crew's ability to actually make an accurate system weapons delivery depended almost solely on the skill of the BN, who had to ensure the delicate computer was getting accurate velocities from the Doppler radar and from the plane's inertial navigation system (INS) and that the cursor on the radar scope was indeed tracking the target. It took steel nerves and an iron stomach for a BN to ride through the flak, turbulence, and maneuvers of the pilot while concentrating on managing a recalcitrant system.

The A-6 was a BN's airplane. Without a skilled BN the A-6 was just a dumb bomber. With one, the A-6 was an all-weather, twenty-four-hour weapons system. As more than one BN remarked, "The pilot's job is to get me to the target so I can destroy it, then get me back to the ship, where the food is."

Once the target—in this case the Dragon's Jaw Bridge—had been identified with the search radar, the BN stepped the computer into the attack mode. The computer began providing steering commands to the pilot, who manually flew the plane as the computer calculated where in space the bombs needed to be released to hit the target. If the plane was carrying unretarded weapons, by now the pilot had popped up to bombing altitude and was trying to hold the plane in level flight to smooth out velocity inputs to the computer. He flew directly toward the bridge as the system released the weapons—right through the barrage fire of all the antiaircraft guns surrounding the bridge, plus anything else the defenders had in order to put bullets into the air, including machine guns and rifles.

The necessity to go straight for the bridge on the bombing run gave the gunners the opportunity to concentrate their fire above it. This was the hellish climax for the bomber crew—they were skimming above a flak volcano.

Once the bombs were gone, the crew was on its own, free to jink if the pilot thought he could avoid flying directly over the bridge but, in any event, getting back down as low as possible as soon as possible as the bombs detonated behind the plane with trip-hammer flashes. With the weight and drag of the bombs gone, the Intruder was soon up to five hundred knots as the crew "got the hell out of Dodge."

Sam Sayers flew four of those night missions against the Dragon's Jaw and four bad-weather day missions. Other A-6 crews flew many more. No doubt night-flying Intruders and Intruders hidden by clouds hit the bridge a few times, perhaps more than a few, but when the BDA came in, the bridge still stood.[3]

CHAPTER 10

FOOLS, DRUNKS, AND LOST FIGHTER PILOTS

In 1966 the Rolling Thunder air campaign entered its second year, although it was never a consistent effort. As noted earlier, "bombing pauses" interrupted the campaign as Lyndon Johnson repeatedly tried to entice Hanoi to bargain by demonstrating "good faith." The pauses were usually McNamara's recommendations as he continued to search for a political settlement. Johnson, McNamara, and their civilian aides and advisers completely misread the North Vietnamese, both in terms of their steely resolve and their enormous patience.

During 1965 the Air Force had launched 26,100 sorties into North Vietnam airspace, including 11,600 fighter-bomber strike flights. The next year, 1966, the total sorties Up North tripled while strike sorties quadrupled, and that did not include 36,500 sorties by Navy and Marine squadrons into North Vietnam.[1]

At the same time Hanoi stepped up its air defenses. During 1966 some twenty-six hundred North Vietnamese went to the Soviet Union for pilot and technical training. It was an intense process because the candidates had to gain minimal Russian-language fluency to attend the courses.[2]

Besides weather, enemy defenses, and restrictive rules, US air operations suffered another problem: a bomb shortage. In late 1965 air planners anticipated that the growing sortie count might outstrip the ability of American industry to provide bombs and other ordnance. During the first quarter of 1966 that fear was realized. General Joseph H. Moore, the senior Air Force officer in theater, notified his childhood South Carolina friend, Army General William C. Westmoreland, that the shortfall represented an "emergency situation." The shortages involved aerial rockets, cluster munitions, and 500- and 750-pound bombs. The latter were especially affected, as huge B-52 Stratofortresses consumed vast quantities of Mark 82s and M117s. A single Boeing could drop forty to eighty or more bombs, usually in dense jungle along the South Vietnam and Laos border where Communist forces often assembled. The "Arc Light" missions could be fearsomely effective—surviving enemy soldiers sometimes were captured in a state of shock—but usage was outstripping production.

Admiral Sharp's Pacific Command headquarters crunched the numbers. Mission strengths could be reduced and allocation of available ordnance equalized among Air Force, Navy, and Marines. Eventually domestic production picked up the slack, but in the meantime Robert McNamara's Department of Defense had to explain why it was purchasing bombs previously sold to NATO countries, most notably Germany.[3]

Canceled missions were significant that spring. In April one-sixth of Air Force sorties were scrubbed due to weather or ordnance shortages, although Tonkin Gulf carriers enjoyed better operating conditions, with only 7 percent of the sorties canceled. May was terrible, however. The Air Force scrubbed 40 percent of the planned sorties, the Navy 25 percent. In real numbers the May figure meant that more than a thousand scheduled Thunderchief flights and nearly 750 Phantom missions remained in the chocks.

Commenting upon the bomb scandal in an article entitled "Any Old Bombs to Sell?" the conservative *Chicago Tribune* sniped, "Defending himself at his press conference against charges of planning failures and shortages in the Vietnam buildup, McNamara insisted that the military had sufficient 'war reserve stocks' on hand to tide it over until new production can fill the gap. This lofty concept fails to jibe with the picture of McNamara scraping up every bit of old war surplus ever unloaded upon Europe to meet the present demands of the battle in Vietnam."[4]

As part of the overall US strategy, attacks on the Thanh Hoa Bridge were drastically diminished during 1966. The Navy continued its occasional small-scale efforts, while the Air Force, stymied at conventional efforts, was thinking far outside the bombing box.

★

Despite ordnance shortages, some units found ways to expand their bombing capability. To optimize their air wing's offensive capability, some Crusader squadrons trained in dive bombing as well as air-to-air and flak-suppression missions. One of those was *Oriskany*'s Air Wing 16, which in predeployment training sent F-8 pilots to the Chocolate Mountains bombing range on the California-Arizona border. Many Navy F-8 pilots cordially detested "Air to mud," although their Marine counterparts regarded close air support of Marine riflemen as their most important responsibility.

Among the *O-Boat* fighter pilots was Lieutenant Commander Richard Schaffert, who flew several strikes against the Dragon's Jaw. He recalled, "The first time I saw it was August 18, 1966. My wingie Bill McWilliams, and I had two thousand-pound Mark 83s apiece and were headed for a smaller bridge in that general area. Couldn't find it—surprise, surprise! But we saw that big one and gave it a try. Luckily we rolled in together and dropped on my mark, looked back to see two great explosions in the general area and an incredible wall of flak. God was still taking care of drunks, fools, and lost fighter pilots."[5]

Although Thanh Hoa received little Air Force attention that spring, other bridges were on the target menu, including Ha Gia and Bac Giang near Hanoi. One pilot recalled, "The North Vietnamese defended them like they were the last two bridges standing in Southeast Asia."[6]

Some Thud drivers said of Bac Giang, "It will be as infamous as the Thanh Hoa Bridge." The bridge was certainly notorious in its own right: a four-span structure twenty-five miles from Hanoi on the key Northeast Railway to China. The combination rail and road bridge had been targeted four times in late April and early May before the Thunderchiefs dropped it in the Thuong River on May 7.

The Northeast Railway extended eighty miles from Hanoi to the Chinese border and was defended as befitted a strategic asset. Aircrews were told that at least a thousand active flak sites of all calibers defended this JCS target. When the Bac Giang Bridge fell, Thunderchief pilots breathed a sigh of relief—the bombers seemed to be making progress.

The Ha Gia Bridge linked Hanoi with the Thai Nguyen industrial area fifteen miles directly north of Hanoi. The bridge lay east of the village, where a dozen or more large gun positions existed. American bombers dropped the southern span on June 12, but the tireless Vietnamese had it repaired in about ten days.

★

During 1966 two of the least-known players in Asian skies were valuable Douglas products: the EF-10B Skyknight and the EB-66 Destroyer. Although their contributions are seldom acknowledged, they were among the combat-support aircraft combat aircrews appreciated most.

The F3D Skyknight was a blunt-nosed, straight-winged, twin-jet design that began life in the late 1940s as the world's first dedicated jet night fighter. In the 1950s a Marine Corps squadron of Skyknights frequently escorted Air Force bombers on night missions over North Korea and claimed half a dozen kills. However, the subsonic F3D lacked the performance for daytime aerial combat and therefore acquired another mission. When the Department of Defense changed aircraft designation systems in 1962, the F3D became the EF-10, for "electronic warfare fighter." The right-seat crewman, previously an RIO, became a "zapper," operating electronic systems to jam enemy communications and radars, including the Fansong radars that guided SA-2 SAMs.

Based at DaNang, Marine Composite Squadron One (VMCJ-1) frequently supported Navy and sometimes Air Force missions Up North. The squadron began operations in 1965, sometimes flying from Takhli, Thailand, to augment Air Force EB-66 Destroyers. With two three-hundred-gallon drop tanks, the Skyknight could stay airborne more than three hours.

Colonel Wayne "Flash" Whitten recalled, "With the two drops, we were left with two internal noise jammers that were typically employed against Fansongs and the Firecan fire-control radar associated with 57 and 85mm antiaircraft guns. Unlike the multi-position EB-66C with nine internal jammers, the EF-10B could not receive or jam the long range Spoon Rest target acquisition radar employed by SAM battalions. Our intent was to temporarily degrade Fansong's ability to acquire and track inbound bomb-laden strike aircraft and hopefully preclude a successful missile engagement. . . . We did not have steerable antennas, which required us to point the nose of the aircraft toward the targeted radar, a tactic that must have been well known by the North Vietnamese Air Defense Command by 1966."[7]

On March 18, 1966, Captain Bill Bergman, with First Lieutenant Whitten (Riverboat One), led First Lieutenants Everett McPherson and Brent Davis (Riverboat Two) on a two-plane mission supporting an F-105 strike against a target ten miles west of Thanh Hoa. It was a high-threat profile, flown inside the "missile ring" defending the bridge, and because of recent MiG-21 activity, two Marine Corps Phantoms escorted Riverboat One and Two.

Bergman and Whitten had flown about sixty missions over North Vietnam and formed a strong team. Whitten recalled, "Bill Bergman was a second-tour aviator and an experienced EF-10B pilot. 'Mac' McPherson had only joined the squadron about a month earlier but quickly fit into our unit. Brent Davis, my hooch mate, was a highly disciplined officer and a well-respected ECMO [Electronic Counter-Measures Officer]."[8]

Nearing the initial point that day, the Skyknights entered an oblong-shaped pattern at about twenty thousand feet, with one jet always pointed at the target area. The tactic was not foolproof, as the powerful Fansong radar could "burn through" the jamming to track an aircraft.

A SAM site near Vinh on the coast south of Thanh Hoa was active during the ingress, repeatedly coming "up" for a look, then shutting down to prevent countermeasures, such as some Yankee air pirate launching a Shrike.

As the F-105s began their attack, Whitten began jamming a Firecan AAA radar, but he could not simultaneously counter the SAM's Fansong. "Things got real busy in the cockpits over the next few minutes. . . . As I remember, we had just made our outbound turn to the west when Bill called my attention to a large fireball to our front in the vicinity of where we expected our wingman to be. They would have likely just rolled out on a heading inbound to the target."[9]

One of the escorting F-4 backseaters was big, enthusiastic First Lieutenant Eugene "Basic Mule" Holmberg, who also saw the explosion. Holmberg's F-4 was now being targeted by SAMs, one of which detonated in the vicinity of the plane.

While the Thuds pulled off target, Bill Bergman called Riverboat Two and got no reply. Riverboat One exited the area westward into Laos before looping back toward DaNang.

The resident SAM unit, the 61st Battalion under the 236th Missile Regiment, had launched several SA-2 Guideline missiles with a valid firing solution. One SAM detonated close enough to McPherson's Skynight to inflict fatal damage. Riverboat Two crashed about twenty miles south of the target area, with Vietnamese villagers later reporting a stricken aircraft descending erratically, trailing smoke. They reported that the Americans had ejected, when in fact the EF-10 had no ejection seats; crews had to exit the plane via a chute that took them out the bottom of the fuselage.

In 1991 a US MIA team found Vietnamese documents related to the missing Skyknight. Davis' remains were returned in 1997, but McPherson's body, although buried at the time, was not recovered. Riverboat Two was only the third Marine aircraft lost over North Vietnam. The first two were an F-4B in December 1965 and a KC-130F in February 1966.

Years later Whitten examined the list of American aircraft lost in Southeast Asia. He identified four—perhaps six—planes known or likely to have been downed by SAMs or AAA south of Thanh Hoa in February and March 1966, probably by the 61st and 63rd Battalions.

The Vietnamese missileers claimed two kills on March 18, apparently believing that a detonation near Holmberg's Phantom was successful. But it was not. Nonetheless, Whitten cites a Hanoi document attributing much of the SAM success to a Nguyen Xuan Dai, a twenty-six-year-old radar tracker of the 61st Battalion. He had been among the first Vietnamese trained in Russia, but his class was hastily recalled due to increasing US air activity in mid-1965. His battery claimed two Voodoos destroyed with one missile on March 7, 1966. (Two F-101s actually were lost on that date.) With these repeated successes, Dai was promoted to missile control officer, and his unit was recalled to Hanoi. There he claimed the A-4 Skyhawk of Lieutenant Commander John McCain in October 1967. Declared a Hero of the People's Armed Forces in 1970, he remained on active duty after the war.[10]

★

The EB-66 Destroyer's capabilities varied according to the model. EB-66Bs were "ground tunable" with electronics that were not adjustable in the air, while C models with fewer jammers could be adjusted in flight based on what the ECMO saw. An electronic warfare officer explained, "The basic issue with the EB-66 was that all of its jammers were omni-directional—they transmitted in 360 degrees, which greatly reduced power over distance. In *Glory Days* author Wolfgang Samuel reported that EB-66 crews envied the Navy's EKA-3Bs, which had directional jammers that broadcast in about a 30-degree cone, greatly increasing effective power. (Think of a garden hose nozzle with a variable stream.)"[11]

Better electronic warfare aircraft were in development back in the States, as well as guided ordnance and some weapons that had promise but might or might not make the first team. The air war against the North was vigorously stimulating American industrial innovation and invention. Wars have always been technological hothouses in America—this one was no different. And, of course, the Americans really wanted that bridge at Thanh Hoa.

CHAPTER 11

CAROLINA MOON

Since World War II Eglin Air Force Base in the Florida panhandle has seen a wide variety of innovative weapons programs, but probably none more so than Carolina Moon. In 1963 Eglin became home to the Air Force Special Air Warfare (SAW) Center specializing in weapons and systems testing. That year a combat crew-training group was established at nearby Hurlburt Field to teach fliers how to use new weapons and equipment. SAW units went to Vietnam in 1963, cycling in and out for the next decade.[1]

Eglin and Hurlburt were hotbeds of cutting-edge ideas and activity. The staff studied electronic countermeasures, how to defeat SAMs, improving conventional munitions, night and all-weather flying—even how parachutists could lower themselves to the ground when snagged atop a jungle canopy.

In the summer of 1965, when it became obvious that conventional ordnance could not topple the Thanh Hoa Bridge, Eglin began work on one of the most innovative concepts of the Vietnam War. Project Carolina Moon took a reverse approach to slaying the Dragon. Instead of bombing it from above, weapons engineers studied how to blow it up from below—from the Ma River. The weapons they settled on were air-dropped mines.

Carolina Moon was conceived and executed in extreme secrecy. The project was so sensitive that it was not included in a classified 1969 report on Air Force Research and Development for Southeast Asia 1965–1967.[2]

Although the Air Force had institutional experience with mines dating from World War II, the challenge of toppling the Dragon's Jaw required a new weapon. Developed by the Eglin armament laboratory, the new mine looked promising . . . and impressive. Each mine was massive: eight feet wide and thirty inches high, weighing almost two tons. Their steel bodies were so large that the Air Force sought assistance from the Atomic Energy Commission to build them. At the Y-12 National Security Complex in Oak Ridge, Tennessee, the weapon bodies were built on machinery designed to produce nuclear weapons parts.[3]

Apparently the explosive was a devil's brew of chemicals designed to enhance the power of the warhead. Ordnance engineers reckoned that the mine's eruptive force could be "mass focused" upward, producing a detonation equivalent of *one thousand tons of TNT* within twenty to thirty feet of the mine. That number was an eye-watering figure: a non-nuclear kiloton detonation. Although the floor of the Dragon's Jaw was fifty feet above the river at normal flow, the engineers thought that a focused explosion of this magnitude directly under the bridge should lift the structure off its foundations and bring it down.[4]

Triggering the mine called for the best fuses the engineers could create. The primary fuse was a radar-activated detonator used in the 1950s' Bomarc surface-to-air missile. A high-altitude bomber killer, Bomarc, officially the CIM-10, was designed to detonate when its on-board radar detected a target aircraft overhead. At Eglin the backroom boys made the fuses smarter by tweaking them to distinguish between a bridge's large structure and lesser items that might appear above the mine, such as birds or a telephone wire. As a backup in case the radar fuse failed, the mines received an infrared sensor that would detonate when it sensed the ambient heat emitted by a large metal structure.

In all, thirty Carolina Moon mines were produced, including ten without warheads for training missions. The mines were expensive: $20,000 each, for a total cost of $600,000 in 1965 dollars, which would be the equivalent of $4.8 million in 2018.

Although Eglin was the Air Force's weapon-testing center, the base had no suitable facility to evaluate the entire mission profile. Consequently Fairchild C-123 Provider and Lockheed C-130 Hercules transports dropped training "shapes" offshore. Retarded by parachutes and dropped from an altitude of four to five hundred feet, the mines splashed into the ocean when the chutes that dragged them out of their airplanes automatically released. At that point engineers observed whether the weapons would float . . . and they did.

Subsequently some mines were detonated beneath test structures to determine what the effects would be on the Dragon's Jaw and other spans. The results were promising, with the blast energy focused along two axes, vertically and horizontally, to achieve maximum effect.

America had a new infernal device.

Now all the Air Force needed to do was put a mine in the Ma River. A specially modified B-52 would be just the ticket, but a B-52 five hundred feet over the Ma River? The airplane selected was the C-130 Hercules.

In the 1950s Lockheed was doing a booming business manufacturing fighters and reconnaissance planes when the Air Force requested proposals for a multiengined transport. Some Lockheed executives, including Kelly Johnson, designer of the P-38 Lightning and F-104 Starfighter and future landmarks, including the U-2 and SR-71 spy planes, doubted there would be much of a market for a combat transport. Despite their reservations, Johnson and Vice President Hall Hibbard inked the contract in 1951.

The C-130 was one of the first aircraft designed to use turbo-prop engines, four of them. Each Allison T56 provided more than four thousand horsepower, enabling the Hercules, the "Herc," to lift its own weight. With reversible propellers, a C-130 could get into short airfields, and its impressive power-to-weight ratio permitted short takeoffs as well. The rear ramp permitted rapid loading and unloading, a quantum advance over side-loading aircraft.

First flown in 1954, the Hercules entered service two years later. Tremendously versatile, in addition to hauling cargo it has served as an aerial tanker, medevac, airborne command post, special operations platform, and paratroop lifter, plus numerous other roles, including aerial firefighter. As the AC-130 Spectre, it served as a gunship in Vietnam. The Hercules was widely exported to some seventy nations, from Afghanistan to Zambia. At this writing in 2018 updated models of the C-130 are still in service in the US Marine Corps, Air Force, Air Force Reserve, and National Guard as well as forty militaries around the world. On the world stage the Hercules starred in Israel's spectacular rescue mission to Uganda in 1976, flying unrefueled twenty-five hundred statute miles to Entebbe, where commandos freed Jewish hostages.

Perhaps the greatest tribute to this amazing aircraft is that the C-130J Super Hercules is still in production—*sixty-four years* after the first Herc took to the skies.

The Carolina Moon project managers began with several possible C-130 crews before selecting two from Sewart Air Force Base in Smyrna, Tennessee. Both crews were led by experienced airlift pilots: Majors Richard T. Remers and Thomas F. Case. Beginning in January 1966 the crews worked under extreme secrecy at Eglin, often wearing civilian clothes off base. In all, the Carolina Moon project involved sixty-nine military and civilian personnel.[5]

The airmen learned that Carolina Moon required more than simply pushing the load out the back of the airplane—delivering mines accurately was a complex operation, calling for a reliable means of opening the parachutes to extract the weapons from the back of a Herc and accurately placing the two-ton weapons in the middle of the river. Because water depth, currents, and wind affected delivery to the desired point beneath the bridge, extremely detailed intelligence was required.

Ordnance and operations officers huddled frequently to refine Carolina Moon tactics. A night mission was obviously required, as flying a transport over North Vietnam in daytime would be suicidal. The ingress and attack profile would need to be flown low, at five hundred feet, to minimize the possibility of discovery by enemy radar. Mission planners chose an inbound leg of forty-seven nautical miles, which would take 18.8 minutes to cover, assuming no navigation errors, as the Herc flew at a speed of 150 knots. Eglin's sprawling real estate afforded training sites resembling the terrain expected near Thanh Hoa. During practice missions Remers' and Case's crews became familiar with what they would likely see during the actual attack.

Each attacking aircraft would drop five mines between one and two miles upstream of the Dragon's Jaw. It was uncertain whether one mine would actually drop the bridge, so multiple weapons allowed a margin for error. In war always go for overkill.

The project team, now down to forty-one men, including four civilians, left for Vietnam in mid-May 1966. At DaNang the maintainers and "ordies" assembled ten mines by May 22. Two crews, two planes, and two loads of weapons seemed optimal in case the first mission failed for any reason.

Carolina Moon was vetted and approved at the highest theater levels, Admiral Sharp's Pacific Command and Lieutenant General Joseph H. Moore's newly established Seventh Air Force. Joe Moore was a pragmatist. As a pursuit squadron commander in the Philippines in 1941, he said the one benefit of war was that "at least we could throw away our damn ties." He was willing to consider innovative solutions to thorny problems. Besides, he had an additional reason: his son, also Joseph, was a Phantom pilot.[6]

Seventh Air Force maintained a steady flow of information to the Hercules' crews. Reconnaissance and intelligence updates showing changes in North Vietnamese gun positions were inserted in the mission plan. The routes in and out were altered accordingly.

But the fliers had ultimate responsibility for their work. Both command pilots believed the Herc's rugged airframe could absorb moderate flak damage, and four Allison turboprops gave them an excellent chance of remaining airborne with one or two engines inoperative.

The aircraft commanders arrived at differing solutions regarding a low-altitude emergency. Because the fliers could not wear body armor and parachutes simultaneously, Remers decided that his men would wear chutes, expecting to be able to climb to a reasonable bail-out altitude if necessary. The airmen would lay their armored vests on the floor as extra protection. Case took the opposite tack: his crew would wear flak vests and store the parachutes.

Shortly after arrival at DaNang the Carolina Moon crews received notice that the first mission was scheduled for May 30. But May 27 brought chilling news. Seventh Air Force reported five new heavy-caliber antiaircraft sites and a huge increase in automatic weapons in the target area. Nonetheless, operations officers and the two command pilots believed the risk was acceptable: Carolina Moon was a go.[7]

To improve the Herc's odds, an attack to divert the North Viets' attention during the mining was laid on. Four Phantoms of the Eighth Fighter Wing at Ubon, Thailand, would attack Route 1A, the coastal highway fifteen miles south of Thanh Hoa. Bombs and flares released shortly before the Herc's target time would certainly attract Vietnamese notice. Additionally, two Douglas EB-66 Destroyers of the 41st Tactical Reconnaissance Squadron from Takhli, Thailand, would jam known Vietnamese radar frequencies for the critical period of the attack.[8]

With planning complete, Carolina Moon needed only one or two nights of good weather with a decent moon. Without a radar to navigate and provide terrain avoidance, Remers and Case needed to be able to see the ground to avoid it, and the navigators needed to see their turn-points. And they would need to see the river and the bridge.

★

At 12:25 A.M. on May 30 Remers and copilot Thomas M. Turner advanced their four throttles and accelerated down DaNang's active runway. The flight engineer, Master Sergeant John R. Shields, monitored the performance of sixteen thousand screaming horsepower. Banking seaward beneath an eight-tenths moon, they stayed at about a hundred feet over the ocean, then turned northbound while maintaining radio silence.

Thanh Hoa lay 220 nautical miles ahead. Seven Americans were off to slay the sleeping dragon.

Both crews had two navigators to increase chances of spotting the primary or secondary drop points. Remers' navigators, Captain Norman G. Clanton and First Lieutenant William R. "Rocky" Edmonson, meticulously noted the time on their charts as they crossed the coast-in point, providing a datum for the leg to the initial point. Remers advanced his throttles, climbing to four hundred feet, then retarded the throttles to slow to the optimum 150 knots.

North Vietnam was quiet. Gauzy moonlight diffused by the ever-present haze reflected from rice paddies as the minutes ticked away at an agonizing pace. Making just two-and-a-half nautical miles a minute, the Herc finally reached the initial point and turned for the first drop point. So far, so good—the Phantom diversion seemed to have achieved its purpose.

There was the river! With the ramp down and the loadmasters ready, the pilots flew down the river toward the bridge. The tension wound tighter and tighter as the seconds ticked away. With no flak at the first drop point, Remers pressed ahead to the second drop point, a mile nearer the bridge.

Suddenly Vietnam lit up with muzzle flashes and tracers.

The gun crews of the 228th Air Defense Regiment heard the throaty drone of four turboprops in the darkness; the command post sent all units to Alert Condition One.

The Herc crew worried that the gunners would see the big, slow transport in the moonlight, distinctive with its high, pointed tail.

Heavy and light AAA fire flashed and flared around the transport, but was poorly directed. The crew reckoned that the nearest gunfire fell hundreds of feet astern: the gunners couldn't see the Herc and were shooting at sound, which meant they shot at where the airplane had been, not at where it was.

On the signal from the pilots Staff Sergeant Aubrey B. Turner and Airman Johnny A. Benoit initiated the sequence of popping chutes to drag the five mines out of the open rear of the aircraft, one by one. Once released from the shackles that secured them, the mines went out easily on rollers. Flying the plane slightly nose-up helped. The parachutes blossomed ghost-like in the Indochina darkness starting about a mile and a quarter upstream of the Dragon's Jaw.

Air Force lore insists that during the bomb run you're on the government clock; on egress you're on your own. With the last mine gone, Richard Remers coordinated ailerons and rudder, turning hard right while descending back to relative safety at a hundred feet above the planet.

When they crossed the pale white ribbon of the beach and achieved the sanctuary of the Tonkin Gulf, the crew was euphoric. From their perspective the mission was a rousing success. Back at DaNang the men posed for an early-morning photo shoot and celebrated with adult beverages. They had *done it* and lived to tell the tale!

Like a Broadway premiere's cast awaiting the reviews before breakfast, Remers' men and their friends stood by for the morning recon reports.

The two early-morning RF-101 pilots returned to DaNang, where the film cassettes were removed from their Voodoos' noses. After immediate processing, the photo interpreters scrutinized the barely dry prints, seeking some sign of damage to the bridge.

Nothing.

In addition, none of the five mines were visible along the bank, upstream or downstream. They had simply disappeared.

According to a North Vietnamese account published years later, "Troops had seen parachutes descending over the upstream ferry crossing, and Colonel Nguyen Van Khuy dispatched soldiers to investigate. They reported mines floating toward the bridge, prompting the commander to order an impromptu response. Four soldiers sprinted to the riverbank, expending all their rifle ammunition on the visible mines. Some of the weapons exploded under accurate gunfire. In the morning engineers from the province military headquarters and some public security personnel retrieved stranded mines and detonated them."[9]

You may believe this nonsense if you wish, but rifle fire probably could not detonate the mines. The fusing was sophisticated—proximity and infrared—and the Viets had no idea of where to aim even if they were accurate. Furthermore, removing two-ton mines from a river was not a job for troops in a sampan—heavy equipment would be required.

Regardless of the truth of the North Vietnamese account, the fact was that the mines apparently failed to detonate under the bridge. Perhaps failing to detonate, the mines were carried by the river on out to sea. If they did explode, they didn't take the structure down.

It is possible that the mines missed the river altogether and fell on land. Another possibility is that the mines plunged too deep into the water when released by their parachutes and buried themselves in the mud at the bottom. However, the most likely scenario is that the swirling eddies of the river washed the mines into shallows, where they were stranded. The unpredictable currents of the river were always the weak link in the plan. If so, the North Vietnamese probably pulled the mines above the high water line.

We are left with the mental image of a North Viet explosive ordnance disposal (EOD) squad detonating one of the captured mines without any idea of its tremendous explosive power. If they did, one suspects they might have been instantly launched into the hereafter, maybe all the way to Communist heaven, if there is such a place, to hang out with Karl Marx, Lenin, and Stalin while awaiting Uncle Ho's arrival.

★

Meanwhile, back at DaNang, the powers that be ordered the second Carolina Moon mission launched *that night.*

The aircrews were incredulous. Even with another diversion and radar jamming support, repeating the mission so soon invited disaster. The North Vietnamese would be on alert and waiting. The aircraft commanders clashed vocally with their superiors, to no effect.

The order stood.

One of Major Case's loadmasters was Airman First Class Elroy E. Harworth, a twenty-four-year-old Minnesotan with nearly six years' service. He had a baby boy and a pregnant wife and confided to his wife in a letter that he and the other crewmen felt that they were going to die in Vietnam.[10]

In the daylight hours remaining, Carolina Moon planners revised the mission profile. Time over target was pushed back half an hour, and ingress-egress routes were altered to avoid repeating the first mission's route. The main difference was Major Tom Case's decision to take one of Remers' navigators. First Lieutenant Rocky Edmondson's experience from the previous night offered an advantage that Case wanted to tap.

The second Hercules, Radium One, tucked its wheels into the wells at 1:10 A.M. on May 31. Due to strict radio silence, no Americans followed the progress of the mission.

The Hercules was expected to return to DaNang around 3:45 A.M., but as dawn broke, hope ebbed. Case's aircraft had disappeared without a word. The diversionary fighter crews reported flak near the bridge followed by a large explosion on the ground about two minutes before the scheduled attack time.

Perhaps twenty aircraft, including Remers', searched for the missing Herc through most of the day but found nothing. Major Tom Case, a thirty-four-year-old Georgian, had vanished with his seven-man crew—copilot First Lieutenant Harold J. Zook, EWO Captain Emmett R. McDonald, navigators Rocky Edmonson and First Lieutenant Armon D. Shingledecker, flight engineer Staff Sergeant Bobby

J. Alberton, and loadmasters Airmen First Class Harworth and Philip J. Stickney.[11]

Again, aerial reconnaissance showed no damage to the bridge. Later search-and-rescue aircraft spotted an empty life raft and some wreckage, probably not from Radium One.

Subsequent aerial photography revealed a cable strung across the Song Ma about fifteen hundred yards upstream. Analysts theorized that the barrier might have blocked some of the mines laid in the river.

Postwar searchers found that the C-130 crashed in virgin jungle well west of Thanh Hoa. According to the North Vietnamese, it had been solidly hit by 228th Regiment gunners near Tho Xuan's (also called Bai Thuong) "Yellow Star" airfield about twenty-five miles upstream and exploded in midair. This account is doubtful. A more likely scenario is that after the Herc was severely damaged by flak over the river, Tom Case turned toward Laos and climbed so the crew could bail out there if necessary. It may or may not have been hit again by flak. In any event, Radium One didn't make it out of North Vietnam. The remains of three crewmen were returned in 1986 and two others in 1998.[12]

At an unspecified date long after the attack, US intelligence officers interrogated a North Vietnamese sailor from a sunken PT boat. He said that four mines from the second attack hit the bridge but caused no lasting damage.[13]

Some official and quasi-official sources state that one of two diversionary Phantoms was lost while supporting the second Carolina Moon mission. The missing F-4C crew from the Eighth Tactical Fighter Wing included Major Dayton Ragland, a Korean War POW who had packed his bags, expecting to rotate home the following day. He was providing a combat checkout for the front-seater, First Lieutenant Ned Herrold, new in theater.

However, neither the timing nor the location of the Phantom loss seems to fit the C-130 mission profile. An official source lists the Phantom down nearly three hours before the Herc, some thirty miles south of the target area. Moreover, an unofficial source says the F-4 took off six hours before the bridge attack.[14]

Major Remers' crew was debriefed at Pacific Air Forces Headquarters in Hawaii, where General Hunter Harris Jr. reigned. An experienced bomber pilot, Harris was reportedly vocal in his displeasure with the decision to launch the second Carolina Moon mission so soon after the first. His ire was certainly justified: if similar conditions of clear sky and moonlight were necessary, the next week was still available. And another weather delay would impose no serious problems. After all, thirteen months had passed since the first F-105 missions against the Dragon's Jaw, and the bridge wasn't going anywhere.[15]

One hopes that General Harris sacked some officers in DaNang, but the historical record is silent. Even if he did, nothing could bring Major Case and his crew back from the dead.

★

Of course, the North Vietnamese propaganda minions rewrote the Carolina Moon story to emphasize the patriotism of the Dragon's Jaw defenders. Here is a 2013 account from the People's Army Publishing House lauding the First Battery of the 231st Anti-Aircraft Artillery Regiment:

> With a burst of twenty-one 57mm rounds the soldiers of the First Battery shot down this aircraft when it snuck in under the cover of night . . . ' Battery Commander Nguyen Quoc Duyet told us (the editors):
>
> "Recently during a night battle, all of us officers and enlisted men, saw with our own eyes civilian residents of Thanh Hoa City who had been killed and wounded by American bombs because we had failed to fire accurately and had not shot down any American aircraft."
>
> The battery had fired on suspected American aircraft flying night missions, but other than perhaps deterring some pilots, the efforts were futile. Barrage fire along the enemy's expected flight path was literally a hit or miss proposition—far favoring the latter over the former.

> We determined that in order to be able to shoot down enemy aircraft at night, in addition to maintaining a high state of vigilance, coordinating together well, and making good preparations for battle, we also would have to be able to spot the enemy at long range and to aim our guns extremely accurately.
>
> On the night: "Recognizing the shape of a bandit aircraft, Do Van Sot, the commander of Gun Crew Three, shouted, 'It's not one of our aircraft!' Following the plan exactly, when the aircraft was at the proper range Sot waved his flag* to give his gun the order to fire.
>
> "The rounds fired by Sot's crew and the rest of the First Battery struck the iron crow, hitting it in its heart. Bright red flames trailed from the aircraft's fuselage. It shuddered as it tried to keep flying, but then this massive chunk of steel slammed into a hillside planted with yams. There was a tremendous explosion, followed by many more. The flames continued to burn throughout the rest of the night."[16]

Another version of the C-130 shootdown was also published in a North Vietnamese news website in 2013:

> An observation post heard five "large and unusual sounding explosions." A large object was seen at river's edge two hundred meters from the bridge, apparently snagged on something.
>
> Engineers began disassembling the mine at 1300 on 30 May, and disarmed it by 1700. The other five [*sic*] had been detonated "by their internal self-destruct mechanisms."
>
> All mines were flung from aircraft upon crash. Two self-detonated two hours later. One was hurled a long way from the crash site and was damaged. The other three remained intact. By June 4 engineers had defused and recovered four intact mines.[17]

For whatever reason, the Vietnamese believed that each attack involved six mines when actually the C-130s each carried five.

---

*One wonders how the gunners saw Sot waving his flag.

★

In the summer of 1966 America's adventure in the Vietnam War had six and a half more years to go. On June 29, 1966, the secretary of defense held a press conference and announced that Navy and Air Force bombers had inflicted heavy damage on three of North Vietnam's petroleum facilities and that an F-105 had been lost during the attacks. What McNamara didn't say was that the Johnson administration had dithered over this decision to attack the petroleum, oil, and lubricants (POL) targets for over a year, and the Communists in Hanoi had used the time well. They had dug underground storage tanks, laid pipelines, and done everything in their power to ensure that when the bomb storm came it would do minimum damage to their ability to fuel trucks making the run down the Ho Chi Minh Trail to the Cambodian and Laotian sanctuaries. By wringing their hands and waiting, the Johnson administration had ensured that when it did give the green light to attack these targets, the results would be militarily and politically indecisive.

In early August McNamara told Congress that his arbitrary date for the end of hostilities in Southeast Asia was June 30, 1967, a mere ten months away.

Having made that bald prediction, he now backpedaled, adding, "At the moment I would not recommend a supplemental [appropriation], although I think some time during 1967 is very likely. The reason I would not recommend it today . . . is that there are still many uncertainties not only as to the duration of the conflict, but also with respect to the level of operations that need to be financed."[18] Apparently the secretary of defense's crystal ball, just so clear a moment ago, had clouded up quickly. The truth was that he was lying to Congress.

★

For the rest of 1966 carrier aviators launched eleven missions against the Dragon's Jaw, including one with twenty-two bombers on September 23 that dropped fifty-seven tons of bombs. The strike destroyed an

The interior of the first Dragon's Jaw bridge at Thanh Hoa. This elegant structure designed and built by the French, was completed in 1904, and in 1945 was destroyed by the Viet Minh, the Vietnamese resistance. The second bridge, completed by the North Vietnamese in 1964, was designed to carry more traffic and was of much stronger construction. (*Author's collection*)

The Dragon's Jaw in 1968, the second bridge at Thanh Hoa. Notice the bridge has a central pillar and is of steel truss construction. (*Author's collection*)

USS *Ranger* (CVA-61) preparing to launch a sleek RA-5C Vigilante and an EKA-3B Skywarrior tanker during 1965 operations. (*Tailhook Association*)

A longstanding member of "The Tonkin Gulf Yacht Club" was USS *Oriskany* (CVA-34), which logged eight Vietnam deployments between 1965 and 1973. Her air wing commander, James B. Stockdale, was shot down on an aborted bridge strike in 1965. (*National Museum of Naval Aviation*)

An F-105D of the Thailand-based 355th Tactical Fighter Wing with full loadout of 750-pound M117 general purpose bombs, often employed against Thanh Hoa Bridge.

Probably more F-105 Thunderchiefs flew against the bridge than any other American aircraft. This cockpit view shows the "Thud's" instrument panel with radar warning receiver mounted upper right. (*National Museum of the Air Force*)

Thunderchiefs from Takhli, Thailand, headed "up north" in 1966, refueling from a KC-135 tanker. F-105s flew all the initial attacks against Thanh Hoa Bridge in 1965. (*National Museum of the Air Force*)

Colonel Robinson Risner after his return from more than seven years of captivity in North Vietnam. He led the first two missions against Thanh Hoa Bridge and was shot down five months later. (*Richard P. Hallion*)

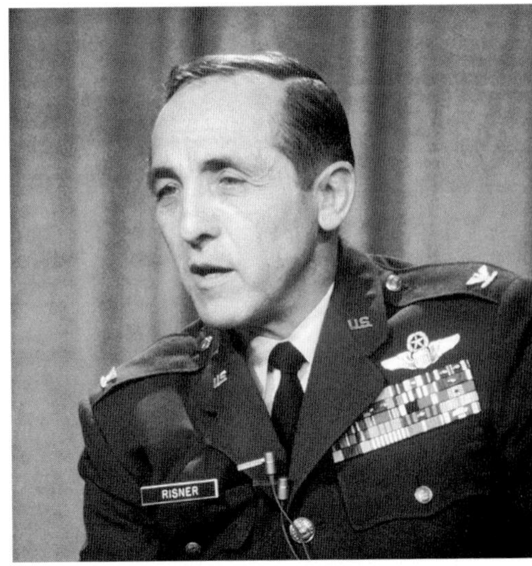

The Navy's first MiG kills were scored on a USS *Midway* (CVA-41) strike against the bridge in June 1965. *Left to right:* Lt. J. E. D. Batson, VF-21 executive officer Cdr. Lou Page, RIOs Lt. Cdr. R. B. Doremus, and Lt. J. C. Smith. (*Tailhook Association*)

North Vietnam's first generation of fighter pilots learned to fly the Korean War vintage MiG-15, here with underwing drop tanks to extend the range. (*Istvan Toperczer*)

On April 4 1965, North Vietnamese MiG-17s shot down two USAF F-105 Thunderchiefs. One of the victors was Lt. Tran Hanh, here receiving accolades of his comrades in a staged propaganda photo. (*Istvan Toperczer*)

The first North Vietnamese pilots to engage American aircraft were Tran Hanh and Pham Ngoc Lan, who encountered US Navy F-8 Crusaders on April 3, 1965.

A pilot's view of the bridge showing the geographic features on each bank and the surrounding terrain that allowed Vietnamese gunners clear shots at US aircraft.

The Dragon's Jaw under heavy attack, demonstrating why accurate bombing was difficult for trailing pilots after the initial hits obscured the target in smoke. Note the flak bursts in the air.

The Thanh Hoa Bridge on April 26, 1967, is very much intact. Photo taken by an RA-5C Vigilante from RVAH-13 aboard USS *Kitty Hawk*, CVA-63.

Lt. Cdr. Sam Sayers in the cockpit of an A-6 Intruder, about 1967. Sam flew 11 missions against the bridge, which the authors believe was the most by any airman. Shot down once near Vinh and fished from the sea by an Air Force rescue amphibian, Sayers was a highly competent professional aviator and a graduate of the Navy's Test Pilot school, retiring eventually as a captain after thirty years of service. (*Courtesy Mary Sayers*)

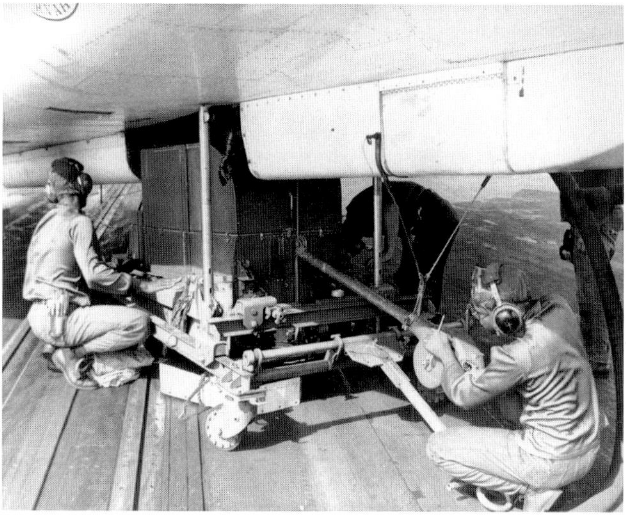

The US repeatedly flew reconnaissance flights over the bridge, monitoring damage and repairs. Here Navy crewmen load cameras into an RA-5C Vigilante for another sortie. (*National Museum of Naval Aviation*)

The most effective American all-weather attack aircraft was Grumman's Intruder, often flying solo sorties against the bridge. These A-6As of Attack Squadron 196 flew from USS *Constellation* (CVA-64) in 1968. (*National Museum of Naval Aviation*)

This reconnaissance photo was taken by an RA-5C Vigilante on January 19, 1968, just before the massive Air Force and Navy assaults of late January, which, like all the others at that stage of the war, failed to drop the bridge. Note the wealth of detail derived from study of the photo, especially using magnifying lenses. Note also the extensive work the North Vietnamese have done to get truck and rail traffic around the bomb craters and across the damaged bridge. Clearly visible in the upper left is a pontoon bridge for truck traffic.

This photo, taken on the same flight as the photo above, shows the southern approaches to the bridge. Railcars are clearly labeled sitting on spur lines. The presence of all these railcars was one reason the heavy attacks of late January 1968 were approved and flown. Also of note are the myriad of bomb craters after two and a half years of aerial assault. Fifty years later, far better imagery is provided by satellites.

Carrier Air Wing 15 flew from USS *Coral Sea* (CVA-41) for most of the Vietnam War. Here an Alpha strike smothers the eastern span in a pre-1969 mission.

North Vietnamese militia survey the remains of an F-105 shot down in May 1968. More Thunderchiefs were downed attacking the bridge than any other aircraft.

An SA-2 Guideline two-stage surface-to-air missile on its launcher. The radar-guided SAM posed a serious threat to American aircraft over North Vietnam but scored few kills against planes attacking Thanh Hoa Bridge. (*Istvan Toperczer*)

Vietnamese soldiers examine an engine from the Lockheed C-130 Hercules that was downed while dropping mines in the Ma River on May 30, 1966. (*Troy Haworth*)

Probably the smallest-caliber defensive weapon deployed around Thanh Hoa was the Russian-built 12.7mm (.50 caliber) "Dishika," here posed with female crew for propaganda purposes. (*Istvan Toperczer*)

The single-barrel 14.5mm ZPU-1 had a low hit probability against jet aircraft, so it was usually deployed in multiples. (*Istvan Toperczer*)

North Vietnam's 37mm antiaircraft gun was the Soviet-designed S61, dating from 1939. One of the eight crew members stands by with a five-round clip for a fast reload. (*Istvan Toperczer*)

North Vietnam's premier Ho Chi Minh visiting a 57mm antiaircraft site, accompanied by a media chorus. (*Istvan Toperczer*)

The Pave Knife laser-designating pod that US Air Force F-4 Phantoms used to guide precision weapons onto the bridge in 1972. (*National Museum of the Air Force*)

In this Pima Air and Space Museum exhibit, a Paveway laser guidance unit is screwed onto a dummy Mark 84 2,000-pound bomb positioned on a loading cart, ready to go under an airplane.

This photo, taken in August 1972, is literally a snapshot of the campaign, after the crippling Air Force strike in May but before the Navy toppled the bridge in October. Many of the bomb craters on both approaches probably are residuals from US efforts to suppress nearby antiaircraft guns.

Reconnaissance flights kept track of the bridge's status after the Air Force strike that displaced the western span in May 1972. This shot was snapped by a USS *Hancock* (CVA-19) RF-8G Crusader on September 8. Note the water-filled bomb craters on both sides of the river. (*USN*)

The ultimate dragon slayers: pilots of Attack Squadron 82, whose combination of "dumb" and "smart" bombs did the deed in October 1972. Left to right: Lt(jg) Jim Brister and Lt(jg) Marvin Baldwin, squadron Cdr. Don Sumner, and operations officer Lt. Cdr. Leighton "Snuffy" Smith. (*Admiral Leighton Smith*)

Intended to replace the Douglas A-4, Vought's A-7 Corsair II did not quite succeed in displacing the Skyhawk during the war, but provided excellent bombing accuracy and greater performance. This A-7C belonged to Attack Squadron 82, which dropped the Thanh Hoa Bridge.

Dragon in the river. A Vigilante recon plane brought dramatic proof of USS *America's* (CVA-66) successful strike in October 1972. (*Adm. Leighton Smith*)

A Vietnamese repair crew rigging lines to raise the collapsed portion of the bridge. The work was not accomplished until after the 1973 cease-fire. (*Doan Cong Tinh*)

The rebuilt Dragon's Jaw Bridge at Thanh Hoa as it exists at this writing, 2019. Once again it is an important transportation asset for Vietnam. (*Theo van Geffen*)

estimated eighty railcars and more than sixteen hundred tons of fuel. Although the bridge was temporarily impassible, as always the damage was quickly repaired.[19]

Some senior officers realized that the fuel and ordnance expended on Thanh Hoa missions and the losses incurred were wasted effort. One was Rear Admiral David C. Richardson, who commanded Task Force 77 in 1966–1967. As such, he was responsible for conducting offensive operations over North Vietnam and other parts of Indochina. Like his predecessors, he was well aware of the Thanh Hoa Bridge's reputation.

Richardson recalled, "The Chief of Naval Operations, Admiral David MacDonald, had changed my orders twice to make me CTF-77. Something prompted that, so I went to see him to find out why. What he told me was, 'Take care of the lads.' Only recently did I learn of the chewing out he and the other chiefs had to endure from Lyndon Johnson that prompted that dictum to me. But after a month in theater and the political lies and nonsense I was then witness to, I fully understood."

Despite the tense political atmosphere, Richardson proved an innovator. A Guadalcanal fighter pilot from 1942, he possessed a rare combination of fleet, aviation, and intelligence experience. That background led him to approach Seventh Fleet challenges head-on.

"In about November 1966 Captain Jig Ramage, my chief of staff, and I took the Thanh Hoa Bridge off the target list, thus forbidding further targeting of that bridge. We did it despite our belief that if the bridge fell, South Vietnam would drift away from the NVN, as we professed to believe that only that bridge kept the north and south physically connected.

"However, Captain Bill Houser, my flag captain of *Constellation* (and the finest skipper I have ever served with and one of the three finest men I have ever known), pleaded with us to allow one more attack. We relented."[20]

A night Intruder mission was approved, but just before launch the go A-6 was scrubbed for system failure. The on-deck spare was manned by Lieutenant (Junior Grade) Ronald J. "Zap" Zlatoper, the junior pilot in VA-65. When the go bird went down on deck, Zlatoper was taxied to the catapult and fired off into the night. At the age of twenty-three he had been among the first five "nugget" aviators to fly Intruders without previous fleet experience. He would have an enviable naval career and, as a four-star admiral, would command the Pacific Fleet. But all that was in the future.

Zap recalled, "Teamed with then Lieutenant (Junior Grade) Dick Schram as my BN, we probably flew a half-dozen strikes against the Thanh Hoa Bridge during our 1966 deployment on the *Connie*.

> I best remember the night when we went from a two-point strike to a Navy Cross and back to a two-point strike in an hour or so. We launched on the night strike against the bridge with five Mark 84 two-thousand-pound bombs. Dick had a good, solid radar lock-on, and we made a good level bomb run, breaking away with fairly heavy flak and escaping back to sea.
>
> After a night carrier landing we debriefed and then went to our stateroom for a libation. Fifteen minutes later the intelligence officer called and asked us to come to IOIC [the Integrated Operations Intelligence Center]. An RA-5C Vigilante had made a side-looking radar run on the bridge ten minutes after our strike, and the picture they brought back showed the bridge was down!
>
> My commanding officer, Bob Mandeville, said, "Zap, that'll be a Distinguished Flying Cross."
>
> Then CAG, Commander J. D. Ward, came in and thought it looked like the bridge was down. He said, "Zap, that'll be a Silver Star." Everyone in IOIC was getting very excited and screaming Navy Cross!
>
> And then the carrier commanding officer, Captain Bill Houser, came in and said, "That looks like a shadow to me." Suddenly everyone agreed with him, and we had two points toward the twenty-point strike-flight Air Medal.
>
> By my rough calculations I personally dropped about sixty thousand pounds of ordnance on that bridge, to no effect.[21]

Admiral Richardson provided perspective: "Bill Houser joyously presented us with the poststrike photos showing the north side of the bridge down. Jig Ramage and I both asserted that the photo showed only a shadow over that end of the bridge that made it look that way. Sure enough, photos taken under morning light showed the bridge still stood."[22]

The Dragon was still standing—as the war was about to enter a new phase.

CHAPTER 12

THE THANH WHORE BRIDGE

Raw numbers of the escalating war told the story of airmen trying to achieve Johnson's military goal: "Don't lose." In 1965 the Air Force launched some 26,000 sorties into North Vietnam, including 11,600 fighter-bombers. In 1967 the total quadrupled to over 100,000 sorties, with almost 55,000 by fighter-bombers. The Navy contributed to the American effort; carrier aircraft pounded North Vietnam around the clock.

Lyndon B. Johnson kept agreeing to bombing halts, usually advocated by Robert McNamara. He had ordered two in 1965, the second one extending until the end of January 1966. In 1967 he was ready to try it again. This time the halt would be in February, coinciding with Tet, Vietnam's lunar New Year. Washington hoped that Hanoi might be willing to negotiate over their holiday since they had ignored the Christian one. Instead, the ever-pragmatic North Vietnamese enjoyed a bomb-free six days to move war materiel to South Vietnam, an amount that one source estimated at twenty-five thousand tons, which is undoubtedly an overestimate. Regardless of the exact amount, a lot of it went south under empty skies. South Vietnam and America's worst enemy wasn't in Hanoi: he resided in the White House and was advised by Robert McNamara, the self-anointed house expert on the application of military power for political purposes.

A week after the Tet ceasefire, on February 20, two *Enterprise* A-4 Skyhawks launched an impromptu assault on the Dragon's Jaw with visually guided ordnance. Lieutenant Commander (later Rear Admiral) Jeremy "Bear" Taylor and Lieutenant (Junior Grade) Jay Greene were diverted from bridge targets in the Vinh area to cover a downed *Enterprise* Phantom about eight miles south of Thanh Hoa.

By the time the two VA-113 Stingers arrived, the ResCAP (Rescue Combat Air Patrol) had been canceled. Later Air Wing Nine aboard *Enterprise* learned that the F-4 pilot had been killed and the RIO captured.

As Taylor recalled,

> So there I was at fifteen thousand feet with Jay, no mission, no target, with four Bullpup missiles and not much gas (we were flying A-4Cs with a heavy load) and not much time since the sun had set as we approached the area. We were at roll-in distance to a North Vietnamese bridge of high and strategic value to Ho Chi Minh, one with a magnetic attraction for every Navy bridge destruction specialist of brave heart and fighting spirit and his equally valiant, highly qualified wingie.
>
> We attacked the Dragon's Jaw in the tradition of Wade McClusky at Midway. Two guys, four runs amid a really impressive, but fruitless, exhibition by the vaunted 37-, 57-, 85-millimeter air defenses of Thanh Hoa.
>
> I got two hits on the bridge, one dead center on the center pillar of concrete, and one on the northeast approach at the end of the bridge ("into the mouth of the dragon," as I explained it to the ensign intel officer back on the big gray boat). Jay got one hit that barely missed the bridge but clobbered the southwest approach.
>
> There was no chance for a fourth missile on target because I waved Jay off due to the increasingly intense and accurate fire of the frustrated NVN gunners that I duly noted (i.e., indelibly imprinted forever) on the pullout from my second run at three thousand feet.

Nevertheless, Jay rolled in, fired, and tracked the missile, but wisely broke off his second run at five thousand feet to let the missile fly itself a little short of the bridge. Who knows where that one went? We hightailed it to feet wet, calling "Winchester" (out of ammo). Duty done. Feeling great . . . adrenaline flowing. What a high!!! . . . NOTHING LIKE IT!

We were out of there. . . . Back to the ship in dwindling twilight for a "pinkie" landing. Two OK-3s from the LSO.

Glory gained? Nope. It was scored two points toward our next strike/flight air medal. My skipper put me in hack and announced in the Stinger ready room that the unsupported attack that had failed to drop the bridge was a "vainglorious exhibition of stupidity." So you say, Skipper. But for Jay and me, we wouldn't trade the experience for anything.

And no PTSD either.[1]

★

In March 1967 the *Bon Homme Richard* joined four other carriers in the Western Pacific: her *Essex*-class sisters *Ticonderoga* and *Hancock*, plus the nuclear-powered *Enterprise* and the upgraded *Forrestal*-class *Kitty Hawk*. They maintained Task Force 77 strength at the desired five flight decks, serving both Yankee Station off North Vietnam and Dixie Station off South Vietnam.

The failure of the Tet bombing pause forced Lyndon Johnson and his inner circle to face the fact that unless they escalated the war, there was no way to force the Communists in Hanoi to the bargaining table. They decided to put North Vietnam's electrical power–generating facilities on the targeting lists.

Skeptics in uniform noted that North Vietnam had essentially an agrarian economy, with only a miniscule industrial base that used electricity. Nevertheless, the power plants had to go . . . for political reasons.

As it happened, Thanh Hoa had one located between the bridge and the city on the south side of the river. Close to the coast, it was one of the first power plants targeted. The *Bonnie Dick* put up an Alpha composed of six A-4 bombers from VA-212. VA-76 and the two fighter squadrons, VF-211 and VF-24, would provide flak suppressors, and VA-212 and VA-76 would provide two aircraft from each squadron for Iron Hand duty. The fighter squadrons provided two sections for combat air patrol (CAP). One KA-3 tanker would be over the ship, and the A-4 squadrons would have a tanker each airborne. This was a typical Alpha from an *Essex*-class carrier.

Stephen R. Gray, in his terrific memoir *Rampant Raider,* tells us how it was. At the time he was the junior pilot in VA-212. He was the strike leader's wingman. It was his first Alpha strike:

> The launch went smoothly, with Commander Marvin Quaid (the XO of VA-212) leading the Alpha strike formation on a large circle above the ship until everyone had joined. I was excited to be part of this great armada. We held the air wing formation for about fifteen minutes, until it was time for the various components to break off and start their runs. Elements continued to split off until our six bombers were alone. We could see the mouth of the Song Ma on the coast as Commander Quaid dropped us low for our pop-up to the bombing roll-in.
>
> We crossed the coast at thirty-five hundred feet over the river mouth and began jinking in formation. Quaid called, "Eagles, arm switches," as we crossed the coast, and I flipped the master arm and station switches on. So far, so good, I thought as we reached the pop-up point without seeing any flak. I watched Quaid's airplane turn belly-up as he began his run. As I continued to wheel and climb to reach my own roll-in point, I was alone for a few seconds with an eagle's-eye view of the target area. Flashes of exploding weapons dotted the ground as the flak suppressors completed their runs, and smoke was rising from distant fires as I pulled the nose down and shifted my scan to the gun sight.
>
> Picking up the outline of the power plant main building, I noted that the rising smoke indicated nearly calm wind, so no wind correction would be necessary. I put the pipper on the south half of

the building and scanned the instruments for bomb release altitude, thirty-degree dive angle, and 450 knots air speed. At four thousand feet I punched the bomb pickle switch three times and felt the little plane buck and jump as the bombs came off the wings. As I pulled out of the dive, the rising Gs started the familiar restriction of vision as gravity pulled the blood supply away from my head. I had about a fourth of my normal field of view left as blackness surrounded by peripheral vision. I moved my head to keep the XO's airplane in my remaining field of view. My vision cleared immediately when I relaxed the G forces and pulled inside the XO's turn to join on him. I looked back at the target and saw that the power plant building was completely obscured by smoke and the last section's bombs were exploding in the transformer field. A few black puffs of flak burst to our right but were too far away to pose a hazard. I joined the XO's airplane and slid under him for the look-over. He was clean. He passed me the lead and gave me the look-over. I was elated! Either we had caught the North Viets napping or the flak suppressors had been really effective, because the few puffs of flak had been the only visible signs of resistance.

The recovery went smoothly, and I flew a good pass to a 3-wire. When we all assembled in the ready room we were ricocheting off the walls. Our adrenaline levels were still very high, and we were all regaling one another with details of our flights. The air wing flight surgeon entered the ready room with a tray of "lollypops," little brandy bottles the size of airline liquor bottles to be passed out to the strike pilots to help settle us down. This exercise and our elation would become a quaint memory later on when we were flying three Alpha strikes a day.

A VFP-63 RF-8 photo pilot had made a supersonic run over the target about five minutes after the strike group retired. His photos showed the main power plant building to be cratered rubble, completely destroyed. One of the steam boilers had been blasted several yards outside the confines of the power plant yard, and huge craters pocked the transformer field. It would be a long time before Thanh Hoa had any electricity.[2]

★

The Navy was also taking another step in the precision weapons revolution. Walleye (originally designated AGM-62, later Guided Weapon Mark 1) was a revolutionary television-guided weapon, often mislabeled a missile when in fact it was unpowered. The TV guidance made it an extremely accurate glide bomb, and its shaped-charge, explosive-mixture warhead provided extra punch. The warhead had the explosive power of 825 pounds of TNT.[3] The weapon had a glass nose for the camera to look through—hence the name Walleye.

Television guidance had originated in World War II, most notably in war-weary four-engine bombers of little future use. The highly classified program was called Project Aphrodite. A pilot and engineer took off in the bomber, armed the heavy explosive load in flight, then bailed out. A guidance aircraft then steered the flying bomb to its destination, keeping the target in the TV screen until impact. But at the time television technology was in its infancy, and arming the bomb load in flight was downright dangerous. President John F. Kennedy's older brother Joe died on an Aphrodite mission in 1944 when the plane blew up before the crew could bail out.

Twenty years later, however, Martin Marietta had perfected television for ordnance delivery. Within range of the target—as much as sixteen miles—the pilot used his cockpit TV screen to designate an impact point, actually looking through the camera in the nose cone of the weapon. Unlike other 1960s ordnance such as Bullpup, Walleye was a "fire and forget" weapon that allowed the pilot to take evasive action and leave the area immediately after launch.

The honor of introducing Walleye to combat fell to VA-212 under Commander Homer L. Smith, a forty-year-old West Virginian from the Annapolis class of 1949 who had already flown over 150 combat missions. The Rampant Raiders, named for their lion emblem, received the weapons in late 1966 during predeployment training. Their A-4E Skyhawks were modified to accept the compatible TV system, and they embarked in USS *Bon Homme Richard* for their third combat cruise.[4]

The Raiders wasted no time once on Yankee Station. With clearing weather—a requirement for optically guided weapons—a few days after the Thanh Hoa power plant strike, on March 11, 1967, Homer Smith's VA-212 conducted the first Walleye attack, hitting the Sam Son army barracks located almost on the coast nine miles southeast of Thanh Hoa. The 1,100-pound glide bombs performed according to the owner's manual and hit their designated aim points. The 850-pound warheads exploding inside buildings proved devastating.

Smith was absolutely determined to drop the Dragon's Jaw, not only for tactical and strategic purposes but also because, in the words of one of his pilots, the air wing that slew the Dragon would become famous.[5]

Homer Smith was smart, astute, and motivated. He held an engineering degree from Annapolis and approached the Thanh Hoa Bridge with a clinician's eye and a tactician's brain. He even made a model of the structure based on recon photos. He concluded that if three Walleyes struck specific support girders simultaneously, the bridge would collapse of its own weight. He convinced his CAG, Commander Jack Monger, who approved an all-out effort.

Mission planning was meticulous. In addition to Smith's studies, the briefing included specific points in the structure selected by Army demolition experts as the best prospects for inflicting telling damage to the bridge. The planners even accounted for the optimum sun angle to provide the best contrast for the TV guidance systems in the Walleyes. The optimum time over target was calculated to be 2:12 P.M.[6]

On March 12, the day after the Sam Son mission, *Bonnie Dick* launched an Alpha strike of some thirty aircraft against Thanh Hoa, all supporting Smith and his wingmen against the Dragon's Jaw.

Smith and his Number Two almost got a free ride down the chute, attacking before the defenders could react effectively. But Number Three came under heavy fire: while concentrating on smooth, steady flying in his five-hundred-knot dive, his peripheral vision recorded what seemed to be hundreds of muzzle flashes around the bridge. Still, all three Skyhawks successfully launched their Walleyes, and each pilot pulled and jinked mightily to get out of the target area without being hit.

One of the A-4 pilots on the mission was Stephen Gray, flying as a flak suppressor. Diving ahead of the bombers, his target was a 37-millimeter site southwest of the main span. Today he was carrying new weapons, six cluster bomb units (CBUs). Designed specifically as antipersonnel weapons, each bomb, or canister, contained around 250 hand-grenade-sized aluminum bomblets, each completely covered with steel pellets surrounding an explosive core. The bomblets had a ridge on them that forced them to rotate when the CBU canister broke up in midair at about a thousand feet above the ground. The rotation armed the bomblets, which would explode on impact. They proved devastating on flak sites, shredding human bodies and damaging guns so badly that they couldn't be fired.

Here again is Stephen Gray:

> The flak suppressors broke away from the Walleye group and began our run-in to the pop-up point. We were at 3,500 feet, and I could see the outline of the Thanh Whore Bridge up ahead as we crossed the coast and armed our switches. Heart pounding and mouth dry, I could see the bridge clearly as we arced up and over to the bombing altitude. The lead pilot split off to begin his attack on his flak site, and I frantically scanned the area south of the bridge for my target. There! There it is, I thought as the first muzzle flashes from the guns outlined the site. The target was directly ahead of me at twelve o'clock, so I had to execute a roll-ahead maneuver, rolling upside down with the nose high and pulling the nose down until the target touched the top of the canopy bow, then rolling upright and finding the target in the gun sight.
>
> The site was winking with muzzle flashes as the guns poured out rapid fire. The flak gunners could figure out an attacker's intent

just as soon as the airplane's nose aimed at them in the dive. At that point it became a them-or-you situation, and they would shift their fire to concentrate on the incoming plane. The easiest moving target to shoot at is a no-deflection shot. All the gunners had to do is aim straight at the diving plane.

The flashes seemed to grow and merged into one continuous flicker as I got closer. White streaks of tracer flashed through the gun sight, and I could hear a staccato *pop, pop, pop* even through my helmet as the supersonic shock wave from near-misses struck the canopy. On reaching release altitude I punched the bomb pickle and felt the plane jump as the bombs came off the wings. I jammed the stick back and rolled hard left as soon as the nose came above the horizon, then hard right for a few seconds, then hard left again to try to destroy their tracking. Rolling left, I looked back to see my hits. I had missed seeing the bomblets explode, but little puffs of smoke and dust dotted the flak site, and the guns were silent. I never saw a flak site keep shooting after a CBU attack.

I was streaking toward the safety of the Gulf to rejoin the other flak suppressors when an ear-piercing, drawn-out, gurgling scream lanced through my headset. Jesus! I thought. Somebody caught one in the throat and is dying over the air. So chilling was the sound I almost pissed my pants. The memory of the scream and the certainty that someone had died lasted until the debriefing when the screamer was revealed to be none other than the skipper, Commander Smith, venting his rage and frustration at the Thanh Whore Bridge.[7]

The Rampant Raiders had put all three of their Walleyes on precisely the girders that Homer Smith had designated. Despite the unprecedented accuracy of the glide bombs, photo interpreters reported that the bridge appeared "undamaged and serviceable."[8]

Commander Homer Smith continued leading the Rampant Raiders for the next two months. Although scheduled to assume command of an East Coast air wing, he wanted to complete two hundred combat missions. On May 20, flying his 197th sortie, he was shot down near

Haiphong and disappeared into the North Vietnamese prison system. He died in captivity; some POWs suspected he had been tortured to death, perhaps for knowledge of the new Walleye precision weapon. His remains were returned without explanation in 1974.[9]

Steve Gray recalled,

> Air Wing 21 had a number of 2,000-pound bombs, the largest bomb an A-4 could carry, and we were saving them for an all-out effort to drop the Thanh Whore's bridge once and forever. It was to be the last combat sortie of the '67 deployment.
>
> We had an earlier strike on the Phy Li bridge complex on which I was one of the bombers. I was disappointed not to be selected for the Thanh Hoa strike, but the skipper selected his best bombers, and the other junior pilot, Terry Reider, edged me out. Terry was probably a better bomber than I was. We were all in the ready room cheering the guys on the strike, everyone giddy with relief and excitement that this very hard and costly cruise was ending. It was July 29, 1967. Just as the pilots got the command to man airplanes, we got the word that USS *Forrestal* was on fire, the strike was canceled, and we spent the rest of the day alongside *Forrestal* taking off her wounded and helping with damage control.[10]

Forrestal sustained one of the three catastrophic fires aboard carriers during the Vietnam War. First had been *Oriskany*, a victim of mishandled flares in October 1966, with 44 dead and 156 men injured; then *Forrestal* in July 1967, with rockets accidentally launched on the flight deck, killing 134 men and wounding 161, and the third incident was aboard *Enterprise* off Hawaii in January 1969, when a Zuni warhead cooked off and started a conflagration that killed 28 men and injured 314.

The combination of live ordnance, hot jet and huffer exhaust, confined space, and jet fuel was a witches' brew that needed the most careful handling. During the *Enterprise* fire at least fourteen major explosions hammered the ship. On all three carriers aggressive, competent fire-fighting efforts saved countless lives and quenched the flames. Nothing speaks more profoundly about the valor and courage of American sailors than the conduct of these crews in these horrific emergencies fighting to save their shipmates . . . and their ship.

★

Between January and March 1967 the Dragon's Jaw was attacked at least twenty-four times by the Navy and six times by the Air Force, without significant result. Nevertheless, Walleyes killed other bridges and soft targets with astonishing regularity. In a seven-month period Navy pilots claimed sixty-five hits by sixty-eight bombs—a 95 percent success ratio. Other operations in less optimal conditions dropped the direct hit figure to about 70 percent—still extremely impressive considering the North Vietnamese defenses and the atrocious weather.[11]

After mastering the twin challenges of reliability and accuracy, the missing ingredient was a knock-out punch. Consequently, there were no more glide-bomb attacks against the Dragon's Jaw until 1972, when a punch would finally become available.[12]

CHAPTER 13

THE BRIDGE CLAIMS ANOTHER VICTIM

In the United States that summer of 1967 Lyndon Johnson was watching his popularity and political position erode as the American public became more and more disaffected by Vietnam. Johnson tried to continue his policy of waging war to a stalemate and still looking like a peacemaker. On August 24 he ordered a twelve-day pause in bombing around Hanoi; he had already ordered a one-day pause earlier on Buddha's birthday in the spring.

Speaking in Texas on August 29, Johnson amended his previous approach—linking a bombing halt to "an indication" that Hanoi would reduce its actions in the South. Now he said the bombing could stop "when this would lead promptly to productive discussions." He added that Washington "would operate on the assumption that Hanoi would not take advantage of a halt to increase infiltration [of South Vietnam]."[1]

Johnson was an atrocious poker player. He held two deuces, an ace, a trey, and a lousy four, with nothing to add to the pot, and he had no credible bluff.

Ho Chi Minh read Lyndon Johnson like a book he had written himself. All he had to do was wait until the inept Texas gambler inevitably folded.

★

The Air Force continued to target the Dragon's Jaw. Their attacks were always bigger than Navy strikes and involved many more airplanes. The base element was usually four flights of four F-105s: twelve planes with iron bombs and four with CBUs to suppress defenses.

Supporting the strikers were two flights of Wild Weasels, four in a flight. The first pairs in each flight were two-seaters with electronics to detect enemy radar, and two were single-seaters with Shrikes to shoot and CBUs to drop.

Rounding out the thirty-two plane gaggles were two flights of Phantoms, eight planes, on MiG CAP.

The Thuds took off at ten-second intervals from their bases in Thailand, quickly joined in flights, and headed for the tanker tracks. Usually tanking was performed "zip-lip," with no radio calls so as to minimize chances of alerting the enemy, which was a forlorn hope at best. Tanking called for a high degree of professionalism from the fighter-bomber pilots and the noncommissioned boom operators in the tankers who guided their probes into the recipients' refueling receptacles.

Each mission usually involved three in-flight refuelings for every airplane in the gaggle. The second came shortly before entering North Vietnam, and the third came on the way home. At the time no other air force performed tanking so routinely, and five decades later it was still largely an American trait. However, no other air force sent tactical aircraft laden with ordnance over the distances that were routine for the US Air Force and Navy or ferried them across vast oceans.

After topping off, the strikers reformed and headed for their targets, generally arriving around 7:30 A.M. or 3 P.M. The predictable schedule eased the North Vietnamese task of anticipating when the Yankee air pirates would arrive, yet the attackers needed daylight to bomb and tank, so the Air Force did the best it could.

Over the bridge the Weasels tried to roll in three minutes ahead of the strikers, concentrating on SAM sites, although gun-laying radars were fair game. Within SA-2 range, the Thuds formed into a "SAM box," or pod formation. At least one plane in each formation was supposed to carry an ECM pod to jam known enemy frequencies. Usually the leader's wingman stepped up and flew five hundred feet away. The second-section leader was five hundred feet out and down, with Number Four stepping up. The goal was to give each pilot space to maneuver to avoid a missile and prevent a SAM burst from damaging more than one plane.

When MiGs were flying, the strikers usually knew they were airborne via "one of the agencies" that was monitoring North Vietnamese radio frequencies and radar emissions. If enemy fighters got past the F-4s, the supersonic MiG-21s often tried an overhead attack to break up a Thud flight, leaving individuals vulnerable to slower, more agile MiG-17s.[2]

Approaching the target at fourteen to sixteen thousand feet, the bombers preferred a wagon-wheel-attack pattern, reaching the dive point from a left-hand turn. The left turn was familiar to pilots because they usually fly left-hand patterns around airports and because most humans are right-handed, making the cross-body movement more natural. Unfortunately, the left-turning tendency made the gunners' job of estimating lead easier.

Trying to ignore bursting flak and the audible warnings of ECM equipment, pilots concentrated on identifying their briefed target and reaching their dive points. Thuds liked to dive at 45 degrees and release at about 550 knots at about 5,500 feet above the target. The pull-out started the instant the weapons were gone, usually a five-G pull that often induced gray-out as the periphery of the pilots' vision faded due to blood draining from the head. In any case, they wanted to avoid bottoming below 3,000 feet to avoid flying metal from light-caliber AAA guns.

That clear-air scenario was rarely achieved. Flights lost integrity in the attack and off-target maneuvering, and weather was always a factor. Even without clouds at intermediate levels partially obscuring the target, visibility in the moisture-laden tropical air over North Vietnam was rarely better than five miles.

With their gaggles of attackers and big tankers, the Air Force gave the bridge everything they had.

But the bridge stood as impervious to explosives as if it were made of kryptonite.

★

Only one American plane was lost on a Dragon's Jaw strike mission in 1967. That misfortune fell to a *Kitty Hawk* Phantom crew on May 14. Air Wing Eleven's original mission was against warehouses in Haiphong, but the mission was scrubbed and the Thanh Hoa Bridge substituted.

As explained by Lieutenant Commander John Holm, a VF-114 pilot who often flew as a flak suppressor for VA-85's A-6 Intruders:

> We carried six LAU-10 rocket pods with twenty-four VT [proximity-] fused Zunis.
>
> On May 14 our new flag decided the way to get the bridge was to wear it down. We launched three cycles back to back with six A-6s and six F-4s in each strike package. I was on the second go. We had excellent recent photos to work with, and we made sure we got someone assigned for each close-in flak site.
>
> We pushed out ahead of the strike and were unloading on the flak sites as the Intruders rolled in. I always fired in pairs, so I got eight Zunis with each pickle push, and I tried to line up the targets so I could cover three sites in one run, beginning with a steep dive angle and flattening out and using a little more lead as I got lower. Point and shoot.
>
> We didn't get down into the automatic weapons fire. There was always opposition, but we got in and out. I've seen the bridge completely obscured by smoke from the bombs, but it was always still there in the next photo.[3]

That afternoon the *Hawk* launched another maximum-effort Alpha strike, its third of the day, composed of more than two dozen jets from the two A-4 squadrons, VA-112 and 114, plus A-6s from VA-85, with four VF-114 F-4s as flak suppressors. Again, the Phantoms were armed with Zuni pods because the high-speed rockets were extremely accurate against relatively small targets such as gun positions.

The mission was carefully choreographed with a dual-axis attack to split the defenses. The fighters would dive from the north about twenty seconds ahead of the first bombers. The suppressors would pull off their targets as the Skyhawks and Intruders rolled in from the opposite direction. The carrier aviators prided themselves on their high degree of professionalism: with proper interval and exquisite timing, three dozen jets could get on and off a target in about one minute or so.

Leading the flak suppressors was Lieutenant Commander Charles E. "Ev" Southwick flying Linfield 201. He was born in Alaska in 1931 and raised in Seattle. After graduating from the University of Washington, he entered the Naval Aviation Cadet program and received his wings of gold in 1955. A career fighter pilot, he flew FJ-3 Furies and F-8 Crusaders before attending the Air Force Fighter Weapons School. He endured a two-year "payback" tour in Washington before returning to flight status. In 1966 he completed transition to the F-4B Phantom, and in February 1967 he reported to the VF-114 Aardvarks, who chose the emblem of an anteater for their squadron based on Johnny Hart's *B.C.* comic strip.[4]

Ev Southwick was among the Navy's MiG killers. On April 24 he shot down a MiG-17 with Ensign Jim Laing in his backseat. Almost immediately their Phantom fell victim to flak gunners or North Vietnam's first ace, Nguyen Van Bay, but the crew ejected offshore and were rescued. In the same aerial combat Lieutenant Denny Wisely and Lieutenant (Junior Grade) Gareth Anderson splashed another "red bandit," making Wisely the Navy's most successful fighter pilot, with two kills to his credit. On a previous cruise he had downed an An-2 Cub biplane with a radar-guided Sparrow missile. Although a biplane wasn't much of a trophy, fighter pilots have to take what they can get.

Southwick's RIO on the bridge mission was Lieutenant David John "Jack" Rollins, also born in 1931. He grew up in California and Nevada, enlisted directly after high school in 1948, and was commissioned in 1960. Trained as an F-4B RIO, he joined VF-114 for the first of two Aardvark tours. In September 1963 Rollins served as an instructor and projects officer at VF-121, the West Coast Phantom school at NAS Miramar, San Diego. Rollins returned to the 'varks in August 1966. Married since 1950, he had three children and a promising naval career.[5]

Approaching the coast northeast of Thanh Hoa, the attack group split. The Skyhawk and Intruder bombers looped southwesterly, while Ev Southwick took his suppressors directly inland to attack from the north.

The defenders were ready, as usual. Before the jets reached their roll-in points in the cube of airspace surrounding the bridge, flak bursts began erupting ahead of the *Kitty Hawk* fliers. They pushed onward through the barrage.

The plan for the flak suppressors was to attack from eleven thousand feet, fire the Zunis in a 30-degree dive at 450 knots, and pull level by three thousand feet. With the sight reticle on the visible AAA positions, which were easy to see because they were covered with muzzle flashes, Southwick ripple-fired the rocket pods and saw the Zunis streak out ahead of Linfield 201.

The Phantom twitched somewhere in its beefy airframe, accompanied by a bang. Rollins craned his head, looking past his pilot, and went wide-eyed. Flames were gushing from the starboard intake. The crew's first thought was compressor stall.

More likely, the jet ingested rocket fragments from a premature detonation of a Zuni warhead. The ordnance manual said that Zuni fuses were made to avoid "fratricide"—the same problem that downed Jerry Denton's Intruder two years before. But whatever the cause, Linfield 201 was in deep trouble.

Southwick scanned his instruments: starboard tailpipe temperature fluctuating and no throttle control; the port engine was also unspooling. Without engines the F-4 would lose electrical power, so the pilot reached behind and pulled the handle to deploy the ram-air turbine. The housing door in the fuselage popped open, extending the air-driven propeller to provide minimum electric power to essential instruments.

Southwick overflew the bridge and banked into a 90-degree left turn, descending toward the ground on the west side of the river. What he desperately needed was altitude, at least fifteen thousand feet of it to get far enough off shore for a possible rescue. Yet altitude was precisely what he didn't have.

Heading southeast in a dying Phantom, Ev Southwick opted for the river. Perhaps the crew could get downstream to the mouth of the Song Ma where a helo might reach them.

When the treetops began passing by at canopy level, the crew was out of options.

It was time to get out.

At perhaps fifty feet Southwick pulled the face curtain over his head, initiating command ejection of both seats and leaving Linfield 201 to its fate.

The Phantom lit mostly level in the mud flats just off the north tip of a small island, about four miles downstream from the bridge. The port wing tip dug in, spinning the aircraft almost 180 degrees and leaving it pointed back toward the bridge.

After a short parachute ride, the crew landed on either side of a creek paralleling the river, out of sight of each other. Ev Southwick got a full ejection sequence. His chute snapped open, and he swung once and landed on his feet about one hundred yards from the creek bank. He was near a banana grove, but the foliage offered no cover.

Jack Rollins had barely separated from his seat when he slammed into a rice paddy, knocking the wind out of him. Worse, his head lay under water with mud clogging his oxygen mask. Barely able to use his hands, he raised himself up, wrestled his helmet off, and took stock. Then he pulled his emergency radio from his survival vest and tried to contact one of the jets still overhead. It was no use—he was stranded in North Vietnam.

Only later did the RIO learn that his back and pelvis were broken.

The crew was quickly surrounded by villagers who followed the now-familiar routine. Unfamiliar with zippers on torso harnesses and G-suits, the Vietnamese began cutting off the flier's outer garments. Somebody cut Rollins' boot laces rather than untie them. As the RIO's hands were bound behind him, another Vietnamese pulled off his wristwatch.

Then an enraged villager dashed at Jack Rollins, raising an apparently homemade knife. Rollins tried dodging the blow but the assailant rammed the blade into his right shoulder, leaving the knife stuck there. Some uniformed personnel quickly arrived—apparently militia—and took charge of the prisoner.

Out of sight of Rollins' view to the west, Southwick also faced a hostile mob. As the Vietnamese closed, the fighter pilot thought he was about to be murdered on the ground.

"Come with me!"

The voice was loud, firm, and unaccented. Southwick looked around to see a man with Eurasian features. The locals deferred to him, and shortly the pilot was immensely relieved to see Rollins.[6]

Tied and blindfolded, they were loaded into a military vehicle that headed north. The fliers entered the Hanoi Hilton late that night.

★

The airborne search-and-rescue (SAR) effort lasted well past dark. Other pilots reported two good chutes but heard none of the electronic *whip-whip-whip* of an emergency beacon. Nonetheless, A-4s remained on station while VA-115 Skyraiders, VA-144 Skyhawks, and an SH-2 helicopter were summoned. The chopper lifted off from *Clementine*, the generic name for the northern SAR ship, but by then it was far too late, and the rescue effort was canceled around 6:30 P.M.

Meanwhile the Aardvark F-4 drew unusual attention. Visible in the estuary, not even the rising tide fully covered the Phantom, which was photographed by a Swedish reporter, Sven Oste. In Hong Kong two days later he mentioned the jet to American authorities, who at first seemed skeptical. But when Oste described the markings, all doubt was removed.[7]

Reconnaissance the morning of May 15 revealed the naked hulk lying on the mud flat. Because Linfield 201 had pancaked in, largely intact, it became a potential intelligence coup for Hanoi—and Moscow. Task Force 77 was especially concerned about the enemy obtaining intact AIM-7 Sparrow missiles, so on the morning of May 16 *Enterprise* launched four Skyhawks of the VA-113 Stinger squadron to destroy the Phantom.

Leading the mission was Lieutenant Commander Jeremy "Bear" Taylor, who selected his own weapons load-out. He recalled,

> I was to strike the hulk at dawn on the 16th. I chose as the weapon for this assignment the Mark 4 gun pod lightly loaded with 400 rounds of 20 mm for one long pass. I planned to shoot from about 3,000 feet down to a thousand. Four hundred rounds of 20 mm high-explosive incendiary will do a lot of damage.
>
> Strafing also remained the most accurate weapons delivery in the A-4 Skyhawk's inventory of weapon choices. A little more hairy, but time was running out to destroy that F-4 and her Sparrows. I led a division of A-4s with Wild Bill Ellis on my wing loaded with Mark 82s [five-hundred-pounders] and my section lead was George Wales, also armed with a Mark 4 gun pod. His wingie was armed with Mark 82s.
>
> Tactics counted on an element of surprise—one division of A-4s popping up from the sea at dawn, hours before the usual Doctor Pepper schedule "10-2-4" the Thanh Hoa gunners counted on. Climb to 10,000 feet and roll-in headed southwest for one long strafing pass with Wild Bill dropping five Mark 82s on my hits. George and his wingman rolling in from the north for a north-to-south pass with about a twenty-second interval. One run, four aircraft. And outta there.
>
> The strike on Linfield 201 went exactly as briefed, except . . . I popped up, climbed to roll-in, eyeballed the F-4 right where it was on the pre-strike photos from the day before, roared down the chute passing 3,000 feet with the F-4 centered in my gunsight, squeezed

> the trigger—and *blap*! One round of 20 mm spit out and a jam [gun jammed]. My two bombers moved a lot of mud and it looked like George's 20 mm were all over the hulk.[8]

Despite the bombing and strafing, the Vietnamese gutted the airframe while making arrangements to transport it to Hanoi. Floated on a bamboo raft, the battered carcass was moved upriver and eventually became a prized exhibit in the capitol's war memorial. Of course, all the damage to the plane was implicitly attributed to the valiant North Vietnamese gunners who shot it down.

★

The perennial nature of the campaign against the Dragon's Jaw—and the Vietnam War—was well illustrated by one pilot in one squadron in one air wing. On September 1, 1966, Lieutenant Commander Richard Schaffert of VF-111, a three-war squadron, had bombed the Thanh Hoa Bridge with his wingman. One year and two days later, still flying from *Oriskany*, the Sundowners and other Air Wing 16 squadrons returned to the Dragon's Jaw. Follow-on attacks were launched on September 11 and 12, all large Alpha strikes. Schaffert said, "On the third strike Old Salt (VA-163) Lieutenant (Junior Grade) Hunter got a huge hole in his A-4's wing but made it back."[9]

On September 23 Task Force 77 launched twenty-two aircraft with fifty-seven tons of ordnance and again inflicted temporary damage: "Some 80 units of rolling stock and 1,678 tons of POL [petroleum, oil, and lubricants] were destroyed in four days, unable to vacate the area."[10]

But the bridge still stood.

★

Astute readers will ask: Despite all the strikes against the Dragon's Jaw in 1967, why did only one attacking aircraft fall—Linfield 201, perhaps a victim of flak, perhaps a victim of its own ordnance? The answer is that the Navy and Air Force were winning their battle with the flak crews. Flak suppressors were decimating the gunners.

The authors have found no North Vietnamese publications describing the casualties the gun crews took from flak suppressors and stray bombs, although the carnage must have been horrific. Zuni rockets, five-hundred-pound bombs, antipersonnel cluster bombs—the suppressors were highly trained professional airmen who knew how to use their weapons. Men serving the AAA guns must have died on nearly every strike. By the dozens or hundreds. When a crew was slaughtered in a gun pit and the weapon destroyed, another gun was rushed into position and another crew manned it. The new crew likely had only rudimentary instruction, didn't have any experience, didn't know how to lead a diving attacker, and died on the next strike or the one after.

Few airmen gave any thought to the human toll they were inflicting. The flak suppressors were trying to "keep the gunners' heads down." If the suppressors did their job, they would save American lives. Their loyalty was to their fellow fliers, their shipmates, their comrades, their fellow Americans. Those few pilots who did reflect on the slaughter thought, *They're trying to kill us, and we're trying to kill them.*

Like the Soviets facing the *Wehrmacht*, the Vietnamese Communists shoved men forward to die in turn. In the States, television announcer Walter Cronkite was telling the American people every night how many Americans had died the previous day in South Vietnam. In North Vietnam no one was counting bodies.

In the terrible math of war every North Vietnamese gunner who died defending the Thanh Hoa Bridge was one less to go south to fight Americans. Yet American airmen didn't think that way. The shattered bridge that wouldn't fall was an affront to their dedication, professionalism, and war-fighting abilities. They wanted that bridge.

The Communist rulers in Hanoi saw the bridge in much the same light. Although that tortured structure was no longer a transportation asset, they must have realized, as did Rear Admiral David C. Richardson, that every American bomb dropped on it or on the gun crews was one less on other targets, such as truck parks, fuel farms, ammo dumps, and troop concentrations. Yet that fact really didn't matter to the politburo. The bridge was the symbol of American impotence and North Vietnamese resistance. It was the flag waving over Fort McHenry in the dawn's early light.

In human affairs *symbols* matter. The battle was all about *the bridge.*

CHAPTER 14

"WE ARE MIRED IN A STALEMATE"

The year 1968 was the midpoint of America's tragic Vietnam experience, four years after the Tonkin Gulf incident. Critics pointed out that during World War II America had defeated Hitler and crushed the Japanese Empire in just forty-five months. The Johnson administration had been waging war in a rice-paddy shithole against a third-world dictatorship without a Navy, one that had to beg the Soviets and China for military equipment, for roughly the same period of time and didn't seem to be making any progress. Still, McNamara and other administration spokesmen always had a cautiously optimistic message. The press called it "the credibility gap."

In 1968 the draft peaked with 296,000 inductees. Military spending reached a "peacetime" high of $198 billion, *10 percent* of the gross domestic product, a figure not matched in the five decades since.[1]

In April civil rights leader Martin Luther King Jr. was assassinated in Memphis. Immediately riots broke out in cities across America. In June a Palestinian assassinated presidential candidate Robert F.

Kennedy, JFK's brother and the heir to Camelot, as he campaigned in Los Angeles. Crime in US cities increased significantly, leading to a "law and order" movement that Republican candidate Richard Nixon tried to make his own.

That year was also when the most Americans died in Vietnam. In one week alone in May 730 Americans were killed in Vietnam, the bloodiest week of the war. During 1967 American troop strength in Southeast Asia topped 500,000. There were 11,363 men killed in action, raising the butcher's list to 20,000 since 1964. Both figures were exceeded in 1968: more than 563,000 American military personnel served in theater, and 16,899 of them were killed. Many more were maimed for life. Men who would have died of their wounds in World War II or Korea came home missing limbs and eyes and faces. What's more, they came home to an angry America that somehow, illogically, blamed *them*.[2]

Part of the problem was the draft, which swept up all those young men who didn't go to college, which was almost all of the black youth, while somehow missing the scions of wealth and privilege who have always found a way to avoid combat in all of America's wars. Almost every young man from the upper-middle class who could find a way to avoid Vietnam combat was assiduously busy at it. Al Gore, son of a US senator, did join the Army but wound up in an engineering battalion in Vietnam and so avoided the mud and blood of combat. Bill Clinton evaded the draft and went off to England to do a Rhodes Scholar gig, smoke pot, and bed English girls. While students publicly burned draft cards and rioted on college campuses, one future Democratic senator, Gary W. Hart, rode out his draft eligibility in divinity school. Antiwar college professors inflated the grades of poor students who might get drafted if they flunked out—the great late-1960s grade inflation. Some young men went to Canada and never returned, although others returned to the United States when President Jimmy Carter offered them a pardon in 1977 if they would apply for it; two hundred thousand of them did.

The black youth of America found the civil rights movement. The Nation of Islam said they were getting a raw deal, fighting the white man's war, although the numbers belie that. Of the men who went to Vietnam 88.4 percent were white, 10.6 percent were black. Of the men who died in Vietnam 86.3 percent were white, 12.5 percent were black. And of the men who were killed in battle 86.8 percent were white, 12.1 percent were black, even though blacks of military age in America were 13.5 percent of the military-age population.[3] Perception is everything in politics, and America's young black men were sure they were getting screwed.

All the foregoing might not have mattered had Vietnam been a cause for which the administration could rally the American people and lead them to victory. Without "victory pure and sweet" as the guide star, the unanswerable conundrum was: What in hell are we fighting for? The corrupt, incompetent South Vietnamese government? Stopping the spread of world Communism? If your son was facing the prospect of getting drafted and being sent to Vietnam, none of that washed.

In 1968 the Air Force had 58,500 personnel in South Vietnam and 47,600 in Thailand, both figures slightly more than the previous year. They supported 1,768 aircraft throughout Southeast Asia, including 218 F-4 Phantoms and 108 F-105 Thunderchiefs.[4]

Meanwhile the North Vietnam defenders were industriously improving their air defenses with guns, ammo, and SAMs donated by the Soviet Union and China and brought into the country through the port of Haiphong and the Northeast Railway. When Rolling Thunder kicked off in early 1965 North Vietnam was thought to possess seven hundred antiaircraft guns of all types, twenty-two early-warning radars, and just four fire-control radars.

In late March 1968 US intelligence reported nearly 5,800 AAA guns throughout the country, including 609 in Route Pack IV, where Thanh Hoa was situated. The guns were largely mobile, capable of using 1,158 prepared sites. The large majority of weapons were 37- to 57-millimeter, while nearly a thousand were 85- and 100-millimeter monsters.

Just prior to the 1968 US presidential election the air defense net had blossomed to more than eight thousand AAA guns, four hundred radar stations, and forty SAM sites.[5]

★

The Navy and Air Force fought a long, bitterly contested conflict in Southeast Asia with each other—the infamous "sortie war"—as service chiefs sought to impress Secretary of Defense McNamara with the number of aircraft launched bearing ordnance. The generals and admirals resorted to numerical subterfuge to run up the count. Air Force personnel at Tan Son Nhut Airbase near Saigon and elsewhere watched F-100s take off with one five-hundred-pounder beneath each wing. Meanwhile carrier sailors saw A-4s launch off the pointy end of the boat with similar load-outs. "It was absurd," recalled one aviator. "We exposed six airplanes and pilots to a threat when the same amount of ordnance could have been delivered by one airplane."

No doubt flag officers angling for another star caused some of this nonsense, but the generals and admirals also had their eyes firmly fixed on the future. This shitty little war would end someday, one way or another, and once again the services would be locked in political combat for defense dollars. The American military has shrunk after every war it ever fought, including the American Revolution. The tide comes in, the tide goes out: this is life in a democracy. Airplanes and ships were wearing out and becoming obsolete. The uniformed services were starving for investment. Nothing less than the future of these services would be the stake in the coming political death scrum.

At the operator level some efforts at cooperation did occur. A rare example came near the end of January 1968, when the gods of weather, politics, and tactics briefly touched hands.

Analysts in the Pentagon knew that previous bombing halts had allowed the Communists to restore their transportation network. Intelligence and recon flights confirmed that lucrative targets were accumulating around Thanh Hoa. Hoping, again without reason, that a heavy blow might bring Hanoi to the bargaining table, Washington approved a joint operation and laid it on. It would be the largest effort since the first strikes in April 1965.

Rarely had the Air Force and Navy coordinated their efforts against a single target. This time Seventh Air Force did the planning—a situation that raised hackles in the Air Force squadrons and wings because officers in Saigon had no skin in the game and sometimes lacked current operational knowledge; it was almost akin to Johnson and McNamara sticking pins in maps at the White House. Yet the "blue suits" were still doing remote mission planning four years later at the end of the war when the Strategic Air Command in Omaha ordained details for B-52 strikes.[6]

Recognizing Thanh Hoa's increasing defenses, Seventh Air Force assigned heavy electronic countermeasures to the mission. The command had three ECM squadrons in the Far East, including two at Takhli. They flew Douglas EB-66 Destroyers—close cousins to the Navy's A-3 Skywarriors that performed tanking and ECM duty from Tonkin Gulf carriers.

Four Destroyers orbited fifty nautical miles (fifty-seven statute miles) off shore with another quartet sixty-five miles west of the target over the Laotian border. The two-phase jamming was successful; the Vietnamese radar system was overloaded, preventing or at least limiting its ability to track strikers inbound or on egress.[7]

As usual, five carriers were deployed in WestPac, including USS *Coral Sea*, the "*Coral Maru*," with Air Wing Fifteen on its third Tonkin Gulf cruise.

Coral Sea aviator Pete Purvis explained, "Based on our recent success in Haiphong, Air Wing Fifteen had a reputation as 'bridge busters.' Our air wing commander, Jim Linder, wanted to burnish that image by going after 'the big one' and dropping it into the Song Ma, once and for all—yet again."[8]

The Navy's end of the operation involved eight A-4E Skyhawks as strikers and eight F-4B Phantoms as flak suppressors and MiG CAP. Tankers, early-warning sentinels, and jamming aircraft rounded out the cast.

The Skyhawks rolled in at noon, beginning three and a half hours of bombing. Last over the bridge to assess bomb damage was the RF-8G flown by Lieutenant (Junior Grade) Jay Miller, escorted by VF-151's Lieutenant Commander Pete Purvis and his RIO, Lieutenant (Junior Grade) Barrie Cooper.

The typical "photo Joe" profile was flown between four and six thousand feet, the choice usually dictated by clouds, pushing six hundred knots—nearly supersonic.

Purvis recalled,

> We orbited just offshore about twenty miles south of Thanh Hoa at fifteen thousand feet and waited for our strike group to clear out and the smoke over the target to blow away. It was Chamber of Commerce weather. Only a few white, puffy clouds blocked the view of a clear horizon—unusually nice weather for this neighborhood. Our plan was to go inland south of Thanh Hoa and clear of the AAA envelope, do a right-hand U-turn, and fly over the bridge heading southeast toward the Tonkin Gulf.
>
> We watched our strike group rain bombs on the bridge through a hail of AAA and then race toward the gulf, "feet wet" and safety. It looked as if someone had hit the whole southern span. The pictures, however, would tell the whole story. Now it was our turn.
>
> As smoke slowly drifted away, Jay pushed over and I followed, sliding into position on his right. I lit minimum afterburner to keep up and to erase my F-4s signature smoke trail. Jay's F-8 had cleaner lines and less drag than my warty F-4.
>
> After our U-turn we rolled out over the river about eight miles upstream and headed southeast downriver toward the bridge. There wasn't any AAA in that neck of the woods, so Jay had a good straight setup.
>
> The usual heavy AAA greeted us as we neared the bridge, but no radar-guided stuff. The gray and black smoke that followed bomb explosions had cleared from the bridge's south side. It was still intact.

> As we neared it, an increasing volume of black, white, and gray flak bursts and the telltale red-orange tracers coming up. . . . It didn't let up until we were a mile from the bridge. Our job finished, we bobbed and weaved our way to the coast ten miles away. Our aircraft didn't seem to be damaged.

Purvis and Cooper anticipated a quick return to the *Coral Maru* when Miller's voice crackled on frequency. "Switchbox 110, Corktip 710."

Purvis feared the Crusader had taken a hit, but it had gotten away clean. That was the good news.

The bad news: Jay Miller had forgotten to flip his camera switch on. Without awaiting comment he added, "Got to go back in."

As Purvis explained, "All three of us had that awful sinking feeling." No sane aviator wanted to make a repeat pass at an alerted target. But there was no way around it if the mission was to be accomplished. If they didn't do it, someone else would have to. Every guy in a flight suit had to pull his weight.

The two pilots exchanged information on remaining fuel and arrived at the conclusion that they would need a tanker upon returning to the Gulf—if they made it back to the Gulf. *Coral Sea*'s strike control confirmed that a KA-3 would be anchored over the southern SAR ship.

They decided to go back up the egress track. Jay Miller shoved up the power and aimed his Crusader at the span, making six hundred knots with the camera running this time. He had to fly straight and level for fifteen to twenty seconds over the bridge to get his pictures. All three aviators anticipated a sky full of flak, as before.

And yet . . . "We chewed up the next few miles to the target," Purvis said, "and then over the bridge, and then a hard left turn to return to the southeast and the safety of the Gulf. Not one flak burst!"

"Coop, did you see any Triple-A?"

"Not a bit. Guess the gomers secured for chow once the photo bird went by, and they stood down until our next strike."

CAG Linder's daily memo summarized, "Today's first large-scale gaggle went against the infamous Thanh Hoa Bridge. The Scooters had direct hits on the left span . . . but it just wouldn't tumble."

The coordinated mission plan called for Korat's 388th Wing to launch the first Thunderchief strike, followed by the 355th from Takhli. In addition to electronic support and flak suppressors, a diversion would precede the actual strikers, drawing Vietnamese attention farther downstream.

Among the Korat Thud pilots was Major Kenney W. Mays, nearing the end of his combat tour. He planned his portion of the mission with a fellow Texas Aggie, Captain Steven W. Long Jr. of the 469th Squadron. Because weather scrubbed the morning launch, leadership defaulted to the 34th Squadron, which had taken the contingency lead.

The straight-line distance from Korat to Thanh Hoa was 415 statute miles, but those who would fly the mission preferred deception over simplicity. Mays recalled that Seventh Air Force planners had put the Thuds on a straight-in run from the refueling track to the bridge. That seemed a far too predictable flight path, so the Korat pilots took it upon themselves to amend the plan. Therefore, the two squadron commanders and the wing deputy of operations decided to ignore the ingress route provided by Saigon. As Mays explained, "We planned the mission like we were headed for a target near Hanoi. When we hit the river that runs under the Thanh Hoa Bridge, we turned down the river and headed for it."

Mays took the lead with Scuba Flight. All four pilots in his flight were seasoned, experienced professionals. All were majors. Major Donald W. Rever led Gator Flight, while Lieutenant Colonel Rufus Dye Jr., on his thirty-sixth mission, led the second section.[9]

★

While the Thuds were inbound to Thanh Hoa, airborne MiGs were vectored northwest by their ground control intercept (GCI) controller.

The revised ingress route achieved its purpose, as the Communist ground controller apparently believed that the target was Hanoi.

The Korat flights entered enemy airspace at the "Fish's Mouth" bend of the Mekong River, about 120 miles west-southwest of Thanh Hoa.

When Mays called "Go hot" on the radio, Scuba Flight pilots began flipping switches to arm their weapons. As Mays later recalled, "Jim Daniel was the deputy mission commander . . . he accidentally hit his jettison button and dropped his stores before we got to the target. I told him he could go back, but he said he was coming along for the ride. He did not want to miss the fun and continued on to the target . . . clean."[10]

Although Mays' pilots scored "good hits" on the bridge, he considered the most important target to be secondary. As he rolled into his dive he spotted train cars in a railyard, apparently waiting to cross on a ferry. He keyed his mike, alerting those behind him and the 355th's strike, still inbound.

Mays summarized, "Takhli also hit the rail cars. With the diversion down the river we had no MiG threat and very little flak. One reason was undoubtedly because the four defense-suppressor fighters concentrated on the 37 and 57mm sites on both ends of the bridge, covering them with CBUs and 500-pounders. As the 105s pulled off, four of the gun positions apparently stopped firing."

Korat's bombers slathered the Dragon's Jaw with M117 750-pounders and nearly twenty tons of M118 three-thousand-pounders. The bombs appeared well aimed, erupting on and around the bridge.

The second wave from Thailand, the 355th Tactical Fighter Wing's strike, was composed of sixteen F-105s. Takhli's aerial armada consisted of Wolf, Bear, Wildcat, and Bison flights armed with 750-pounders and twenty-six three-thousand-pounders, basically duplicating the Korat strikers' load-out. Wolf Two was unable to plug during the prestrike refueling and returned to Takhli. The other fifteen fighter-bombers flew the mission as briefed and attacked in midafternoon, diving through light-caliber AAA at eight thousand feet. Considering that flak suppressors had worked over the gun sites twice already that day, it was a wonder that the North Vietnamese managed to get any flak at all into the air to greet the third wave of attackers.

The pilots estimated that all their ordnance hit in the target area, with extensive impacts on the road immediately east of the bridge. Some egressing pilots counted sixty or more railcars combined on both sides of the bridge but had no time to assess damage.[11]

Nonetheless, the weight of the ordnance delivered was exceptional—about three bombs every four-and-a-half minutes for three and a half hours.

Every jet over Thanh Hoa got away clean. The only American plane lost that day throughout Indochina was a prop-driven Air Force T-28 trainer on a noncombat mission.[12]

As usual, the last American over the target was a photo-recon pilot, flying "unarmed and unafraid." The F-101 Voodoo got its pictures and scorched out of the area as fast as its Pratt & Whitneys would propel it.

Initial estimates were optimistic: "All ordnance reported on target and doing extensive structural damage."

During debriefing at Korat and Takhli the Thud pilots awaited BDA from the photo interpreters. At length the official verdict arrived: "The eastern approach was interdicted, rendering the rail line unserviceable to rolling stock."[13]

Closer inspection of the pictures revealed "only superficial damage to the superstructure of the bridge, although girders were twisted and bent. The southern approach to the bridge was severely damaged. Rail tracks, twisted and torn, lay beside the rail bed, which was no longer recognizable because of large bomb craters. The harsh truth was a bridge temporarily unusable, but one that would be operational again in the future."[14] Actually, given the North Vietnamese's abilities at bridge repair, the very near future.

★

The following day, January 29, 1968, the Americans stood down on a thirty-six-hour bombing pause during the Vietnamese Tet holiday, one called by the ever-optimistic Lyndon Johnson. The weather swept away any thoughts of a restrike on the bridge as the monsoon moved in, bringing low clouds and reduced visibility through the April 1 bombing halt in most of North Vietnam. Not that it mattered: on January 30 the North Vietnamese Army (NVA) and Viet Cong launched their offensive in South Vietnam during the holiday to which Lyndon Johnson thought he should make obeisance.

More than 150,000 Viet Cong, backed by 130,000 NVA regulars who poured out of Laos and Cambodia, attacked five major cities in South Vietnam, including Saigon and the American embassy, along with more than a hundred other towns and cities across South Vietnam in what came to be called the Tet Offensive.[15]

A key component of the Communist offensive was terror. Defense analyst William J. Luti said, "Thousands of government officials, schoolteachers, doctors and missionaries were rounded up and executed."[16] Throughout history dedicated fanatics have seemed to have little trouble murdering the defenseless.

Without the aid of the US Army and Marine Corps, South Vietnam would have collapsed. US and South Vietnamese forces held fast and fought back and, by late March, had achieved a decisive military victory. The three-phase campaign, lasting until September 1968, cost the United States and South Vietnamese some 10,500 killed or missing as well as killed unknown thousands of South Vietnamese civilians. Although the US press didn't know or report it, Tet was a military disaster for the Communists. The prolonged siege of Khe Sanh provided the US Army with an opportunity to do what it did best in Vietnam—deliver massive firepower on a concentrated enemy. Combined North Vietnamese Army and Viet Cong losses for the entire campaign are unknown but probably approached fifty thousand dead or missing, plus sixty thousand wounded. The Viet Cong never fully recovered.

Yet it wasn't reported that way. Luti continued, "Journalists wrongly portrayed the Tet Offensive as a military defeat and never corrected the record."[17]

But then, in the age of television, with its constant stream of pictures and commentary, how *does* one correct the record? Arguably television's portrayal of events becomes reality, regardless of the truth. It would be two generations before the American public began to realize that television and newspapers fighting for advertising dollars slanted their reporting to reflect the prejudices of the producers and editors and the perceived tastes of their audience. Only then did the public lose faith in the media.

Although the Tet Offensive was a tactical American victory, the contrast between the Johnson administration's happy talk and the severe military bloodletting that came to pass made both the press, however biased and incompetent, and the public treat it as a strategic defeat, which is precisely what it was. Under the press pummeling, Johnson's low popularity plummeted even farther. His ambivalence, lies, and "no victory" strategy had come home to roost. The Tet Offensive was the final nail in the coffin of Lyndon Johnson's presidency.

Yet the North Vietnamese Communists had made their first serious mistake. By committing the Viet Cong and the bulk of the North Vietnamese Army to open combat with the Americans, they were playing a game they couldn't win. American air power and overwhelming firepower could finally be brought to bear, not on roving bands of guerillas but on massed enemy combatants in the open: the result was a slaughter. Never again would the Viet Cong be a powerful military force. Within two months, by the end of March, they were essentially wiped out.

General Vo Nguyen Giap and Ho Chi Minh in Hanoi recognized the greater truth: Tet was a strategic victory over the hearts and minds of American civilians.

The Communist shock-and-awe campaign left Washington stunned. CBS news anchor Walter Cronkite interjected a personal opinion in a late February newscast, saying, "We are mired in a stalemate."

Watching the program, Johnson reportedly exclaimed, "If I've lost Walter I've lost Middle America."[18] Finally—finally—the Capitol Hill arm twister grasped the fact that he could not hustle the hard-eyed pragmatists of the Hanoi politburo.

Out in the heartland nonpolitical Americans with a visceral dislike for Communism had to face the fact that their government had apparently bitten off more than it could chew. The vultures began circling: this sitting president faced challengers in the Democratic primaries for the presidential nomination for the November election.

The one bright spot in all this angst was that Robert McNamara departed, eased out by the president, with his last day at the Pentagon on February 28, 1968. He officially departed on July 1 to become president of the World Bank.

Savaged by the press, "Johnson buckled," Henry Kissinger said years later. Ever the fool, Lyndon Johnson decided to try another bombing pause, even though the previous ones had been abject failures. This time he would do it with a twist: on March 31, 1968, he announced, "Tonight, I have ordered our aircraft and naval vessels to make no attacks on North Vietnam except in the area north of the Demilitarized Zone where the continuing enemy buildup directly threatens allied forward positions and when the movements of their troops and supplies are clearly related to that threat.

"The area in which we are stopping our attacks includes almost 90 percent of North Vietnam's population and most of its territory. Thus there will be no attacks around the principal populated areas, or in the food-producing areas of North Vietnam."

Johnson ended his speech with these words: "I shall not seek, and I will not accept, the nomination of my party for another term as president."[19]

Johnson had just admitted that his leadership of America's effort in Vietnam had failed. The air campaign over North Vietnam, which McNamara's Whiz Kids had orchestrated, Johnson also believed to be a failure. And the way he and McNamara had run it, it certainly was. Unwilling as ever to fight hard enough to win in Vietnam, Johnson began trying to extricate America from the Indochina quagmire. But it was too little, too late: America was in to its neck.

The irony is that the military campaign had actually begun to bear fruit. Tet was a military defeat for the Communists and arguably should have been followed up with all the military pressure it was possible to apply. In his book *White House Years* Henry Kissinger remarked, "There is much evidence that at the time of the 1968 Tet offensive Hanoi was on the point of exhaustion when saved by our unilateral bombing halt. There is no doubt in my mind that the resumption of bombing in May 1972 hastened the end of the war."[20]

And then, miraculously, just three days after Johnson's announcement of the bombing halt, the North Vietnamese agreed to negotiate in Paris. Americans soon realized that the Communists' move to the bargaining table was a Pyrrhic victory. Months were spent arguing about the shape of the conference table—square or round? When that was finally settled, Hanoi made its demands: the United States must leave Vietnam and overthrow the South Vietnamese government. There was nothing to negotiate: Hanoi demanded an American surrender. This farce continued for years, making it politically very difficult for the Americans to resume bombing while "negotiating." This was the political impasse into which Lyndon Johnson had adroitly maneuvered America.

★

The bridge missions on January 28 were the Vietnam War in microcosm: American technology and persistence pitted against Asian patience and resolve.

When Johnson's announcement of the end of bombing came two months later it was anticlimactic. The Americans had done everything possible to drop the Dragon's Jaw and had nothing left to throw at the bridge.

Since the start of the war at least twelve aircraft had been lost on missions against the bridge: six F-105s, two F-4s, two A-1s, an F-100, and a C-130. Thirteen fliers were dead or missing in action and seven captured. Only one man, F-105 pilot Major Robert E. Lambert, had been rescued, back in May 1965.

★

In August in Chicago the Democrats held their convention to nominate a presidential candidate. As the nation watched on television, antiwar protesters rioted outside the convention hall as clouds of tear gas wafted through the downtown and leaked inside.

In October the last bomb fell on North Vietnam. Rolling Thunder was over.

In November the Democrat nominee, Hubert H. Humphrey, the "Happy Warrior," lost the presidential election to Republican Richard M. Nixon.

At year's end *Apollo Eight* orbited the moon and returned to earth. It was an amazing irony: America couldn't defeat Ho Chi Minh or extricate itself from Vietnam but was well on its way to putting a man on the moon.

On the Ma River at Thanh Hoa the twisted, blackened, scarred steel of the Dragon's Jaw Bridge still stood.

CHAPTER 15

"COURAGE IS FEAR THAT HAS SAID ITS PRAYERS"

Former Republican vice president Richard M. Nixon was handily elected president in November 1968. Nixon's victory was won partly on the basis of his "secret plan" to end the war.

The policy was "Vietnamization"—turning over the heavy lifting to Saigon while America gradually pulled troops from the country. Anyone who read newspapers realized that without the US Army and Marine Corps, South Vietnam would have collapsed under the Communist juggernaut at Tet in 1968. If and when the United States pulled its soldiers and Marines out of South Vietnam, the Republic's days were numbered unless a political settlement could be reached that North Vietnam would honor.

So Lyndon Baines Johnson left the White House in January 1969, following Robert Strange McNamara, the number-crunching Whiz Kid from Ford, out the door. McNamara's gradual application of military pressure had been a spectacular failure. He ultimately came to the conclusion "that we could not achieve our objective in Vietnam through any reasonable military means" and told the president just that. "President Johnson was not ready to accept that. It was becoming clear to both of us that I would not change my judgment, nor would he change his."[1] Johnson sent McNamara to the World Bank and, after Nixon took office, went back to Texas.

★

Rolling Thunder ended on November 2, 1968, forty-five months to the day after it began in March 1965. In stark contrast, America's involvement in World War II against Japan, Germany, and Italy also lasted forty-five months, from December 1941 until August 1945. Johnson's vacillating policy had involved seven partial or complete bombing halts lasting days or even months. The total respite Johnson had given North Vietnam was an amazing twelve of those forty-five months.

Part of the problem seems to have been racial or cultural condescension in Washington. Certainly the Air Force and Navy airmen who flew against North Vietnam's air defenses fully appreciated their opponents' courage, competence, resiliency, and dedication. Lyndon Johnson was apparently ignorant of the writings of Renaissance Italian theorist Niccolò Machiavelli, whose advice to the prince was: "Never do your enemy a small injury." Machiavelli practically defined the school of realistic statecraft; LBJ flunked the course.

Make no mistake, the Rolling Thunder air campaign against the North had caused the Communists severe damage: the Air Force claimed destruction of 1,305 bridges and damage to nearly 1,800. The airmen also reported destroying or damaging 2,800 AAA sites, 170 SAM sites, and 260 radar sites. Yet the air war was geographically limited: North Vietnam's vital population and industrial centers of Hanoi and Haiphong were immune from attack for much of that period. Even worse, for political reasons the United States refused to make the effort required to win air supremacy over North Vietnam. Some MiG bases were bombed in the spring of 1967. Runways were cratered, some planes were destroyed on the ground, but Washington vacillated, as usual. The effort came to little.

An eyewitness account of the conditions in North Vietnam after Rolling Thunder was provided by John Colvin, a British intelligence agent and diplomat in the region dating from World War II. He wrote, "My traveler told me that there had been, as a result of the bombing, only one undamaged bridge between Hanoi and Thanh Hoa in the southeast of the DVR (Democratic Republic of Vietnam). . . . Between Phu Ly, a town along the main route to the South which had been largely evacuated in 1966 and later almost totally destroyed, and Thanh Hoa, he saw electric lights on two occasions only. . . . He saw no piped water supply in any town or villages of the area. The center and the main streets of Thanh Hoa had been heavily damaged; shops open sold little more than oil, salt, cloth and, occasionally, cigarettes."[2]

Still, militarily, the destruction had been insufficient. The hard truth remained: before Rolling Thunder North Vietnam was an agrarian society barely on the verge of the modern era, and the air campaign had not set it back much. After the air campaign most villagers lived precisely as they had before—without electricity, telephones, or running water and working in the rice paddies, tending small gardens, and fishing in coastal waters. Manufacturing, such as it was, was accomplished by hand or animal power.

Yet the most important fact was that North Vietnam was an absolute dictatorship. Any Vietnamese who lived north of the 17th parallel who thought that the politburo should discuss peace terms with the Americans and stop the bloodshed kept their mouths firmly shut.

That was not the case in America, and the Communists understood that the war would be won when the American public refused to allow it to go further. They fought with every weapon available to influence American public opinion in their favor. As Kamejiro Senaga, a Japanese Communist politician, said, "We will create hate for your soldiers in the minds of your people."

Offensive wars are always difficult for a democracy to wage. Lyndon Johnson should have read the masterwork of the ancient Greek, Thucydides, *History of the Peloponnesian War.* This account of democratic

Athens' thirty-year war against Sparta, which Athens lost, should be required reading for every politician.

History and hindsight tell us Johnson made several mistakes. First, regardless of John F. Kennedy's commitment to Vietnam, Johnson should have reevaluated and asked the basic question: Is a military adventure in Vietnam in America's national interest? Arguably, even in the middle of the Cold War, it wasn't. If there is historical evidence that the Johnson administration ever addressed this basic policy question after JFK's assassination, the authors are unaware of it.

Secondly, once Johnson decided to get into a shooting war with North Vietnam, he made the egregious error of not getting a declaration of war from Congress when it could have been his for the asking. When he needed it to keep the nation rallied around a national cause, such a declaration was beyond his grasp.

His third error was persistently refusing to solicit or follow the advice of the military professionals on the Joint Chiefs of Staff. If anyone in Washington knew what military arms could and could not accomplish, it was those men. Certainly it was not Robert S. McNamara nor his civilian "Whiz Kids."

★

Military aviation attracted some of the nation's best, brightest young minds in post–World War II America. On July 21, 1969, two military aviators, Neil Armstrong and Buzz Aldrin, walked on the moon. They had both been fighter pilots who logged combat time in Korea. Neil Armstrong was a junior naval aviator who flew from a carrier. Upon leaving the Navy he completed his engineering degree at Purdue. He was a highly skilled, experienced civilian test pilot when NASA selected him for astronaut training. In 1970, after his moon walk, he earned his master's in aerospace engineering from the University of Southern California. After leaving NASA he went on to become a professor of engineering at the University of Cincinnati.[3]

Buzz Aldrin, born Edwin Eugene Aldrin Jr. (he later legally changed his name to Buzz), went to the Air Force upon graduation from the US

Military Academy. Flying F-86 Sabre jets, he shot down two MiG-15s over Korea. He earned a doctorate in astronautics from MIT in 1963. A career fighter pilot, although he was not a test pilot, he was accepted as an astronaut after NASA dropped the test pilot requirement. Aldrin served twenty-one years in the Air Force, retiring in 1972 as a colonel. Despite having no test piloting experience outside of NASA, his last posting was as commandant of the Air Force Test Pilot School. Like Armstrong, Aldrin too ultimately went into academia. He joined the University of North Dakota's faculty in 1985, helped develop the university's space studies program and recruited its first department chair from NASA.[4]

But few of America's military aviators would walk on the moon; several hundred of them were imprisoned in Hanoi. And the Vietnamese Communists fully intended to use them to manipulate American and international public opinion.

Prisoners of war (POWs) possessed military information that was usually time limited. Aircrews seldom knew upcoming targets and could claim—truthfully—that such information was never passed down to their level. Technical data had a longer lifespan, but much of it was generic. Pilots didn't design, manufacture, or maintain weapons systems. Interrogators were far more likely to torture prisoners for political advantage, especially propaganda statements.

The North Vietnamese interrogators had plenty of help. Russians participated in some sessions. Cubans tortured a dozen or more POWs and beat at least one American to death. Upon repatriation, surviving prisoners were told by their own government not to mention third-world interrogators due to "diplomatic ramifications." When the Obama administration normalized relations with Cuba in 2016, no mention was made of Fidel Castro's staff in the Hanoi Hilton nor the Cuban MiGs that murdered four Americans in international airspace in 1996.[5]

In addition, committed leftists, such as American Trotskyite writer Mary McCarthy and actress Jane Fonda, were given access to the POWs. Later McCarthy wrote that she considered Robinson Risner "a gaunt, squirrel-faced man" who "had not changed his cultural spots." In other words, he resisted Communist extortion. Yet at the time of their enforced meeting she exhibited some concern, asking the guards if she could send prisoners a Bible and some food. The turnkeys said Bibles "would cause problems" and the air pirates received "plenty of wholesome foods." In truth, many prisoners were sick and emaciated. Their diet frequently consisted of rice with boiled pumpkin or cabbage soup.[6]

Jane Fonda's behavior was so special it earned her the nickname "Hanoi Jane," which she has carried with her through the date of this writing and will probably be featured in prominent headlines in her obituaries. She went to Hanoi in July 1972, where seven POWs were paraded to interviews with her for propaganda photo ops. She claimed they asked her to tell their friends and family to support presidential candidate George McGovern because they feared they'd never be freed during a Richard Nixon administration. Back in the states Fonda said about the torture the POWs endured that "these men bombed and strafed and napalmed the country. If a prisoner tries to escape, it is quite understandable that he would probably be beaten and tortured."[7]

Symptomatic of the passions the war unleashed, "[I]n March 1973 the Maryland state legislature held a hearing to have Fonda and her films barred from the state. William Burkhead, a Democrat state delegate from Anne Arundel, said, 'I wouldn't want to kill her, but I wouldn't mind if you cut her tongue off.' . . . She continued to openly question the accounts of the US government and American POWs, who told devastating stories of the torture they endured at the hands of the North Vietnamese."[8]

Fonda had a gift for infuriating people. In the eyes of many Americans her greatest sin was posing with a North Vietnamese 57-millimeter gun crew, seated in the gunner's seat. The photo was reproduced in almost every newspaper on the planet. She apologized for that photo in the years that followed, but it still defines her. She was an actress who lent her celebrity to far-left causes without understanding them. In fact, she defines the stereotype.

Several leading lights among the POWs had been shot down attacking the Thanh Hoa Bridge or in the vicinity. Smitty Harris had been downed on the second bridge strike in 1965 and was instrumental in efforts to resist the Communists in prison. With three others he implemented the tap code that POWs used to communicate with each other.

Bob Peel, the Tennessee athlete and F-105 pilot, found, like many POWs, that faith and humor were essential in Hanoi's extortionist pressure cooker. He explained,

> This faith helped POWs to maintain a sense of humor that carried them through dark hours of torture. When doors would slam, and tramping feet would notify each prisoner that some new punishment was at hand, one of them came up with the statement, "If you don't like it, you shouldn't have joined." This would ease the tension and help us face with a smile whatever was in store for us.
>
> Another example is the ability it gives you to laugh for a while during torture. This is something the captors in North Vietnam could never understand. During beatings or other forms of torture you would be told to say you are a criminal, you are a criminal. You answer, "You are a criminal, you are a criminal," and it blows his stack. How can you make fun of him when you are powerless to resist anything he wants to do to you? It helped our morale, as on the Hanoi march, many heads were "bloody, but unbowed."[9]

Ray Merritt, also an F-105 pilot, was shot down on the same day as Robbie Risner, September 10, 1965. Like so many prisoners, he found an upbeat aspect to a terrible situation: "In one way, [being a POW] was a positive. You know that you can survive. You can dig down deep to find whatever is necessary to keep you going, whether it is military training or schooling or your God. . . . We knew that even if we were shot down, our job was not done. We knew that if we could tie up the enemy's assets that they would have to deal with us instead of shooting at our planes."[10]

He added, "I was imprisoned nearly seven and [a] half years. I never had any doubt that someday I would return home again. With a philosophy of living for today and let tomorrow take care of itself, plus the kind and encouraging words of other POWs, long days were turned into short weeks and short years. My faith in God never wavered and His will was that I return home again."

The prisoners exploited for Vietnamese propaganda included Thanh Hoa Bridge survivor Jim Stockdale, who broke a window pane and disfigured his face to avoid being paraded before an international press corps to demonstrate "the lenient and humane treatment" the Communists claimed.

A few prisoners found more public methods of resistance. Commander Jerry Denton, whose Intruder was blown out of the sky by its own bombs near Thanh Hoa in 1965, was dragged before socialist film crews. He was told what to say: "I get adequate food, adequate clothing, adequate medical care." He did, then added, "Whatever the position of my government is, I support it." All the while he was blinking his eyes in the Morse Code pattern T-O-R-T-U-R-E, confirming for US Naval Intelligence for the first time that American POWs were in fact being tortured.[11]

The guards moved the prisoners frequently, some as many as six times in seven years. Often the Americans did not know their actual location, so they gave the dozen or so prisons names of their own. Most common was the "Hanoi Hilton," which was actually the old colonial Maison Central, with integral compounds called "Heartbreak Hotel" and "New Guy Village." Other locales were "The Zoo," "Dogpatch," "The Briar Patch," and "The Plantation." Some were more than a hundred miles from Hanoi.

The Vietnamese were especially attentive to senior men and hardcore juniors. Eleven of the blackest criminals—dedicated communicators and resisters—fetched up at the Zoo, a separate compound near the Hilton. Seven had been captured in 1965, so their reputation as recalcitrants was well established. These eleven were kept in solitary confinement from 1967 to 1969, the boredom broken only by repeated torture sessions. In time the "Alcatraz Gang" defined the nature of torture. The prisoners distinguished between mistreatment—merely being kept in solitary in leg irons—and genuine torture. Being hung from the ceiling with ropes, with their arms nearly pulled from their sockets, made the torture list.

Air Force Captain George McKnight and Navy Lieutenant (Junior Grade) George Coker staged an extremely rare escape in October 1967, swimming downstream in the Red River one night until they were recaptured. Severely beaten, they went to Alcatraz for two and a half years.

Eight of the "gang" were Navy, and some knew each other. Jim Stockdale and Harry Jenkins were friends from *Oriskany*'s Air Wing 16. Stockdale and Jerry Denton had both been test pilots. Bob Shumaker and Nels Tanner were from the same *Coral Sea* fighter squadron, although they had been shot down nineteen months apart, in 1965 and 1966. Commander James Mulligan, an *Enterprise* Skyhawk pilot, had been captured in 1966. Rounding out the Thanh Hoa connection, Howie Rutledge had ejected from his crippled *Bon Homme Richard* Crusader west of the city in late 1965.

Ten of the eleven "gang" members survived the ordeal, including Air Force F-4 pilot Sam Johnson, a future Texas congressman, Skyraider pilot George McKnight, and George Coker. Major Ron Storz, an Air Force forward air controller (FAC), died in captivity in 1970.

As the first Navy pilot downed over the Thanh Hoa Bridge, for a time Commander Bill Franke was the senior prisoner at "Heartbreak Hotel." A SAM had shot down his Phantom in August 1965. A "new guy" in the "Thunderbird" prison (named for the Vegas casino) related an eerie experience to Franke. "I went to your memorial service on the *Midway* flight deck a few days after you were killed in action. I want you to know the chaplain prayed you right into heaven."[12]

At "Heartbreak" torture was rare, but the pressure was ever present. To alleviate the tension, Franke entertained his men at the expense of a guard dubbed "Dipstick." The Phantom skipper would say, "Good morning, Dipstick. It looks like a beautiful day for a bombing."

Besides the massive changes involving loss of freedom, like many POWs Franke missed the little things, like simply being able to turn a doorknob or having a milkshake.[13]

Among the blackest offenses a POW could commit was communicating with another American. The guards glimpsed Risner tearing up a note but could not prove it. When he refused to produce the remains, he was taken to "quiz," as the prisoners called interrogation. When he refused to admit he had been communicating, he was accused of "an aggressive attitude" as "an active combatant."

A guard forced Risner onto the floor, turned him on his stomach, and expertly applied the ropes. "In a matter of minutes one arm was completely wrapped and the same incredible pain had begun. When he started on the other arm, it triggered all the agony of that night in the past."[14]

At Hoa Lo, Risner was tortured for thirty-two days before his strength failed him. He was coerced into signing a "confession" of war crimes. But he returned to his leadership position among the POWs despite three years in solitary, maintaining contact via the tap code.

A pillar of the POW community was *Oriskany*'s CAG, Commander Jim Stockdale, downed on a weather-aborted strike briefed against the Dragon's Jaw in 1965. Bill Franke, who followed Stockdale into captivity a month later, was encouraged to learn that his fellow test pilot was in the same prison. He considered Stockdale "the smartest human being I have ever known." Some effective leaders led largely by example; Jim Stockdale was a tough customer who led by both example and intellect.[15]

As the only wing commander to survive a combat ejection, Stockdale was selected for special treatment. "I got handled roughly because they knew I was putting out instructions on how to resist." He spent about four years in solitary but maintained leadership via the tap code. He was tortured fifteen times and learned the nuances of "the rope trick."

"They had a trained guard who put you through it," he recalled. "No American ever beat the ropes." Some died in the torture room, and some were simply murdered by a Cuban sadist.

The torturers broke Stockdale's left leg, but he charitably wrote it off as unintentional. With rare objectivity he wrote, "'Pigeye' was a good reliable worker who had common sense, the sort of guy you would like to share heavy work on the farm with. He was even that way as a torture guard, seldom erratic. I always thought he felt sorry for breaking my leg."[16]

Stockdale added, "The main thing was to shut off blood circulation in your upper body. They'd weave manila ropes around your arms until you were smitten with pain, your shoulders distended. In time they'd proceed to bend you double as they pulled the ropes up. You realized you wouldn't be able to tie your pajama strings for a month because of the nerve damage in your arms. There's the pain and the mental problem of knowing that, if you want to save the use of your arms, you have to give up at some point. And finally, he puts his foot on the back of your head with your face down on the concrete so you have claustrophobia and you're puking. So somewhere you say, 'I submit.'"[17]

Through it all Jim Stockdale lived with the persistent dread of discovery: the Vietnamese might learn of his role in the second, imaginary Tonkin Gulf incident. "If my captors had read my name in almost any American newspaper . . . after the Tonkin Gulf episodes, the simple confession they might be able to torture out of me would be the biggest Communist propaganda scoop of the decade: 'American Congress Commits to War in Vietnam on the Basis of an Event That Did Not Happen.'"[18]

As Stockdale capsulized, "L. B. Johnson hoodwinked the United States people and Congress into passing a joint resolution giving him war-making powers in Southeast Asia on the basis of an event that never took place."[19]

In September 1969, four years after his shoot-down, Stockdale, the Stanford philosopher, realized that no matter how dire the situation, there was always an option. He opted out.

Previously Stockdale had disfigured himself to prevent the Viets from parading him for propaganda purposes. He suffered terribly for his rebellion. But now, with another senior officer purge pending, he felt he could resist no more. He broke a window, grasped a shard of glass, and began cutting his veins. As the blood flowed, he collapsed.

The guards found Stockdale bleeding out onto the filthy floor. Rather than let the senior air pirate die, which would have caused them much grief from their political masters, they took him to the dispensary, where he recovered. Jim Stockdale's attempted self-sacrifice may have convinced the Communists that brutality had its limits.

Ho Chi Minh died that month, and the torture ended shortly thereafter. One wonders whether Ho had been the driving force behind the torture. We shall probably never know.

The prisoners faced more than three additional years in Hanoi, but they had the tempered emotional steel to survive. Their mantra was "unity over self." Among them were men like Air Force Captain Guy Gruters, a FAC shot down twice in two months. He was captured in December 1967. Gruters told his fellow POWs, "Courage is fear that has said its prayers."[20]

While the US government tried to ignore or minimize the POW issue, their brothers in arms always remembered the prisoners. VA-56 adopted one unique method during *Midway*'s 1972–1973 cruise: every pilot's name on an A-7 Corsair II was matched with the name of a POW stenciled below, starting with the skipper's jet. On Commander Lew Chatham's NF-401 was the name of Lieutenant Paul Galanti, a former *Hancock* A-4 squadron-mate of Chatham's shot down in June 1966.

Galanti, Stockdale, Risner, Franke, Gruters, and the other surviving POWs returned from North Vietnamese captivity in February 1973 and gradually got on with their lives when their physical and emotional injuries had healed into scars.

At the same time the Chinese released Lieutenant (Junior Grade) Robert J. Flynn, an A-6 BN shot down in northern North Vietnam on August 21, 1967. Three of the four A-6 Intruders VA-196 launched from USS *Constellation* that day were shot down during an Alpha strike into the Hanoi area, two by flak and one by a MiG. Flynn was one of the three crewmen to survive.* He was marched into China and imprisoned in Beijing. Tortured and alone, he spent five and a half years in solitary confinement.

"Of the 2,032 days he spent in captivity, 2,030 were in solitary confinement, longer than any US military service member in history, according to the POW network. It was his faith that kept him sane and courageous in dire, painful circumstances, he told the *Pensacola News Journal* in 2008. . . . Three times, Flynn endured extended handcuff torture—periods of seven, 30, and 60 days with his hands twisted behind his back.

"'I figured out what I had to do my job,' he said. 'I had to remember God, duty, honor, country, family and self. Without God, there's nothing. And if I couldn't face my country, then I'm no good to my family or myself. So I worried about God, and the rest fell into place.'"[21] Although he suffered severe emotional problems for years, Flynn stayed in the Navy, retired as a commander, and died in May 2014 at the age of seventy-six.

The POWs' shipmates, brothers in arms, and their families were absolutely delighted to have them back. Their valor amidst the most trying circumstances and physical degradation was one of the few bright and shining moments of the entire American Vietnam experience.

---

*The squadron CO, Commander Leo T. Profilet, and his BN, Lieutenant Commander William M. Hardman, were captured and imprisoned by the North Vietnamese. They were released in 1973. Killed were Lieutenant Commander Forrest G. Trembley and his BN, Lieutenant (junior grade) Dain V. Scott, and Flynn's pilot, Lieutenant Commander Jimmy D. Buckley.

Two Air Force F-105s were also shot down about the same time that day over Hanoi and the pilots were killed: Major Merwin L. Morrill and First Lieutenant Lynn K. Powell.

CHAPTER 16

NIXON AND KISSINGER

The Dragon's Jaw was still standing when Richard M. Nixon was inaugurated president of the United States in January 1969. Nixon's goal was to gradually pull America out of Vietnam. In effect, he wanted to perform a military maneuver known as an "armed withdrawal." To do so effectively, the Americans needed to keep applying military pressure to keep the forces that remained from being overrun.

Nixon had built his political career as a staunch anti-Communist, so his focus was foreign affairs. He brought with him into office in 1969 as his national security adviser a Harvard political scientist, Dr. Henry Kissinger, who was a believer in realpolitik. Nixon and Kissinger saw opportunities to improve relations with the Soviets and the People's Republic of China (PRC). With Kissinger's help, "he would play China against the Soviet Union, the Soviet Union against China, and both against North Vietnam."[1]

Nixon and Kissinger took personal control of American foreign policy, largely cutting Secretary of State William Rogers and Secretary of Defense Melvin Laird out of policy discussions. "So closely did the two work together that they are sometimes referred to as 'Nixinger.'

Together, they used the National Security Council staff to concentrate power in the White House—that is to say, within themselves."[2]

Kissinger knew something about Vietnam. He had toured South Vietnam for two weeks in October and November 1965 and spent ten days there in July 1966 and a few days in October 1966 as a guest of US Ambassador Henry Cabot Lodge Jr., who was an old friend. Kissinger came away convinced that military victories in Vietnam were meaningless "unless they brought about a political reality that could survive our ultimate withdrawal." In 1967 he mediated a peace initiative between Washington and Hanoi. Nothing came of it, of course, but Kissinger was learning the players.[3]

Kissinger was a naturalized American citizen. With his family, he fled Nazi Germany at the age of fifteen in 1938. He learned English—all the rest of his life he spoke with a serious German accent—and grew up in Upper Manhattan. After high school Kissinger enrolled in the City College of New York, studying accounting and working part time to pay the tuition and support himself. He excelled as a part-time student but was drafted into the US Army in 1943 at the age of twenty. On June 19, apparently while still in basic training in South Carolina, he became a naturalized citizen. Recognizing brains when it saw them, the Army sent Private Kissinger to Lafayette College in Pennsylvania to study engineering. The program was canceled, and he was assigned to the 84th Infantry Division, where his fluency in his native German got him into military intelligence. He saw combat during the Battle of the Bulge.

As the American army advanced into Germany, *Private* Kissinger was put in charge of the administration of the city of Krefeld. Within eight days he established a civilian administration.[4]

Promoted to sergeant, he was assigned to the Counter Intelligence Corps (CIC) and put in charge of a team in Hanover to track down Gestapo officers and other saboteurs. He performed so well that he was awarded a Bronze Star. Still a sergeant, Kissinger was made commandant of the Bensheim metro CIC detachment responsible for the de-Nazification of the district, with absolute authority and powers of arrest. He was just twenty-two years old.[5]

After his discharge from the Army in 1946 Kissinger went to Harvard, earning an AB, an MA, and a PhD. As a faculty member, he consulted on foreign policy with various government agencies, including the Johnson administration.

As Kissinger saw it, America's foreign policy problems were Russia, China, and Vietnam. Strategic disarmament talks had been scheduled under the Johnson administration, but the United States pulled out to protest the Warsaw Pact invasion of Czechoslovakia in August 1968.

In February 1969 Kissinger entered into secret negotiations with North Vietnamese representative Le Duc Tho, the fifth-ranking member of the Hanoi politburo, at a villa outside Paris. Negotiations revealed how far apart the two sides were. The North's position was that the United States must unconditionally withdraw on a fixed date and abandon the South Vietnamese government of President Thieu as a precondition for further negotiations. The United States proposed a mutual withdrawal of military forces, the neutralization of Cambodia, and a mixed electoral commission to supervise elections in South Vietnam. The sides were so far apart that the weekly meetings came to nothing. "We did not yet understand that Hanoi's leaders were interested in victory, not a cease-fire, and in guaranteed political control, not a role in free elections."[6]

In the hope that the Soviets could somehow be induced to help influence the North Vietnamese, Kissinger suggested to Nixon that an approach be made to Moscow "on a broad front. But the Vietnam War was a major obstacle." It turned out that the Soviets were very interested in beginning negotiations with the United States regardless of what happened in Vietnam, but this approach led nowhere. Kissinger summed up, "The aborted Vance mission showed that Moscow would not risk its relation with Hanoi—and the leadership of global Communism—to engage itself in ending the war. And, in truth, its influence was limited. Hanoi would not circumscribe its freedom of action by negotiating under Soviet tutelage with the risk that Moscow might sacrifice some of its interests for superpower relations."[7]

The truth was that Hanoi felt it had a winning hand. On August 11, 1969, Communist forces attacked more than a hundred cities, towns, and bases across South Vietnam. There was a war on and no diplomatic exit looming in the shadows. Nixon stopped the troop withdrawals and met with American domestic outrage. This played to Hanoi's sense that eventually America's military efforts in Vietnam would become politically impossible . . . in the United States.[8]

★

At the time the United States didn't even have diplomatic relations with the People's Republic of China. The Communists under Mao Zedong had won the Chinese Civil War in 1949, driven the Nationalists to the island of Taiwan, and proclaimed a People's Republic. But the United States continued to recognize Chiang Kai-shek on Taiwan as the legitimate ruler of China.

Some of the groundwork for talks with China were laid well before 1971, when Communist Party of China Chairman Mao Zedong invited the US National Table Tennis Team to visit China after a tournament in Nagoya, Japan. Mao wanted a larger place for China on the world stage, which would require some kind of warming of relations with the United States. The visit received favorable worldwide press coverage. Dr. Kissinger went to China on a secret mission in July 1971, after the table tennis team, to confer with PRC Premier Zhou Enlai, then in charge of Chinese foreign policy. Kissinger returned in October 1971 and this time negotiated a visit to China by President Nixon in July 1972. The announcement of the trip worried the North Vietnamese, who correctly assumed that China was going to place their own interests ahead of those of Communist North Vietnam.

In April 1972 Nixon received the Chinese National Table Tennis Team in the White House, again to great international publicity. The press dubbed the visits "Ping-Pong Diplomacy."

In July 1972 President Nixon went to China and discussed with Zhou and Chairman Mao normalizing relations between the PRC and the United States. There were many stumbling blocks, not the least of which was the American relationship with the nationalists on Taiwan. Still, the Chinese and Nixon began the process of normalizing relations, ending twenty-three years of diplomatic isolation and mutual hostility and tacitly forming a strategic anti-Soviet alliance. Although full normalization would not occur until 1979, the first steps had been taken. "In a stroke the trip reshaped the international geopolitical map, altered the balance of the Cold War, jolted alliances of both our countries in East Asia, and laid the groundwork for China's opening to the world."[9]

While the diplomats laid the groundwork for the historic July 1972 meeting between Nixon and Mao, most of North Vietnam remained off-limits to US airpower. If the flow of men and war materiel into South Vietnam was going to be slowed at all, it had to be done in Laos. The NVA responded by moving AAA guns to Laos. The Air Force, Navy, and Marines lost 233 fixed-wing aircraft in combat in 1969—a 40 percent reduction from 1968—with about two-thirds falling in Laos.[10]

Despite the putative total bombing halt in North Vietnam, US combat sorties there slowly increased, from fewer than three hundred in 1969 to eleven hundred in 1970 and nearly seventeen hundred in 1971. In those three years the Air Force logged two-thirds of the total sorties Up North.[11]

Washington kept sending reconnaissance flights into North Vietnamese air space to monitor enemy activity. But from 1970 onward air defense sites in the North could be attacked for threatening aircraft over Laos. Lucrative targets near SAM and AAA sites were also on the approved list. Yet in late 1971 the Air Force began falsifying reports to justify "protective reaction strikes" when direct opposition had not occurred. The policy was implemented to reduce threats to aircrews properly operating over the North, a distinction lost on many critics in Washington and elsewhere.[12]

Retaliating for Communist attacks in the South, Nixon authorized the first strikes north of Route Pack I since Rolling Thunder ended in March 1968. Operation Proud Deep Alpha, from December 26 to 30, 1971, was limited to targets south of the 20th parallel, an area that included Thanh Hoa. Air Force and Navy aircrews logged 1,025 sorties against logistics and transport targets in that five-day period. Due to weather most of the bombing was done "on top" by radar or with LORAN electronic navigation aids. Evaluation showed disappointing results—only about 25 percent of the bombs struck near enough to damage the targets.[13]

On the day after Christmas 1971 the air defenses around Thanh Hoa claimed another victim. The Eighth Tactical Fighter Wing at Ubon, Thailand, launched a flight of four Phantoms against a storage complex near Thanh Hoa. Captain Larry G. Stolz and First Lieutenant Dale F. Koons were Number Three, the element lead, in Coach Flight. Stolz was in his second combat tour in Vietnam and was breaking in Koons as his backseater, or weapons systems officer (WSO), which was the Air Force appellation that meant the same as RIO in the Navy.

The flight became separated in the target area, and Coach Three was last seen climbing into the overcast a mile or two away. SAM radars were active, so there may have been a missile launch. Coach Three was never heard from or seen again.

The next day the Vietnam News Agency, the Hanoi house organ, announced the loss and produced photos of the crew's singed identification cards. After the war American investigators saw other artifacts in Hanoi that appeared to come from the crew of Coach Three, including a pistol and some US dollars.

One version of this shoot-down passed by the North Viets to Dutch journalists said that the F-4D crashed into the Thanh Hoa Bridge, although no evidence was provided to back up that claim. The American searchers at the time thought the presumptive shoot-down location was about six miles north of the Dragon's Jaw.

Although we will never know what happened to Coach Three, the most likely scenario is that the crew found themselves in clouds when the North Viets launched an SA-2 at them. Unable to see the oncoming missile to outmaneuver it, they would have been in very serious trouble.

Stolz's and Koons' remains were turned over to American authorities in 1988 and positively identified two years later. When they died, Larry Stolz was barely twenty-six and Dale Koons was only two weeks past his twenty-fifth birthday.

As noted, in October 1971 Nixon's visit to China in July 1972 was announced to the press. The next spring, in 1972, Hanoi launched another major effort to conquer South Vietnam, the Easter Offensive. One suspects this all-out push was a direct result of North Vietnam's dismay at the upcoming talks between President Nixon and the PRC leaders in Beijing. Hanoi also had to worry about the years of American diplomacy with the Soviets that seemed as if they might soon bear fruit, a Soviet-American summit. If Nixon went to Russia, a strategic arms limitation treaty was on the table along with numerous other points of the superpowers' relationship. A Russian-American and Chinese-American *détente* would give the Americans more room to escalate the war in North Vietnam, and no doubt the members of the politburo in Hanoi knew it. Despite the massive American troop drawdown underway south of the DMZ, they must have felt "now or never" pressure. Given the way Communists write history, we will probably never know.

Beneath an umbrella of AAA and SAMs, the NVA had stockpiled supplies and positioned huge assault forces north of the 17th parallel DMZ. The US Air Force counted more than fifty SAMs launched at reconnaissance flights, with three Phantoms and a Thunderchief shot down in just two days. A campaign study revealed that "[P]ilots reported that the intensity of antiaircraft fire in the DMZ was equal to that encountered during earlier raids in the Hanoi area. In addition to the 23mm, 37mm, and 57mm antiaircraft weapons used in the past, the North Vietnamese introduced 85mm and 100mm guns into the

DMZ. Also, in the final weeks before the offensive, SA-2 SAMs were emplaced and on occasion fired, in volleys, from multiple locations. This progressive buildup of an air defense system, which conformed to Soviet doctrine, placed in formidable threat an umbrella over the North Vietnamese assembling invasion forces."[14]

On March 29, 1972, General Vo Nguyen Giap pulled the trigger on Operation Nguyen-Hue. Named by the North Vietnamese for the Vietnamese emperor who repelled an eighteenth-century Siamese attack, the invasion was aimed at nothing less than the violent "reunification" of the two Vietnams.

Hanoi had planned well, prepared extensively, and still caught the American leadership in Saigon by surprise. Giap launched a three-pronged attack into South Vietnam, one driving across the DMZ and the other two coming from sanctuaries in Laos and Cambodia. Over the next two weeks at least ten NVA divisions smashed into South Vietnam, a military force that may have totaled 150,000 Communist soldiers.

Leading the Northern assault across the DMZ was the 308th Division, bearing battle honors from Dien Bien Phu in 1954. The attackers were supported by main battle tanks and amphibious vehicles plus mobile artillery and antiaircraft weapons.

The Vietnam conflict was no longer a large insurgency—it was a conventional war between rival armies. Nixon responded by widening the air war over North Vietnam and mining the North Vietnamese harbors. Despite this, the Soviets wanted a summit. And Nixon's invitation to China still stood.[15]

The message to Hanoi could not have been clearer: Hanoi's ambitions and intransigence were not going to stand in the way of the Soviet Union's or People's Republic of China's perceived interest in improving relations with the United States.

After four years of "negotiations" with the North Vietnamese, Nixon and Kissinger understood that only military reverses would force the North Vietnamese to seriously negotiate. To his everlasting credit, Richard Nixon was prepared to supply the military pressure—in an election year—despite the howls of the politicians who mirrored their constituents' war weariness. He and Henry Kissinger had patiently prepared the ground. "We were in the process of separating Hanoi from its allies," Kissinger said.[16] Neither the Soviets nor PRC would intervene militarily to aid the North Vietnamese Communists.

The bogeymen under the bed were dead.

CHAPTER 17

"YOU AIN'T HIT THE TARGET YET"

In bombing, the measure of accuracy is the circular error of probability (CEP), the distance from the aim point within which half the ordnance will strike. Not all . . . *half.* During World War II the Army Air Force strove for a thousand-foot CEP in level bombing—which was a goal more than an achievement. Yet even in the early 1960s there was little reason for optimism. Circa 1965 fighter-bomber pilots typically scored a CEP of 750 feet in combat. As one survey concluded, "It was sufficient for the impact of a tactical nuclear weapon but is far from adequate for conventional weaponry." During Rolling Thunder, from 1965 to 1968, F-105s typically scored 5.5 percent direct hits, with a CEP of 450 feet. Later, technique and equipment cut the previous CEP in half, to a still unsatisfying 365 feet. Photo interpreters counting bomb craters and measuring distances derived the numbers.[1]

Before you decide that combat aviators were incompetent dive bombers, remember that attacking bombers dropped their dumb bombs in a string, or "train." The mil setting the pilot put into the bombsight was a number derived for the middle bomb in the string, or if an even number of bombs were dropped in one pass, the average of all of them. If one bomb in the string was a bull's-eye, all the others in the string missed by varying distances. The average miss distance of all the bombs in the string, divided by two, was the CEP, or the distance from the target at which half the bombs fell inside.

Still, any way one approached the problem, there were a lot of bomb craters scattered all over the landscape, with precious few bull's-eyes.

Then the precision millennium dawned.

★

The dream was ancient: sky-borne gods who would fling unerring thunderbolts earthward to punish or destroy evil doers. During World War II cities were pounded into oblivion by rains of explosives carpeting them. Accuracy was the quest, a technological goal seemingly beyond man's reach. American and German engineers produced television- and radio-controlled weapons that could strike with impressive accuracy . . . some of the time. The Luftwaffe was notably successful, deploying radio-guided ordnance that could strike—and sink—targets as small and as impressive as battleships.

After that war, precision-guided weapons remained more a theory or dream than a reality.

Yet in 1965, at the time of the first frustrating swipes at the Dragon's Jaw, a quiet revolution was underway near Dallas, Texas. An innovative engineer named Weldon Word led a small development team at Texas Instruments (TI). He reversed the conventional wisdom: rather than employing lasers as weapons (Jules Verne and H. G. Wells had dreamed of "death rays"), why not use them to guide weapons onto pinpoint targets?[2]

Like radar (radio detection and ranging), "laser" is an acronym for "light amplification by stimulated emission of radiation." Albert Einstein had envisioned something similar in 1917, but it took until 1960 before Hughes Research Laboratory in California produced the first operating laser. Experimentation suggested a variety of uses.

Because they operate on a single frequency, lasers are small, tightly focused beams that retain their dimensions at extreme distances. Consequently, the "standoff" capability that a laser-aiming device would give aircrews seemed promising. Combat aircrews could launch their weapons from distances previously undreamed of, all the while staying safely outside of the range of many of the enemy's defenses.

The Air Force was already interested—or part of the Air Force, that is. Under Project 1559 the Research and Development Office sought "short term translation of technology into new or improved weapons systems." Laser-guided bombs (LGBs) featured prominently.[3]

In 1965 Weldon Word's supervisor had lamented the miserable accuracy of US Air Force bombing, with a thousand-foot CEP. Long afterward Word recalled, "I said, 'Well, how about laser-guided stuff? We never built any, but we're sure talking the hell out of it.'"

Thirty-four years old, Word came from a rich military background: he was a Navy brat and had served in the Army. One of his TI projects was eighteen months on a naval-industry team perfecting antisubmarine sonars. He also contributed to the Shrike antiradar missile.[4]

Sent to Washington to sell the brass on the idea of using lasers to aim bombs, Word found a defensive attitude among the generals. "They took great offense at our 'Buck Rogers' idea," he said. "[But] you have bomb-damage assessment photos with 800 craters and you ain't hit the target yet."

However, Word and his team found a valuable ally in Colonel Joseph Davis from Eglin Air Force Base. Eglin was the service's weapons system development facility, and Davis' group, Detachment Five, was interested in precision strike. After hearing Word's presentation, Davis offered a one-time good deal: his office would support the laser-guided bomb if it could be developed in six months for less than $100,000.[5]

Weldon Word was the right man in the right place. A better man to develop the technology could not have been found.

A laser-guided bomb was a binary system. It needed a projector to "illuminate" a spot for the ordnance to guide upon. With the seeker on the nose of the falling bomb detecting the reflected energy on a compatible frequency, the weapon could ride the invisible beam all the way to impact. So the attackers needed two aircraft—one to illuminate and one to drop, or launch, the weapon.

Although Texas Instruments won the nod against North American, which was also vying for a contract, limited funding put a bite on Word's crew. Even in the mid-1960s $100,000 only covered a limited number of engineering man-hours to design a system, not to mention the cost of actually producing hardware.

An important subcontractor was Ford Aeronutronic, at the time a division of Ford Aerospace, in Newport Beach, California. They meticulously produced the high-quality lenses required for LGBs. The first six Pave Knife laser pods, weighing twelve hundred pounds each, were hand-built under the scrutiny of Reno Perotti, a widely respected optical engineer.[6]

Scrimping wherever possible, TI bought parts off the shelf at home and abroad. When wind-tunnel testing looked too costly, Word and company built scale models of the weapons for fluid testing in a swimming pool.

TI developed "screw-on" kits for the seeker and guidance systems to be installed on existing ordnance. The Mark 80 series of bombs, ranging from 250 to 2,000 pounds, had been developed by Douglas Aircraft in the 1950s. With a uniform aerodynamic shape regardless of weight, they provided far better ballistic properties than the previous "fat bombs" of World War II and Korea fame. The Mark 80 series were the ideal teammates for laser-guided technology. M118 3,000-pounders were fitted with guidance kits in 1969. The M118 provided 50 percent more bang than the Mark 84 and three times as much as a Mark 83.[7]

In 1967 the LGB was dubbed Paveway, an apparently poetic choice, as the laser paved the way through the sky for the weapon. Reputedly "Pave" was an acronym for precision avionics vectoring equipment; however, industry and scientific sources state that "Pave" referred to the overall Air Force project under which LGBs were developed.[8]

Regardless of the origin of the name, Paveway was a spectacular success, meeting contract requirements for a twenty-five-foot CEP and 80 percent guidance reliability. The weapon sold itself. The original order was for fifty seeker kits. Then, in June 1968, the Air Force paid $4.7 million for 293 more LGB kits. The airmen soon bought another thousand.[9]

Aircrews appreciated the high prices of LGB and electro-optical bombs, the latter running $17,000 or more each, four times the cost of the initial batch of Paveways. But the unit cost of Paveways continued to drop as production increased.[10]

A Paveway I involved three elements: a bomb, the AGM-45 Shrike antiradar missile's control activator, and the laser seeker. The TI system included rear-mounted cruciform airfoils on the bomb for stabilization in flight and moveable canards up front to steer the weapon to its target dot of laser light.

When dropped, the unpowered glide-bomb entered a laser capture area, or "basket," from which it followed its natural trajectory earthward as it steered toward the laser dot target. The basket was the open end of a cone, with the small end on the laser dot.

In flight an LGB described a shallow sine wave toward the laser-dot target. As the dive angle changed, the weapon's canards compensated accordingly. When the bomb's flight path took it above the perfect trajectory, the weapon's canards tipped down to lower the nose. If the weapon descended below the perfect trajectory, the canards rotated upward to raise the nose, as per any well-behaved aircraft. Similarly, it would adjust left or right to respond to wind drift.

However, unlike an aircraft, the canards were an all-or-nothing proposition, slamming full up or full down with no intermediate position. Fliers and ordnancemen called it a "bang-bang" arrangement—rough but effective. And it happened quickly, multiple times per second. The flipping back and forth of the canards robbed the LGB bomb of kinetic energy in its downward flight—creating more drag than a slick bomb—so it required a fairly high release altitude and a lot of airspeed to give the weapon sufficient energy to reach the target.

Too little energy imparted to the weapon when it was released meant that it would literally fall out of the cone—and miss the target. A release below ten thousand feet of altitude was almost pointless. During theater evaluation the Eighth Tactical Fighter Wing began releasing LGBs at twelve thousand feet after a 45-degree dive from twenty thousand.[11]

The Paveway system required a designator aircraft to lase the target. The original AVQ-9 laser designators were optical telescopes mounted in a Phantom's rear cockpit, fixed to the left canopy frame and aimed by the backseater, the weapons system officer (WSO). Visually aiming the laser through the optic, he activated the laser beam with a trigger. The gadget, officially called Pave Light, was dubbed the "zot box" after Johnny Hart's cartoon aardvark that liked to "zot" ants.

Although effective in clear air to ten or twelve miles, the box imposed onerous limits on the designating aircrew. Because the box was fixed to the airframe, the pilot had to fly a pylon turn around the target, presenting the AAA defenders with a predictable flight path. The WSO had to keep the target illuminated by the laser as the bombs fell, so his pilot had to fly a smooth, steady course with no evasive action that would jiggle the WSO's aim off target. Furthermore, the backseater could not eject with the box in place, requiring precious seconds to remove it before pulling the yellow and black handle.[12]

Clearly, the in-cockpit box was only a stopgap—the replacement was already on the way: a twelve-hundred-pound Pave Knife designator pod that was carried on one of the designator aircraft's weapons stations. The gimbaled designator was installed on the lead aircraft in the flight, allowing the Lead to bomb and his wingmen to drop simultaneously. As long as Lead's WSO kept the designator painting the target with laser light as the pilot maneuvered, all the bombs would take the same airy route to their destination. One pass, four bombs, and it was time to return to base for a beer at the club.

Initially twelve Pave Knife pods were manufactured, with three kept stateside for the test program. Three went to the Navy for specially wired A-6A Intruders. The other six went to Thailand, yet two of those were lost on downed Phantoms. The remaining four were retained for use on high-priority targets only.

Although astoundingly accurate, Paveway had serious operational limitations. It was largely ineffective at night, and laser light could be scattered by smoke, rain, fog, and low clouds, diffusing the clarity of the target dot or causing a false image. Still, the pinpoint accuracy airmen had dreamed about for sixty years was finally achievable . . . on a clear day. And although clear days in Vietnam were few and far between, they did come around occasionally.

The Paveway project accelerated quickly. Initial flight testing began in April 1965 as a kit on a 750-pound M117 bomb. Field tests began in Vietnam in 1968, but opportunities were limited by Lyndon Johnson's bombing halt that spring.

Nonetheless, that year an in-theater survey concluded that fighter-bombers armed with LGBs could destroy more than twenty times as many targets for the same number of jets dropping six M117s each. Despite the added laser-incurred expense, there was a huge difference in cost per target destroyed not only because fewer weapons were required but also because attacking aircraft suffered far fewer losses. Cost-benefit analysis . . . McNamara's Whiz Kids must have loved that report.

The Air Force already had another precision weapon, Rockwell's Homing Bombing System, or HOBOS. Like the Walleye ineffectively used against the Thanh Hoa Bridge in 1967, it was an electro-optical weapon, yet it had far more punch because it was mated to a Mark 84 two-thousand-pound bomb. HOBOS had the advantage of also being a "fire and forget" weapon—once the TV seeker was locked onto the target, the firing aircraft was free to maneuver and escape the target area. Deployed to Vietnam in 1969, it proved generally effective, even though it needed a high-contrast target and required modifications to the carrying aircraft. There was also the cost. A HOBOS kit cost more than $20,000 in 1972 dollars versus a Paveway I guidance kit, which cost $2,700.[13]

Anticipating increased need if the war resumed Up North, in 1971 the Air Force authorized production of Paveway guidance pods at a rate of 920 per month, nearly half for Mark 84 bombs. Seeker kits were one thing, however, and the Pave Knife targeting pods were quite another. By April 1972, when North Vietnam launched the Easter Offensive, the large-scale invasion of the south, the new Pave Knife pods were still scarce.[14]

The laser-guided bomb systems were soon put to use. From February 1972 to February 1973 some 10,600 LGBs were dropped in Southeast Asia, more than 90 percent being Mark 84 one-ton bombs. In medium-packed soil a Mark 84 left an impressive calling card: a crater thirteen feet deep and forty feet in diameter. LGBs were credited with a combat CEP of less than twenty-five feet, with 48 percent direct hits, and an 85 percent reliability rate. On a clear day an LGB seemed like the finger of God flicking down to smite the enemy.[15]

"We used to say we were dropping a Cadillac," Colonel Dean Failor recalled. "They were very accurate, and I guess compared to other munitions of the time [they were] cheap, but to us 'crew dogs' they were Cadillacs. They were worth a Cadillac, too, because they worked. We really didn't like the electro-optical guided bombs because they didn't always work."

Failor described the Paveway/Pave Knife accuracy: "We took a bridge out with laser illumination. The first bomb hit the bridge, the second hit the abutment and blew that end off the bridge, the third bomb hit the middle and dropped that span in the river, and the fourth bomb hit the abutment on the other end and blew that up. When we left there was nothing but ripples in the water."

Describing pilot-WSO coordination, Failor explained, "You had to be good at what you were doing. There had to be cooperation between the guy in back and the pilot and a general understanding of how the bomb worked. Once you got that down though, it went well. When you used it properly the laser-guided bomb was so much better than a regular iron bomb that there was just no comparison."[16]

Paveways were truly precision weapons. Failor recalled pinwheeling a bulldozer along the Ho Chi Minh Trail in Laos. It had been stashed in a bomb crater, presenting a difficult angle to an attacker. One LGB destroyed it.[17]

Paveway I was a rousing success. Texas Instruments had designed, tested, and deployed the system in an astonishingly short time, and it was extremely accurate. Combat CEPs were as little as *eight feet.*

To put that number in proper perspective, most "iron bombs" had a built-in error of six mils, or twenty inches of dispersion from the aim point for every thousand feet of fall. Imperfect casings and non-uniform explosive content, plus dents and dings in the bomb fins, accounted for that. An unguided dumb bomb was not a rotating sniper bullet. So the most perfectly aimed dumb bomb released in a no-wind environment from a slant range of 9,000 feet could miss the target by 15 feet. With five hundred pounds of high explosive on a medium-hard target that was as good as a direct hit. Yet half the dumb bombs missed by *more than 450 feet.*

The bad news was that the Paveway had completed its combat evaluation in August 1968, well after Lyndon Johnson's ban on bombing north of the 19th parallel that year. His subsequent prohibition on attacks anywhere in the North left Paveway all dressed up with nowhere to go. There simply were not enough worthwhile LGB targets in South Vietnam or Laos.

But that changed overnight when General Giap led his NVA army across the DMZ on March 29, 1972, the Easter Offensive.

★

In the years of the Johnson bombing halt, the Vietnamese, probably with the help of Chinese construction crews, had worked continuously to keep the vital bridge across the Song Ma open while repairing bomb damage. Between 1968 and 1972 eight concrete piers reinforced the approaches for greater resistance to explosives. The span itself still featured a one-meter-gauge railway along the twelve-foot center, with twenty-two-foot concrete roadways supported by cantilever structures on both sides. By the spring of 1972 the Dragon's Jaw was renewed, refreshed, and well defended. It was as if the innumerable attacks from 1965 to 1968 had not occurred.[18]

With the Easter Offensive going full blast, another round with the Dragon was inevitable. Some veteran fliers were reflective about the Dragon's Jaw. One *Constellation* Phantom pilot recalled, "We thought of calling Hanoi and saying we'd push three A-4s overboard if they would just blow up that damn bridge."[19]

CHAPTER 18

BACK TO NORTH VIETNAM

Washington's immediate response to the North Vietnamese Easter Offensive invasion of South Vietnam was Operation Freedom Train, initially with heavy naval aviation support. Subsequently, when President Nixon approved wider air attacks in early May, Freedom Train morphed into Linebacker, which targeted all of North Vietnam.

Much had changed since the end of Rolling Thunder in later 1968. From 1969 through 1971 US troop strength in Southeast Asia had dropped from over a half a million men to 156,000. By then an additional 20,367 US servicemen had died in theater, although the 1971 toll of 2,414 was the lowest since 1966. The Nixon administration was pulling Americans out of Vietnam just as quickly as it could be safely done—or even faster.[1]

Many of the combat units still in country were advisers to the Army of the Republic of Vietnam (ARVN) and the Vietnamese Marine Corps. The North Vietnamese conventional invasion in the spring of 1972, with 150,000 men in three striking columns, spearheaded by tanks and backed by artillery, meant that American and South Vietnamese defenders were badly outnumbered at the points of contact.

Despite the NVA buildup in the DMZ and southern North Vietnam, the American military leadership in South Vietnam was caught with its pants down. For several days the US military command in Saigon refused to believe that a major attack was in progress. As usual during the monsoon, low ceilings prevented help from American tactical airpower.

James H. Webb Jr. summarized, "In five historic days combat bases were overrun and abandoned, South Vietnamese units ceased to exist, the largest bridge in the northern part of South Vietnam was destroyed against higher orders in order to stop a tank assault, and B-52s were diverted seconds before they erroneously bombed the besieged US advisers. And, most importantly, despite the chaos the South Vietnamese not only stopped the attack, but were able to counterattack a short time later."[2]

It was a stunning military victory for the South Vietnamese and their American allies, yet political support for the war in the United States had eroded too badly for the American government to change its direction, even if it had had the will. The Johnson administration's lies, obfuscation, irresolution, and incompetence had come home to roost. Nixon and Kissinger were working for some kind of political solution to protect the South Vietnamese from the Communists, but the writing was on the wall: the hard, cold, brutal fact was that with or without a political resolution, the United States was leaving.

★

The 432nd Tactical Reconnaissance Wing was one of those deployed with Paveways. Possibly the most junior flier at Udorn was First Lieutenant Ron Rowen, a distinguished pilot graduate of flight training the previous August, with a wife and twin boys back in Utah.

He related,

As I was returning from an early-morning mission, I was met by Major Ivy McCoy on the flight line. He asked if I had experience dropping LGBs at Nellis.

The answer was no, but before I could get it out he said, "Say yes." Then he told me that there was an imaginary basket of delivery parameters that was wide at altitude but narrowed close to the ground. He told me that if I dived directly over the target straight down in afterburner from at least eighteen thousand feet that the "Zot" would designate the target and call *ready, ready, pickle* at the appropriate time in my dive. Ivy mentioned that I could expect asymmetric flight characteristics if I delivered one of the two bombs being loaded on the plane, then the other on another pass.

With that flight-line brief, my WSO and I manned up and launched. Unfortunately, when we got to what was supposed to be the rendezvous point and were in contact with the OV-10 "Nail FAC" configured with a laser designator, we couldn't find the guy visually. Lead put me opposite him in a wheel pattern so we could both scan. After two or three trips around the circuit, I spotted a glint several miles north and low. I asked our FAC to reverse his turn and saw another glint, so I confirmed a tally-ho. Lead told me not to lose sight of the FAC. As I came around the turn to the north I was forced to roll out and proceed north to keep the Nail in sight. After two or three minutes I had joined with the FAC, but my lead was still circling "no joy" to the south.

The Nail pilot suggested that I go ahead and hit the target while Lead was trying to find us. Having never before delivered a bomb in a 90-degree dive going Mach 1 with afterburners cooking, the sight of Mother Earth straight ahead as I roared downward was unsettling. Several thousand feet went by very quickly, and the Nail FAC seemed like he had a slow southern drawl, "R-e-a-d-y . . . r-e-a-d-y . . . r-e-a-d-y . . . *Pickle!*"

On the pullout I pulled five or six Gs instead of the customary four as Vietnam rushed up at me, which seemed judicious, and I was surprised. No asymmetrical loading! On my way back upstairs

I realized that I had pickled both bombs. The F-4E switchology was slightly different from the F-4D I was accustomed to flying. Select all stations and bombs singly in the E-model, and you get one bomb off all stations. Select bombs single and all stations on the D-model, and you got one bomb off one station, sequencing from station to station on subsequent pickles.

Needless to say, smoke and dust from those two-thousand-pounders went several thousand feet high, and the hapless bridge target was vaporized. My flight lead had no problem finding where we were and soon joined the party.

The two of us RTB'd [returned to base]. The debrief with bomb damage assessment was curt and abrupt. "Rowen, I should court-martial you for leaving the flight! However, Sierra Hotel BDA! Nothing further needs to be said about this!"

So there you go. No formal training, no formal briefing, just a verbal description of what needed to take place and that was it.

Ron Rowen's tenure in Thailand was hectic: he flew ninety-one missions, mostly nocturnal, in 181 days.[3]

★

The Navy was deeply involved in the wide renewal of air attacks north of the 20th parallel. At the time of the Easter Offensive USS *Hancock* and USS *Coral Sea* manned Yankee Station off North Vietnam; USS *Constellation* and USS *Kitty Hawk* soon joined them. The four carrier air wings brought some 250 aircraft to the fight.

Meanwhile Air Force reinforcements were inbound from the States. Beginning in early April Operation Constant Guard launched two squadrons totaling thirty-six F-4s from Seymour Johnson AFB, North Carolina, to Ubon, Thailand. They were accompanied by four EB-66 Destroyers from Shaw Air Force Base in South Carolina. A dozen F-105G Wild Weasels accompanied the group and landed at Korat. The planes were in Thailand by April 15.

The next day two more squadrons of Phantoms from Eglin and Homestead Air Force Bases in Florida launched to fly the Pacific to Udorn, Thailand.

Constant Guard III was the largest movement of tactical air command aircraft: 72 F-4Ds from Holloman Air Force Base in New Mexico, with three thousand men and sixteen hundred tons of equipment and supplies.[4]

The ensuing campaign lasted nearly six months. By whatever name, the renewed air campaign demonstrated America's global strength. She was a creature of the sea and sky, bringing firepower to bear in numbers and capability unmatched anywhere on the planet.

★

Among the major players in the renewed air campaign was an old-timer: the Eighth Tactical Fighter Wing at Ubon, Thailand. Inheriting the mantle from the legendary Robin Olds was Colonel Carl Miller, a forty-two-year-old professional fighter pilot with fifty-seven F-84 missions to his credit in Korea. He had flown a previous Southeast Asia tour with 278 sorties in F-100s during 1966–1967. He became vice commander of the Eighth Wing in September 1971, then assumed command in February 1972. He flew 189 Phantom combat missions, for a total of 467 in Southeast Asia.[5]

Miller earned his troops' loyalty. One of his squadron commanders said, "Colonel Miller was a great leader. . . . He would fall on his sword for his men and women, and we all knew it. If he said Go, we would go, period."[6]

The 1972 campaign involved a curious role reversal for the Eighth Wing. Previously the Wolfpack was lauded as the champion MiG killer wing, with 45 percent of Air Force victories through 1968. During Linebacker the Ubon Phantoms prided themselves as the Bridge Busters and were credited with destroying or seriously damaging more than one hundred spans throughout North Vietnam.[7]

Commanding the wing's 433rd Tactical Fighter Squadron was Lieutenant Colonel Rick Hilton, an "old head." A thirty-eight-year-old Oklahoman, he led "Satan's Angels," whose squadron history went back to World War II as a top-scoring P-38 squadron. He had already flown one combat tour by the spring of 1972. Hilton said, "I was privileged to command the 433rd and flew with great warriors like J. D. Franks. J. D. was the expert in laser designators . . . and I believe he would be hard pressed to recall all of the targets he destroyed.

"The squadron employed both the 'Zot' [Pave Light] and Pave Knife laser designators in North Vietnam, but the limitations of the Zot made it less desirable in high-threat environments. The Pave Knife pod was more useful but had two shortcomings: the tracking was accomplished by the GIB [Guy in Back] but the rate-aided feature of the pod design was not robust enough to keep up with the need to pull up to avoid the ground and get out of Dodge. The second problem was that we only had six pods and one of them was in Eglin for continued testing. We had the other five units."[8]

First Lieutenant James "J. D." Franks was a twenty-five-year-old Texan with an aerospace engineering degree from A&M. He graduated from Weapon Systems Operator School in 1971—commanded by Colonel Carl Miller—and that May became one of the Eighth Wing's few WSOs—instead of backseat pilots—qualified on laser weapons.

The Nellis Fighter Weapons School provided a two-week LGB course, forming crews that would proceed to Southeast Asia. Franks and his front-seater, Captain Pete Bracci, were ticketed for the 433rd with Major Vaughn Wells and Captain Rick Mugg.

Once in theater the selected crews flew several training missions "prior to being turned loose in combat with Paveway Zot or Pave Knife," Franks recalled,

> I worked in the squadron weapons office as an additional duty, and we tracked the number of LGBs delivered, who delivered them, and the CEP of the bombs. Records were informal and probably not retained in official USAF histories, but we were dropping quite a few LGBs after I arrived in May 1971.

> The majority of the targets were road cuts, bulldozers, occasionally a bridge, and trucks along the trail. Of course AAA guns were a big favorite, especially if they were shooting at you during a delivery. There was one period when we were fragged with five-hundred-pound Mark 82 LGBs. They were more erratic because of their lighter weight, and that caused the CEP to increase to about thirty feet from the zero feet that was our standard. The Mark 82s did not destroy guns if they didn't get a direct hit. Sometimes they just flipped the gun over. Once I remember someone got tasked on a North Vietnamese tank. The film was memorable in that the tank turret came flying out of the smoke. We kept a "greatest hits" video that was shown in "new guy" school.[9]

Morale was seldom a problem at Ubon. In fact, some troops from South Vietnam opted for R&R in Ubon rather than the fabled fleshpots of Bangkok. Each squadron assigned to the Eighth Wing maintained a "party hootch." Custom beer mugs plus "Sierra Hotel" party suits and hats in squadron colors were de rigeur, and woe betide the new guy who forgot to remove his hat upon entering: the miscreant was forced to stand on the bar and "drink his hat." As one backseater described it, "This entailed filling it with everything behind the bar, including mustard, ketchup, bitters, etc., and serenading the new guy while he stood on a pedestal drinking the concoction. After he finished everyone stomped on the hat to make it look as bad as possible. He then wore it for a year, dropping it over enemy territory from the speed brakes of his Phantom on his last mission."[10]

★

One of the new backseaters at Ubon was Captain Bill Thaler, who experienced a giddy transition from stateside to combat. He had joined the 523rd Tactical Fighter Squadron at Clark Air Force Base in the Philippines but was sent back to Seymour Johnson Air Force Base in North Carolina for more training, arriving there on April 1, 1972. Meanwhile in

Vietnam the Easter Offensive had begun. At Seymour Johnson Thaler flew one training mission and wryly noted, "My second ride at SJ [Seymour Johnson] was a couple of days later and was a 10.5-hour flight to Hickam AFB, Hawaii. I didn't know the guy I was flying with (Larry Shane) and, in fact, didn't even meet him until we got to the airplane. We launched eighteen F-4Es and arrived at Ubon, Thailand, three days later. I still didn't know the names of half the guys in the squadron."[11]

The 523rd lived a gypsy existence that month, with detachments at Ubon, Udorn, and DaNang. However, on April 21—three weeks after alighting in North Carolina—Bill Thaler was flying over North Vietnam on his way to the Dragon's Jaw, the Thanh Hoa Bridge. It was his seventh combat sortie and his first Up North.

The April 21 mission was ambitious in content and scope. It was planned as a dual-axis attack, with the Thailand aircraft attacking from the west after the first wave from South Vietnam had hit the bridge. The briefing noted that upward of one hundred aircraft were involved, including tankers, escorts, and flak suppressors. As Thaler recalled, "I don't know for sure how many participated, but I do know there were tons of us up there."[12]

Lieutenant Colonel Crawford "Sock" Shockley, an early F-100 pilot, led Utah Flight with Captain Larry Henry behind him. Captains Doug P. Brown and WSO Larry W. Peters were the Number Two.

Leading the second section as Utah Three was Captain Larry Shane with Bill Thaler. Utah Four was Captain Bob Harcrow and First Lieutenant Rich Sroka.

One of the problems with a large, complex plan is that early glitches can unravel the whole thing. That began to happen on April 21. The KC-135s were late, requiring some fighters to divert to other tanker tracks. By the time the strike force approached the target area the schedule had turned to hash. Utah flight, carrying unguided bombs, was slated to be among the last to attack from the west, but owing to the tanker screw-up, they were among the first inbound.

Thaler takes up the story:

Intel briefed us on the location of SAMS and the extent of the SAM rings. I never paid any attention to another Intel briefing the whole time we were over there! We were about fifty miles outside of the supposed western extent of the SAM ring when SAMS started coming up, apparently aimed at the eastern wave of attackers since they were not coming close to us at all. We found out later that the eastern wave commander aborted their mission due to target area weather.

I had never seen a SAM before. While the ground was obscured due to a scud layer, above the layer was crystal clear. I was mesmerized by missiles streaking to sixty thousand feet or so at Mach 3. It's an impressive sight. My front-seater, Captain Larry Shane, who had a hundred north, gently reminded me that those weren't the ones that were going to hurt us. So I returned to my main job at that time, which was visual lookout.

We were Number Three in a four-ship flying "pod" formation because no one trusted the ECM pods to begin with. We were stepped up and down on Utah One. So we were about twelve to fifteen hundred feet off each other as we turned inbound. . . .

As we got closer to the target area the SAMs in front started coming our way. They weren't getting too close, though the radar homing and warning [RHAW] gear was going nuts, as it did anytime we had the pods on. I had no signals indicating tracking.

I did not see Utah Two get hit. I was checking to the outside of our formation, and as I turned my attention back to the inside I saw a hole open up in the top of his number-two engine. He had fire coming from under the engine, out the top of the engine, and out the burner can.

We were still twenty or so miles outside the briefed extent of the SAM ring, and it came up from *behind* us. Almost immediately after seeing the hole appear in Two's engine bay, I caught a glimpse of the second missile just before it exploded. It went off probably fifty to a hundred feet below us and almost directly between us and Doug and Larry.

The brain tends to capture every detail of certain events, particularly those that are potentially life threatening. I can still picture the intact missile, followed by the conical fire and black smoke after it exploded. How neither we nor Two were hit, I will never know.

After a couple of exclamations from both cockpits and we realized we had not been hit, we turned our attention to Utah Two. The four-ship formation stayed together to make sure they got to feet wet, where Doug and Larry ejected.

According to Bob Harcrow, Utah Three and Four got vectored toward MiGs. It must have been a short vector because I have no recollection of it. Apparently after not finding any MiGs and being low on fuel, we headed south for home. The search-and-rescue was already underway since the Navy responded very quickly.

No one from our flight expended ordnance. I think we jettisoned the ordnance over water, but I can't remember for sure. Fortunately most of the missions over North Vietnam were not nearly so eventful.[13]

The efficient rescue service that retrieved the crew of Utah Two was an HC-7 Sea Devil HH-3 helicopter, call-sign Big Mother. Two HH-3 Sea Kings had launched from USS *Midway* that morning, motoring forward to operate from USS *Denver* (LPD-9).

Denver launched the two helos at 9:20, standing by while Air Force strikes went in—about twenty minutes later the helos heard a Mayday call. Aboard Big Mother Six-One was Lieutenant Franklin Pinegar, who recalled, "We then heard a call of 'two chutes,' and a position with latitude and longitude was given. My copilot was flying so I plotted the position on our 'flak charts' and determined that we were in a good position for a recovery."[14]

A few minutes later the shipboard controller cleared Big Mother Six-One to proceed.

The Air Force fliers were down about three miles northeast of Hon Me Island, five miles off the coast and twenty-five miles southeast of Thanh Hoa. Heading inbound at 120 knots and forty feet, Pinegar veered left and right off course to confound enemy radar tracking, as the Viets had antiaircraft sites on Hon Me.

Only fifteen minutes after leaving *Denver* copilot Lieutenant John Kennedy sighted a survivor in an orange raft roughly a mile ahead, just as the helo received a radio call on Guard from the other survivor, who reported the pair were about three hundred yards apart.

The helo's swimmer went into the water and swam up to the first survivor. As the aviator was going up in the hoist collar, the swimmer saw that the raft was still attached to the flier's vest. The weight of the raft dragged the man out of the hoist collar, and he fell back into the ocean. The chopper went over to the other survivor and hauled him aboard, then returned for the first guy and the swimmer, who were now ready to be winched up.

Aboard *Denver* Doug Brown and Larry Peters were treated to a survivor's red carpet examination, complete with refreshments.

Peters and Brown were delivered to DaNang the next day, then airlifted back to Ubon in a T-39 Saberliner. Upon arrival they were greeted by a raucous Wolfpack crowd, including Colonel Carl Miller, the wing commander. As Bill Thaler explained, "There were a few free drinks that night."[15]

CHAPTER 19

POUNDING THE NORTH

After their salt-water baptism, the Air Force Phantom crew of Doug Brown and Larry Peters went back to Thanh Hoa for another round with the Dragon on April 27, 1972, as part of a three-flight mission carrying Paveway LGBs and two HOBOS electro-optical weapons. Four chaff F-4s were scheduled but failed to arrive on time, and coastal fog defeated any effort to employ the LGBs, as the mist diffused the laser beams. Several HOBOS one-ton Mark 84s hit the bridge but failed to drop it.

Meanwhile the Wolfpack went against other bridges in North Vietnam. In May Carl Miller's Phantoms struck the Kien An, Cao Nunh, and Lang Bun Bridges, dropping them entirely or partially.

In South Vietnam the Easter Offensive attack had been stopped and NVA units were retreating. Richard Nixon's trip to China was still on for July, and Washington believed the Chinese were ready to improve relations. Still, President Nixon would have been at a disadvantage in negotiations if the United States and its ally, South Vietnam, were militarily defeated in the northern province of South Vietnam, Quang Tri, before he went to Beijing.

Even though 85 percent of North Vietnam's imports came through the port of Haiphong, the Johnson administration had always rejected the option of mining the harbor and cutting off the flow of fuel, weapons, and ammunition for fear of provoking intervention by China or the Soviets. But the Easter Offensive and Nixon's overtures to China changed the political calculus. The order to mine the harbor—Operation Pocket Money—was given in Washington and passed down the chain of command until it arrived at USS *Coral Sea*. CAG Roger "Blinky" Sheets planned the mission with Lieutenant Commander Harvey Ickle, the VA-22 operations officer, and Marine Captain William D. "Charlie" Carr. *Coral Sea*'s A-6 squadron was VMA-242, and Charlie Carr was its most experienced BN. Sheets would lead the strike with Charlie Carr in the right seat.

The multiservice operation began the morning of May 9. The Air Force sent a Lockheed EC-121 early-warning aircraft flying up the Gulf from DaNang. At dawn four destroyers—USS *Richard S. Edwards, Myles C. Fox, Buchanan,* and *Berkeley*—steamed in and shelled the Haiphong Harbor air defense batteries with a thirty-minute bombardment from their five-inch guns.

The guided missile cruisers USS *Long Beach* and USS *Chicago* were stationed forty miles from Haiphong to protect the mining planes from enemy fighters. To avoid exposing US Phantoms to Haiphong AAA, the cruisers were given a fire-free zone to engage approaching MiGs with Talos missiles.

USS *Kitty Hawk* launched seventeen planes for a diversionary attack on the Nam Dinh railyard, but bad weather forced them to hit secondary targets.

Three Marine A-6s from *Coral Sea*, each carrying four of the thousand-pound Mark 52 mines made runs into the harbor below five hundred feet and laid the mines in the positions the planners said would do the most good. Six VA-22 A-7s, carrying four five-hundred-pound Mark 36 acoustic mines, placed them in the outer portion of the channel. The mines were all retarded by parachutes, slowing them greatly and allowing them to splash into the water without damage.

While the mining aircraft were chugging into the harbor with their heavy, high-drag loads, an EA-3 provided electronic-countermeasures support overhead.

The North Vietnamese launched MiGs from the sanctuary airfields around Hanoi. They were in a holding pattern awaiting vectors toward the incoming bombers when *Chicago* launched two Talos missiles at them. One of the MiGs was destroyed.

The mines were all in the water by 9:01 local time, when CAG Sheets radioed "mission complete" back to the ship. *Coral Sea* sent the message on to Washington, where President Nixon was delivering a speech to the nation. It was the evening of May 8 in America. The timing of the speech and the mining operation were not coincidental.

Handed a note that said the mines were in place, the president then said, "I have ordered the following measures, which are being implemented as I am speaking to you. All entrances to North Vietnamese ports will be mined to prevent access to these ports and North Vietnamese naval operations from these ports. United States forces have been directed to take appropriate measures within the international and claimed territorial waters of North Vietnam to interdict the delivery of supplies. Rail and all communications will be cut off to the maximum extent possible. Air and naval strikes against North Vietnam will continue."[1]

The Navy and Marine bombers dropped more mines on May 11 and kept reseeding them as they randomly exploded or safetied themselves after 180 days in the water. Over eight thousand mines were put in coastal waters and three thousand in inland waterways.

There were thirty-six foreign-flagged vessels in Haiphong harbor the morning the mines were laid: sixteen Soviet, five Chinese, five Somalian, four British, three Polish, two Cuban, and one East German. The mines had a time delay of seventy-two hours before they would become active to give these ships time to leave the harbor. One British and four Soviet ships put to sea. The rest sat in the silting-up harbor for three hundred days until the war was over and the Americans had swept the harbor.[2]

★

The next day, Wednesday, May 10, the Air Force attacked the fabled Long Bien Bridge in Hanoi, better known as the "Paul Doumer" for an early French governor. The structure was huge. It spanned the mile-wide Red River flowing through northern Hanoi and was a vital link on the Northeast Railway logistics route from China. F-105s had first attacked the Doumer in 1967, inflicting damage that was soon repaired. Subsequent missions frequently attacked the span, damaging it yet again. Because the bridge was so vital, the North Vietnamese quickly repaired the damage. Now, with the port of Haiphong mined, the railroad was one of the last ways for Hanoi to get war supplies into the country.

The Eighth Wing flew a complex, multifaceted mission against the Doumer and executed almost flawlessly. The bridge attack was combined with a strike against a nearby railyard. The Air Force committed 120 aircraft, including twenty KC-135 tankers, plus radar jammers protecting thirty-two bombers and flak suppressors.

Sixteen F-4Ds hit the Paul Doumer Bridge with dumb bombs and two dozen one-ton LGBs. A four-plane chaff flight led the way into North Vietnam, scattering metal foil that clogged Vietnamese radar screens with useless returns. The only flaw in the mission was the lead flight's HOBOS bombs that malfunctioned or missed their targets; the other elements came together. For their part, the North Vietnamese knew the stakes and pulled out all the stops. They launched some *160 SAMs* at the strike force. Still, Phantoms armed with Paveway laser weapons and dumb bombs hammered the bridge and got away clean.

Photo analysis showed one span dropped into the river and four damaged. The downed span stopped rail traffic across the Red River. The Wolfpack returned the next day with more LGBs, dropping three more spans into the Red River. Restrikes foiled repair attempts and kept the Doumer unusable through the ceasefire in January 1973.

★

Elsewhere in North Vietnam, May 10 was a landmark day in air-to-air action. The Communist leadership ordered a maximum effort with their fighters against the Yankee air pirates.*

On that day a Navy Alpha strike from USS *Constellation* against the Hai Duong Railyard, southeast of Hanoi, ran into a swarm of MiGs.

Navy Lieutenant Randall W. "Duke" Cunningham and his RIO, Lieutenant (Junior Grade) William P. "Willy" Driscoll, were flying as flak suppressors carrying Rockeye cluster bombs.[3] Their squadron's call-sign was Showtime, and the F-4J they were flying carried side-number 100, so they were Showtime 100, or, as the Navy flight-crews used it, "Showtime One Double-nuts." Duke and Willy were on a roll—they had previously shot down two MiGs, tying the Navy record.

After delivering their ordnance, Cunningham and his wingman, Lieutenant Brian Grant, with RIO Jerry Sullivan, were bounced by a gaggle of MiGs. Jumped by two MiG-17s, Cunningham turned sharply into one shooting at him and forced an overshoot. He reversed and launched a Sidewinder, which connected.

The victim's wingman was on Cunningham's tail. As Cunningham tried to drag him out for Brian Grant, Grant said he had two on his own tail and couldn't help. Both American pilots plugged in their burners and accelerated away from the MiGs, then pulled into the vertical and went over the top at fifteen thousand. Jettisoning their external belly tanks, they started down . . . to find eight MiG-17s below them in a defensive wheel, with three F-4s mixed in.

The VF-96 executive officer, Commander Dwight Timm, came squirting from the furball with three Communist fighters hot after

---

*That there were still MiGs operating from fields around Hanoi is one of the most amazing stupidities of the Vietnam War, a direct result of the Johnson, then Nixon administrations' refusal to allow American air power to target the airfields. American fighters were still battling MiGs eight years into the Vietnam War. The Americans had willingly forfeited air supremacy over North Vietnam, which was absolute folly. The first airfield attacks were only approved in 1967 and remained erratic thereafter.

him, two MiG-17s and a 21. Cunningham slid in behind, hoping to destroy a MiG before it shot down Timm.

Meanwhile four MiGs were after Cunningham. Driscoll called them out. When the North Viets opened fire, Cunningham reversed hard, and the trailing fighters overshot to a trail position, just a bit too far to shoot if he kept his speed up.

He was trying, yet he had to somehow get the MiG-17 trailing Timm. Above this drama four MiG-21s were watching. Driscoll kept an eye on them.

Finally, after repeated calls, Timm broke hard right, and Cunningham launched another Sidewinder. Jim Fox, in Timm's backseat, witnessed this 'winder kill, which he said traveled the length of the silver fighter and blew it to bits. The pilot ejected behind Timm's F-4 and Cunningham had to jink hard to miss the falling body.

Above them the four MiG-21s were rolling in to join the fight. Cunningham turned under them and ran out behind them, accelerating and diving. Commander Timm was already on his way east. Although the F-4s were grossly outnumbered, other American pilots were also knocking down MiGs.

As they headed for the coast, Cunningham told Driscoll, "It sure is a shame to quit when we have all this gas and there are all kinds of MiGs." At that time the whole aerial action had taken approximately two minutes.[4]

Randy Cunningham and Willy Driscoll now had four MiGs to their credit, including the two they shot down earlier in the year.

As they headed for the coast, another MiG-17 appeared dead ahead, heading straight for them. What followed was amazing in its rarity, a classic jet-age dogfight between dissimilar aircraft. As Cunningham said, "The enemy liked to fight in the horizontal for the most part, or just to run, if he didn't have an advantage."

The MiG could out-turn its opponents below about four hundred knots, and its three guns in the nose were deadly. The F-4, like all American fighter-bombers, had more fuel capacity and had to be able to carry ordnance, so it was larger, heavier, and had more powerful engines, which means it could out-accelerate the MiGs and go faster. What the Phantom couldn't do was get into a turning fight with a more maneuverable airplane. And the Phantom had no guns, only heat-seeking Sidewinders and radar-guided Sparrow missiles.

Each pilot attempted to use the advantages his plane had over his adversary to get into a position that allowed him to kill his enemy. It was strength versus agility in mortal combat.

When the approaching MiG opened fire, Cunningham pulled into the vertical, intending to go straight up and come back down on his circling enemy. To his amazement the MiG pilot came into the vertical after him. In an instant they were canopy to canopy in a vertical scissors, a position that would allow the slower MiG to get behind the F-4, so Cunningham disengaged by plugging in his burners and powering ahead, only to find the MiG pilot blazing away behind him.

Cunningham went over the top and accelerated away toward the MiG's six o'clock, a classic disengagement. Then he turned around and started back in.

The two fighters ended up in another vertical scissors, this time going slower and slower. Cunningham disengaged again, and came back for a third time. Now, as the MiG joined him in the vertical climb, the American pulled his power to idle and popped his speed brakes. The MiG-17 shot out ahead of him for the first time.

Apparently the Vietnamese pilot stalled, because his nose fell through and he started straight down toward the earth. Using his afterburners, the F-4 pilot held his steed aloft and ruddered it around. The Sidewinder growled. He fired, and even though the missile was looking down at the heat of the earth, it tracked.

The 'winder exploded against the MiG-17, which continued down at a 45-degree angle until it smashed into the earth.

Victim number five. Cunningham and Driscoll were aces, the only Navy flight crew to achieve that status in the Vietnam War.

But they weren't home yet. They were still hanging it all out over North Vietnam amid a swarm of enemy fighters.

As Cunningham told it in his book *Fox Two*, Driscoll shouted on the intercom,

> "Duke, check ten o'clock: MiG-17 rolling in on us!" Irish had his eyes open. We had 550 knots, so I pulled nose high into the attacking craft and told Willy, "Here comes number six." Just then Matt Connelly, who had been watching the fight, yelled out, "Duke, get the hell out of there! There are four 17s at your seven o'clock."
>
> I saw Matt with his nose on us, just as he fired a missile. I thought, "Matt, Jeez, you're shooting at us!" His Sparrow went right over our tail and back to our seven o'clock . . . where four 17s were in pursuit! Matt's desperate missile shot did the trick as the Sparrow went sailing into the center of the formation—they looked like fleas evacuating a dog, splitting off in every direction to get out of the way.[5]

Still trying to get out of North Vietnam, Cunningham and Driscoll headed for the coast. Incredibly, the Phantom was bounced by three more MiGs. They used their F-4's raw power to escape and continued east for the safety of the ocean. Then SAMs were in the air. One exploded near Showtime 100. Cunningham continued to climb in afterburner.

After an estimated forty-five seconds the Phantom yawed hard right. The hydraulic systems were losing pressure quickly. As Cunningham said, "Fear, that ever-present companion, wanted to run the ship. 'What now, Cunningham?' raced through my mind."[6]

At that moment the pilot remembered how another Navy F-4 pilot had handled a similar loss of hydraulic pressure. He jammed the stick full forward, locking the stabilator in a slightly nose-up position. Without control of the stabilator, he began rolling the aircraft using rudder and power.

Cunningham and Driscoll barrel-rolled twenty miles through the sky, trying for salt water as the aircraft burned just aft of the cockpit. An explosion rocked the fighter, but they were still over land, corkscrewing along.

Accompanied by other F-4s and A-7s, they crossed the coast as they lost their last utility hydraulic system and another explosion racked the burning fighter. Now the rudder was useless. The F-4 stalled and began spinning.

Driscoll initiated command ejection. Much to their horror, Cunningham and Driscoll found themselves descending into the muddy mouth of the Red River. While still in the air, they heard on their emergency radios the welcome voice of helicopter pilots inbound.

As other American planes discouraged North Vietnamese small boats, the chopper scooped up the wet crew and took them to USS *Okinawa* (LPH-3). From there they were flown back to the *Constellation* to heroes' welcomes.

Within a few days Randy Cunningham and Willy Driscoll were flown to Saigon for a press conference, and from there they went to Washington to be decorated with Navy Crosses. Their war was over.

The third and final victim of Showtime 100 that busy May 10 was a MiG-17 supposedly flown by a NVAF ace, Colonel Nguyen Toon, also known as "Colonel Tomb." Well after the war the "Tomb" character was revealed as bogus, probably the result of poorly translated radio intercepts. But whatever the MiG-17 pilot's name, he was wounded or killed when a Sidewinder hit his plane. Even if the missile explosion had only incapacitated him, he died when his shattered MiG struck the earth.

Fighter combat in the skies has been called the greatest game. It's played for blood, kill or be killed, up there in the sky where there is no place to hide.

On May 10 other American fighters were also scoring against MiGs. The Navy added five more, for a total of eight, and the Air Force downed three while losing one of their own. In all, eleven MiGs were slain that day in three engagements, for a loss of two US fighters. That one-day total was the American record in Vietnam, and it has not been matched, forty-six years later.

And it was on May 10 that Air Force Captain Steve Ritchie, flying with the 555th Fighter Squadron from Udorn, Thailand, scored his first kill in an F-4. He would go on to score four more that summer, becoming the Air Force's only Vietnam pilot ace. Ritchie's May 10 backseater, Captain Chuck DeBellvue, would help another pilot shoot down MiGs and wound up credited with six, the highest total in the Vietnam War.[7]

★

There was no rest at Ubon that week. On Saturday, May 13, with improved visibility, the Eighth Tactical Fighter Wing's Wolfpack flew toward the Dragon's Jaw. It was a complex, global mission—the sort of work at which the US Air Force excelled. As novelist and analyst Tom Clancy related, "It took everything the ordnance shop and contractor tech-reps at Ubon could put together, including some specially-built three-thousand-pound LGBs."[8]

On the flight line Colonel Miller's ordnance crews had armed sixteen Phantoms with nine three-thousand-pound M118 LGBs, fifteen one-ton Mark 84 LGBs, and forty-eight Mark 82 five-hundred-pound iron bombs.[9]

They also loaded all five Pave Knife laser-designator pods. The first two flights each carried two pods, on the leader's and Number Three (second element) aircraft. The fifth pod went to the third flight leader.

As Lieutenant Colonel Rick Hilton explained, "The M118s had soft cases and would not survive a delayed detonation, so they were set to instantaneously detonate upon impact, with the hope of weakening the upper structure. The Mark 84s were set to delay detonation to achieve some penetration before exploding. Since the leader and Number Three had the Pave Knife pods, they each carried two Mark 84s and one M118. Flight members Two and Four each carried two M118s and two Mark 84s."[10]

The briefing warned aircrews of reduced visibility in the target area: hazy with some cloud cover. The prevailing wind was forecast from the west—contrary to the normal on-shore flow—so each flight commander and his wingman would target the bridge's east abutment. Numbers Three and Four would hold high until the lead element bombed, allowing smoke and dust to settle or blow away for improved visibility.[11]

Colonel Richard G. Horne, wing director of operations, led off early that morning as the leader of Jingle Flight. Pilots ran their throttles full forward, pushing both throttles through the detent into full afterburner, and rocketed away from Ubon's Runway 05-23 into the Siamese sky.

Taking off next was Captain David L. Smith's Dingus Flight of the 433rd Squadron, while the squadron CO, Lieutenant Colonel Rick Hilton, was third with Goatee Flight—as Hilton put it, "batting cleanup" for the precision munitions. Lieutenant Colonel D. C. Vest's Cowslip Flight from the attached Fourth Tactical Fighter Wing comprised the caboose at the end of the aerial freight train, flying F-4Es, each carrying a dozen Mark 82 five-hundred-pound iron bombs. The aerial armada set course for Thanh Hoa, 339 nautical miles away.

The bombers were supposed to follow four Phantoms with chaff dispensers into North Vietnam while other fighters trolled for MiGs. However, the two chaff flights, Brenda and Bertha, had trouble with the tanker rendezvous and arrived too late to participate. Meanwhile Jingle Four aborted with a flight-control problem, leaving fifteen strikers to continue the mission.[12]

Eight minutes out from the Dragon's Jaw Bridge the strike force saw that the weather was marginal. As predicted, the Tonkin clouds sided with the defenders, obscuring the target, worse than predicted at briefing.

While the strikers stalked the area, awaiting a chance to attack, the chaff flight checked in with Colonel Horne, who did not want to wait for them amid an alerted defense. "Jingle, confirm you don't want Brenda and Bertha in."

"That's right, babe. It's too late."

The chaff leader, Major Robert Blake, replied, "Roger, making a port turn down here."

"That's right, get out of here. . . . You can loiter a little bit in case we need you for something else." Horne wanted the chaffers outside Thanh Hoa's SAM belt, or envelope.

At length Horne thought he saw an opportunity and rolled in. But partway down the slide he aborted his run and told his second section to drop. Apparently Jingle Three and Four missed the bridge; circling overhead, Rick Hilton and his backseater, Bill Wideman, in Goatee One, looked for hits but saw none. Wideman advised, "Triple-A coming up at us."

All the while flight leaders tried to keep track of one another. Probably Horne's backseater asked, "Jingle [Flight], are you off target?"

"Jingle Three and Four are off."

Then Dingus Flight, led by Captain Dave Smith, requested clearance to roll in. As Hilton explained, "D. L. must have had the same question that Bill and I had: Where is our leader and his element, and what are they going to do now?"

But Horne said, "If you have the target, you are cleared in."

"Dingus Three, are you off?" Smith asked his element leader.

"Three and Four are off."

Hilton recalled, "I do not know if it was D. L. or his element's good results, but I saw two bombs hit the center of the bridge. Unfortunately, the bridge was still intact."

And the visibility was getting worse. Hilton said to his guy in back, Wideman, "I can't see it. Can you?"

"I think it's about nine o'clock."

"I know where it is, but I can just barely make it out."

In one of the great understatements of the war, Wideman replied, "It's gonna be a bastard."

Circling protectively nearby, the MiG CAP Phantoms continued tracking the mission's progress.

"Jingle Flight, where did you go in from?"

Colonel Horne answered, "From twenty-two [thousand]. Jingle is still at the target, holding high."

In Goatee Lead, Hilton and Wideman hunted the Dragon through the gloom. By now the clouds and haze were so thick that patches of the ground were obscured. Still under fire, Goatee Flight added "an orbit or two to find the bridge."

Wideman muttered, "Come on, Bridge, where are ya?"

At that point an electronic screech intruded from the Phantom's radar homing and warning (RHAW) gear. Hilton told Wideman, "I hope the RHAW works out."

Then . . .

"There it is! Right . . . there!" Hilton exclaimed.

"Okay, I got it," Wideman replied. "I can barely see it, but I got it."

The plan Hilton had briefed was that he and Wideman would roll in on the bridge and drop their three bombs. Then, circling at ten thousand feet, they would continue to illuminate the western span while Goatee Two dropped his four weapons. Numbers Three and Four would complete the attack.

But the cloud cover changed all that. So Hilton improvised, instructing his flight, "Okay, tighten it up. We're all going in together."

And they did just that. The four Phantoms dived through the murky air toward the bridge as the laser pods shined down their death rays. Each pilot punched off his weapons, and Hilton continued down, illuminating the bridge for the LGBs.

Then the Dragon disappeared in a succession of flashes. Hilton tightened his pullout. Watching from the backseat, Bill Wideman exclaimed, "Okay, there's an impact!"

Actually, there were about fourteen impacts.

Hilton radioed, "Good job, fellows."

Meanwhile a MiG CAP Phantom called, "Who's that at nine o'clock? About three miles."

A wingman replied, "He's in a dive, so probably a bomber."

The timing indicates this was Colonel Horne, perhaps making another effort. If so, apparently no additional hits resulted.

Meanwhile, in Goatee One, Rick Hilton and Bill Wideman exchanged thoughts. "God, it was almost impossible to see in that haze."

"Yeah, very tough but I had it. When you said 'I got it' . . . we were going through 10,000 feet and I was holding it [the laser] as well as I could. Well, I got it back just in time for an explosion. I don't know. Want to take another orbit around it?"

"Uh, yeah, just to look at it."

"Boy, there's a hell of a lot of smoke . . . "

"Sure is."

Meanwhile Lieutenant Colonel D. C. Vest, leading Cowslip Flight with iron bombs, reported, "We're about two miles out."

Horne asked, "You're the last flight, right?"

"Rog . . . "[13]

Cowslip Flight plunged for the bridge. Straddling the span, four dozen Mark 82s—five hundred pounds each—added their explosive power to the damage the LGBs had done.

At the west end the Dragon emitted a shrieking, mournful howl as high-tensile steel warped, buckled . . . and failed.

As the F-4s screeched away, clouds of smoke and haze prevented immediate assessment. Still, Colonel Miller was confident enough that when the Phantoms got on the ground back at base he sent a "flash message" to Seventh Air Force headquarters and the Joint Chiefs in Washington stating that the western span "might be interdicted."[14]

★

At Ubon the aircrews were exultant. They knew they had delivered the Dragon a mighty blow. Eleven Phantoms with LGBs—fifteen Paveway one-ton Mark 84s, nine laser-guided three-thousand-pound M118s, and forty-eight dumb five-hundred-pounders—had walloped the bridge and left it badly damaged. Best of all, the strikers got away clean despite lingering in the flak zone.

After debriefing, Rick Hilton went to his trailer to tape record a special message for his wife. He had barely begun when the telephone rang. Dick Horne, the mission commander, wanted the squadron leader to know that the 433rd had buckled the west end of the bridge. Hilton allowed the tape recorder to keep running:

"Well, as you know, sir, I've bounced a few off the top of that thing before, and it was almost personal."

Horne replied that the Air Force had lost many planes and pilots over Thanh Hoa.

"Yes, sir, and some of them are good friends. I'm happy we finally did it."

The boss hung up and Hilton said into his recorder, "Well, love, that was Colonel Dick Horne, who said that we dropped the Thanh Hoa Bridge today."

With that, Hilton adjourned to "The Inferno," the squadron's party hooch, where he indulged in a cherished tradition: he rang the party bell.[15]

Poststrike photography verified the claim. The western end of the western span was in the river. Seventy-two bombs, both smart and dumb, had accomplished what thousands had previously failed to do.

Consulting their bombing tables, Air Force weaponeers estimated that thirty-three times as many unguided bombs would have been required to achieve the same result. As Hilton reflected, "Twenty-nine tons of LGBs at the west end of the bridge broke it. Plus twelve tons of iron bombs. After all the years of pounding, and the lives lost, we finally broke the Dragon's Jaw, and did so without the loss of life or airplane."[16]

With the recon photos in hand, Seventh Air Force's General John Vogt said,

> It was this sort of precise tactic that enabled us to achieve the success we had against the railroad bridges in those high-threat areas. . . .
>
> We discovered, for example, that the effectiveness of the laser-guided bomb was much greater than that of the conventional bombs. One day, for example, we went up and knocked out five bridges on the Northwest Rail Line with a laser strike, and when PACAF [Pacific Air Force] ran that through the computers, they determined that where we used twenty-four total bombs, it would have taken 2,400 bombs to do that by the old method. So there was a tremendous breakthrough in technology and applied tactics.

> Both the Northeast and Northwest rail lines were interdicted within a few days, cutting to a trickle the amount of supplies coming from Communist China . . . we had fifteen bridges out on each railroad at any given time—as fast as they would build them, we would knock them out again.[17]

★

Somewhere far, far above the contrail level another celebration may have begun. Surely the shades of Giulio Douhet, Boom Trenchard, and Billy Mitchell hefted a heavenly brew to mark the arrival of the airpower prophets' dream of lightning bolts flung from the sky with unerring aim.

★

The next day, May 14, *Constellation* launched a recon flight to assess the Air Force's claims of damage to the bridge. A standard two-plane sortie was assigned: an RA-5C Vigilante flown by Commander C. R. Jones, skipper of "Heavy Eleven," escorted by the VF-92 Phantom crew of Lieutenants Russ Ogle and Bart Flaherty.

It was a typical recon flight, an hour and a half: "Short and sweet and back to a ready deck after an Alpha strike," Ogle recalled.

Flaherty said, "As I recall, this was an 'add on' to photo-recce mission on an Alpha strike to some truck park. After the standard intel brief, we (the Viggie crew and Russ and I) were told to remain. It was then we were told that we were to continue as a flight of two to intercept the river and fly downriver to take photos of the bridge. So what we thought would be a trip to a 'goat farm' suddenly got *very* interesting.

"We were blowing down the river at a pretty high rate with us jinking around above the Vig and trying to keep up. As we got close, C. R. went into standard 'straight and level take pictures mode' (SLTPM). We didn't have any indications of SAM activity and, at first, didn't see any AAA. Then we noticed the winking around the bridge. I don't remember if it was Russ or me that looked up and saw what looked like a scene from *Twelve O'Clock High* above us. Nice big black puffs. Lots of 100-millimeter, fortunately quite a ways above us.

"Russ called the Vig and told them about the flak. No reaction—still SLTPM. He called a second time and still nothing. Finally I called and said, 'C. R., they're shootin' the shit outta you!'

"Suddenly the Vig started jinking and must have plugged the burners in. Proof once again that a Phantom with 4+4 [missiles] and a centerline tank was no match for a clean Vigilante. We exited feet wet and RTB [returned to base].

"The pictures were great—proof positive that one span of the bridge was, indeed, partially down."

Ogle added,

> I do remember rolling over to take a look at the bridge and seeing all the twinkling lights and taking a microsecond to realize they were muzzle flashes and thinking that the people on the ground seemed really pissed off.
>
> I also remember having the feeling that we were suspended right over the bridge and not really moving and looking down at the throttles to make sure I had them all the way forward. I did, of course, but I still kept trying to push them forward and wondering why the old girl wasn't going any faster.
>
> Lastly, I looked behind us to check six and realized that our whole plane, from the intakes back, was enveloped in thick vapor from our shock wave. We must have looked like a supersonic cloud from the ground.
>
> Well, that's it, just another day at the office in those days. By the way, I always liked escorting C. R.; thought the guy was Mr. Cool personified. And those Viggies were beautiful machines.[18]

Indeed they were. Originally built as a supersonic nuclear bomber, the bomb bay was between the twin engines, so the bomb was supposed to be ejected out the rear of the plane. The Navy quickly discovered that that method of dropping a bomb, nuclear or otherwise, didn't work: the bomb tended to be trapped in the airflow around the plane and followed along for a while until sooner or later it fell free in an unpredictable trajectory. So the plane was converted to a photo-reconnaissance bird.

The Vigilantes looked fast just sitting on the deck. A large plane with a needle nose, rakish tail, and swept supersonic wings, Vigilantes were bitches to land aboard ship, inspiring the respect of every pilot in the air wing. In Vietnam their mission of photo recon after a strike meant that they got shot at a lot and shot down too often. That fact raised the respect level of Vigilante crews to extraordinary heights. The nose wheel was behind the cockpit, so watching one being maneuvered about a flight deck at night by the yellow-shirt taxi directors who took the nose wheel to the deck edge, then signaled the pilot to turn as his cockpit hung out over the dark ocean, bred awe. Those guys had brass balls. There, but for the grace of God . . . pilots of Vigilantes were masters of courage and self-discipline.

Mr. Cool? Every Viggie pilot and NFO was regarded as the best of the best on every ship fortunate enough to have them aboard.

CHAPTER 20

"WE DROPPED THE BRIDGE"

Keeping track of bridge repairs was a standard mission for reconnaissance squadrons. Especially after the Air Force strikes in April and May, the Pacific Command wanted to monitor enemy efforts to repair the Thanh Hoa Bridge.

Although the gunners around the Dragon's Jaw had taken plenty of casualties, they had gotten so much practice that they were still the best in the business. The idea of catching them napping was a fantasy. The North Vietnamese well knew that photo reconnaissance was a strike-planning tool for the Americans.

On June 16, 1972, Lieutenant Paul "Worm" Ringwood drew a photo mission aboard USS *Midway*. He was on his second combat deployment. He had earned his wings in 1968 and went to F-8s as his fleet assignment. He ejected from an F-8B over Okinawa in January 1969.

The photo birds were sleeker and faster than F-8 fighters. Flying his seventieth combat mission, Worm Ringwood knew the risks. In Vietnamese skies the predictable photo mission was considered the most hazardous, exceeded only by single-plane night bombing missions by A-6 Intruders.[1]

Ringwood often envisioned "Nguyen the AAA gunner down there, totally relaxed and smoking a cigarette until the smoke from a strike cleared. He would then calmly put the butt out and rip into us like clockwork." Ringwood described the gunners around the bridge as "the A team." He had flown recon sorties over Route One before, and in May he had seen Thanh Hoa's brand of flak up close. Muzzle flashes lit up the area on both ends of the bridge.

Most recon flights were escorted, and on this June day Ringwood's RF-8G, "Baby Giant 601," was joined by a *Midway* Phantom flown by Lieutenant Victor Kovaleski, who would score the Navy's last aerial kill of the war.

Recalling June 16, Ringwood said, "My mission that day was a river recce ending just three or four miles south of the bridge. Those gunners were so good that they could aim with accuracy that far away."

Because recon pilots had to fly straight and level to get their pictures, no evasive action was possible. But once they were "off government time," aviators tried to complicate the gunners' problems as much as possible. After he had his photos, Worm broke into a turn at 4,500 feet, making 450 knots or 760 feet per second—a tough target. Then he felt something strike his jet. He had taken a 37-millimeter shell in the tail, setting it afire. He said, "The irony and testament to those gunners is that I got hit with my wings temporarily level and while jinking significantly."[2]

Aviation wisdom held that it was undesirable to bail out over people you had just bombed. The Vietnamese were similarly uptight about pilots who took their picture. With his fire warning light illuminated, Worm shoved his throttle through the detent into afterburner and turned seaward toward the blessed sanctuary of the gulf. Kovaleski radioed a terse call, confirming the fire.

Fire or no fire, Worm Ringwood was going for salt water. Apparently the 37-millimeter round had severed afterburner fuel lines. If the fire burned through the controls for the stabilator, he would lose control of his mount. Or maybe the ass end of the plane would blow off.

Maybe the whole damn plane would explode, frying him to a crispy cinder.

The beach went under him and Ringwood kept going, climbing. When he reached ten thousand feet, the optimum bailout altitude, and was about ten miles offshore, he decided he had tempted fate long enough. He braced himself in his seat, reached up with both hands, grasped the face curtain handle, and pulled downward, hard.

The Martin-Baker seat fired as advertised, rocketing Ringwood out of "Six Oh One." The parachute blossomed and the pilot was jerked upright, suspended in the sky. His adrenaline rush at successfully ejecting vanished a moment later. "I was peacefully descending when I noticed a school of sharks below me. The more I pulled on the lanyards to steer away, like they taught us in Pensacola, the faster I descended toward the school of sharks."

He hefted his survival radio and tried to contact some A-7 Corsairs to strafe the vicious predators before he dropped into the water—to no avail. And strafing sharks would have been a bad idea, perhaps sending the surviving sharks maddened by the smell of blood into a feeding frenzy.

"I landed in the middle of a circle of them and quickly (probably setting a world's record) got into my raft."

In a few moments Ringwood realized that the sharks were actually porpoises. He was swept by a tremendous flood of relief, only to have that dissipate in a twinkling as he spotted several small craft headed toward him. Worm instantly went back to *oh-shit* mode.

Moments later an A-7 came swooping in and dropped a five-hundred-pound bomb amid or in front of the fishing fleet, with the desired result. "They were putt-putting toward me, and after that water geyser shot up a few hundred feet—very impressive—they made a fast 180-degree turn and putt-putted away, never to return."

The Navy's dedicated rescue squadron was HC-7, the Sea Devils, and it was spread across several warships at a time. Big Mother 67, a Sikorsky HH-3A Sea King that had taken off from USS *Long Beach*, a nuclear-powered cruiser, got the call about Baby Giant 601. Flying the chopper was Lieutenant James S. Kelley with copilot Lieutenant (Junior Grade) Early H. "Hank" Frazier and two aircrewmen, Aviation Machinist Mates Richard J. Tinsley and Jimmy C. Keeney.

Big Mother 67 plucked Ringwood from the water and logged him as the squadron's 105th save. Five months before, in January, the same crew had rescued Lieutenant Vic Kovaleski, who had just directed them to Ringwood. Most of the rescued fliers were undoubtedly spared years of captivity or a slow death on the merciless sea.

After his rescue, Kelly's crew deposited Ringwood on the northern SAR destroyer, where he imbibed a nonregulation adult beverage. A few hours later he was returned to *Midway*. He flew another mission the next day.

In the finest traditions of Naval Air, Ringwood endured a couple of days of merciless kidding about his "shark" adventure until another unfortunate captured the attention of the alpha-male pack in the ready room.

When Ringwood was sent back to photograph the Dragon's Jaw in October, he said, "Needless to say, my speed was greatly increased more than usual since the memory of the previous Thanh Hoa flight was vividly etched on my mind. I think I was at five hundred knots that day."[3]

★

The Americans kept pressure on the Dragon after the May 13 strike. During the summer and fall, before Linebacker ended in October, the Navy flew an additional eleven missions against the Thanh Hoa Bridge and the Air Force another two, ensuring that the Dragon remained dormant.[4]

Increasing operating tempos required more carriers than the Pacific Fleet could maintain in the Tonkin Gulf. Two East Coast carriers were deployed that fall: USS *Saratoga* (CV-60) and *America* (CV-66).

America was on her third Tonkin Gulf deployment. She had alternated with Pacific and Mediterranean cruises since 1968, most recently with Air Wing Eight. She left Norfolk bound for the Tonkin Gulf in June 1972, commanded by Captain Burt Shepherd, younger brother of astronaut Alan Shepherd.

Leading the Marauders of VA-82 was Commander Donald Sumner. During predeployment workups the squadron had briefly trained with small Walleye bombs, TV-guided fire-and-forget weapons. There had been little opportunity to train thoroughly with different variants in the Mark 80 series of dumb bombs.

Sumner's operations officer was Lieutenant Commander Leighton W. "Snuffy" Smith Jr. Smith had spent two years as a production test pilot flying the A-7 at Vought's Dallas, Texas, factory. VA-82 deployed with A-7Cs, an older model of the Corsair, even though the ultimate "Echo" version was already flying in the fleet.

After growing up near Mobile in rural Alabama, Snuffy Smith was certain he did not want to be a farmer. He had seen his father work to exhaustion far too often and sought something else. A family member showed a way: his uncle, Page Smith, had graduated from Annapolis in 1924 and retired as a four-star admiral commanding the Atlantic Fleet. Young Smith accumulated five dozen letters of recommendation, enough for a congressional appointment to the Naval Academy. He entered Annapolis in 1958.

Smith's academic career got off to a rocky start. The commandant of midshipmen, Captain William F. Bringle, turned things around when he invited the lad in for a talk. At first glance Smith found the four-striper "looking every bit the warrior, except for his eyes. There was a gentleness in his eyes."

"Bush" Bringle was indeed a warrior. He had led one of perhaps four carrier squadrons to fly against both Germany and Japan, earning a stellar reputation for leadership. Bringle spoke to the youngster softly, earnestly—and convincingly. He said, "Midshipman Smith, you can do this."[5]

And he did. Smith graduated in 1962, beginning a thirty-four-year naval career.

Leighton Smith was designated a naval aviator in 1964 and entered the war as a VA-22 A-4 pilot flying from *Coral Sea* in 1966–1967, with a subsequent cruise aboard USS *Ranger* in 1967–1968. He first bombed the Thanh Hoa Bridge in September 1966.

America arrived off Vietnam in July 1972 and launched hundreds of sorties over the next three months. Then, on October 4, Snuffy Smith got another shot at the Dragon's Jaw, six years after his first effort. The squadron CO, Don Sumner, was temporarily grounded, so as operations officer, Smith planned and led the mission. It was probably the first time the Navy used large Walleye bombs.[6]

Smith explained, "When we rolled in, my weapon came off, but it got hit by a 37-millimeter shell. It disintegrated as soon as it left my airplane, or at least became stupid." The other bombs missed or inflicted no damage, requiring the attackers to regroup, replan, and restrike.

Two days later, on October 6, *America* launched a strike against the bridge, with Smith again leading the strike element. Skipper Sumner was back flying but chose to lead the second section because Smith had planned and led the first strike. Smith said, "I had a good relationship with Don, and we always worked well together." Additionally, Smith had "a gut feeling" that the sixth would be The Day.[7]

Smith's division launched with a larger strike targeting a railroad facility. While the other aircraft created a diversion, Smith, Sumner, and their wingmen headed for the Thanh Hoa Bridge.

The Marauders' load-out was a mixture of smart and dumb bombs. Smith and his wingman, Lieutenant (Junior Grade) Marvin Baldwin, each carried two two-thousand-pound Walleyes, while the other two pilots, Commander Don Sumner and Lieutenant (Junior Grade) Jim Brister, carried two two-thousand-pound dumb Mark 84s.

The two elements split for opposite approaches from east and west, forcing the defenders to divide their gunfire. The aviators barely noticed, but the AAA batteries erupted in both barrage and radar-aimed fire, from 37-millimeter on up.

From sixteen thousand feet the A-7s nosed into 30-degree dives toward the bridge.

In the attack Smith was completely focused on the target. He was aware of the black puffs from flak shells but refused to glance at the ground, where muzzle flashes often captured pilots' attention.

"We rolled in simultaneously," Smith recalled. "Pulled the power back, popped the speed brakes, and got our scopes locked on the bridge. I called 'Lock-on.' Once Marv confirmed that he had locked on, I counted 'Three, two, one, launch," and Marv and I both pickled them at the same time. Then Don and Jim popped up and began their roll-in. They hit the bridge on the west side of the center piling."[8]

After bomb release the Corsair pilots rammed on full power, sucked up the speed brakes, jinked madly, and headed for the ocean. At least five bombs struck the bridge, impacting along the length of the western span: ten thousand pounds of ordnance, concentrated around the aim point where the bridge had visibly sagged from Air Force Paveways.

Circling out of range of the North Vietnamese defenders, the Marauders awaited events. After a few minutes Don Sumner announced that he wanted to check results and was returning for a poststrike inspection. Smith had reservations but responded that he would wait for the CO to rejoin.

Sumner headed westward, inbound at about fourteen thousand feet. He found the bridge still obscured in smoke. As Smith related, "There was so much smoke and crap down there, we really didn't know how much damage we'd done."[9]

All the Corsairs returned to *America;* broke into the racetrack pattern; dropped hooks, wheels, and flaps; and trapped aboard. The pilots thought they had struck the Dragon a heavy blow but had to await confirmation from reconnaissance photos. After their debrief in IOIC, Sumner, Smith, and company adjourned to the ready room to have their approaches critiqued by the LSOs and to relive the mission.

That evening Snuffy got a call from IOIC. He hurried to the intelligence center, where a staffer showed him a freshly developed photograph. Smith noted the time over target—17:02—which was barely two hours previous.

As Smith recalled, "The photo was taken by a Viggie pilot (Lieutenant Wes Rutledge of RVAH-6—Reconnaissance Heavy Attack Squadron Six) whose primary mission that day was in Hanoi. He knew we had gone after the bridge again so decided to swing by the bridge to get a photo."

The entire western span of the Thanh Hoa Bridge was clearly in the river.

Smith was pumped. He told the intelligence officer, "The section that is in the water was hit pretty much simultaneously with a two-thousand-pound Walleye and four two-thousand-pound bombs."

Years later Smith recounted, "I called our skipper, Don Sumner, and shouted, 'You ain't gonna believe this, but we got that mother-fucking bridge!'

"Shortly thereafter we were called to Rear Admiral Jack 'Big Coolie' Christiansen's cabin. When we came in he said, 'I've been waiting for seven fucking years to see this. If we weren't on a Navy ship, I'd buy you guys a drink.' Then, without pausing, he said, 'What the hell, I'll buy you one anyway.' He ordered a pitcher of grapefruit juice and we all had vodka and grapefruit juice in his cabin."[10]

★

The Vigilantes of "Heavy Six" were busy that day. Another RA-5C pilot who shot the bridge was Lieutenant Commander Joseph Satrapa, covering a strike on the Thanh Hoa railyard. Known as "Hoser" for his love of 20-millimeter cannon, Satrapa was a legendary F-8 pilot who had been pulled from his beloved Crusaders against his will and sent to Viggies. But with his navigator, Lieutenant (Junior Grade) Robert Rinder, he reveled in the Viggies' power and grace. He recalled, "Seems like the gomers usually shot two or three thousand feet behind us 'cause we were going at the speed of heat. How fast is that? Well . . . that's classified . . . except, it's really cookin'!

"I got hit about five times over the beach in F-8s—one aircraft was a 'strike' that couldn't be repaired. Only got a single hit in a RA-5C down at Chu Lai."

Satrapa's photo of the bridge showed that the North Vietnamese had activated a smoke screen to foil laser or electro-optical guidance weapons, yet the image clearly showed the entire western span was down in the river.[11]

★

The VA-82 Marauders of USS *America* had completed the execution begun by the Wolfpack from Ubon back in May. It was a bittersweet moment, capping hundreds of missions by hundreds of Air Force and Navy pilots and flight officers who had written their own stories in blood in the long saga of the most prestigious target of the Vietnam War.

Although October 6 had been *America*'s last day of the line period, Smith monitored message traffic while the ship was en route to Singapore for a port call. The next day he was surprised to see the bridge on the target list for October 8, which made no sense—the Vigilantes' photographs clearly showed the western span in the Song Ma. The naval aviators attributed the message to a mix-up at Seventh Air Force, which usually controlled targeting. No matter. Upon arrival in Singapore Snuffy Smith met his wife, Dottie, with, "I'm glad to see you—we dropped the bridge."[12]

★

Smith's Distinguished Flying Cross citation—it should have been a Silver Star—summarized the action:

> Lieutenant Commander Smith brilliantly planned and led a section of Walleye-equipped aircraft against the heavily defended Thanh Hoa railroad and highway bridge. . . . Due to critical requirements of the weapons, he was required to make a low-angle, gliding delivery over numerous firing antiaircraft artillery guns which were using both barrage and radar tracking in their attempts to thwart his attack. Disregarding enemy fire, he steadfastly continued his run, concentrating entirely on obtaining the most optimum release parameters.

> Lieutenant Commander Smith's exceptional timing and perfect delivery in the face of heavy enemy fire resulted in his section's weapons impacting almost directly on the pre-briefed aim points. Post-strike photography confirmed that this vital link and frequently struck target had at last been completely severed and rendered useless to the enemy. Lieutenant Commander Smith's perfectly planned, superbly executed attack, courage and devotion to duty reflected great credit upon himself and were in keeping with the highest traditions of the United States Naval Service.

The citation was signed by Admiral B. A. Carey, Commander in Chief, US Pacific Fleet.*[13]

At last, after seven years the Thanh Hoa Bridge, the Dragon's Jaw, was destroyed, with one of its spans in the river, beyond repair.

*Leighton W. Smith Jr. went on to a distinguished naval career. As a four-star admiral, he became commander in chief of US Naval Forces Europe and concurrent NATO commander in chief, Allied Forces Southern Europe (1992–1996) at the height of the Yugoslavian conflict. In December 1995 he assumed, at the same time, command of the NATO-led Implementation Force (IFOR) in Bosnia, a position he held until August 1996. He was made a Grand Officer of the National Order of Merit by the French government and a Knight Commander of the Order of the British Empire by Queen Elizabeth II.

CHAPTER 21

THE VIOLENT CRESCENDO

The Vietnam War didn't end when the Dragon fell, of course. Yet American air power had slammed all the doors shut on the North Vietnamese. Haiphong Harbor was mined, and ships could no longer enter or leave. The bridges on the two major railways to China were down. The Dragon's Jaw was down. The raw materials of war donated by the two Communist powers, the People's Republic of China and the Soviet Union, could no longer reach the North Vietnamese in sufficient quantity to fuel their conquest of South Vietnam, nor could they defend themselves from American bombing. North Vietnam was out of options and sooner or later would be forced to the negotiating table.

Richard Nixon went to China in July 1972 and began the process of normalizing American diplomatic relations with the most populous nation on earth. That initiative, and the SALT I treaty with the Soviet Union that followed, greatly lessened the danger of nuclear war between these two powers and the West, which was precisely the reason John F. Kennedy and Lyndon B. Johnson gave in the 1960s that America had to stand firm in South Vietnam. Nuclear war now looked more and more remote.

Those two masters of realpolitik, Richard Nixon and Henry Kissinger, finally had the game going their way. That summer the Republican Party nominated Richard Nixon to run for another term as president. Thinking they might get a better deal before Nixon was reelected than after, the North Vietnamese finally went to the bargaining table in Paris and began serious negotiations. Kissinger met with them there on October 8, 1972.

The North Vietnamese position had changed dramatically. Hanoi no longer demanded that South Vietnamese President Nguyen Van Thieu be removed from office. The North proposed a ceasefire and an exchange of POWs. Interestingly, the North also wanted all three Vietnamese combatant governments—the South, the North, and the Provisional Revolutionary Government of South Vietnam (PRG), which was the Viet Cong—to remain in place. Both Washington and Hanoi could continue to resupply their allies or forces on a parity basis, yet no new North Vietnamese forces were to be infiltrated from the North. The United States agreed to extend postwar construction assistance to the Communists in Hanoi. In addition, there was to be a loosely defined National Council that was to work toward local elections and general elections in South Vietnam, but not the North.

When the two sides met again on October 17 there were only two sticking points: periodic replacement of South Vietnam's weaponry and the release of political prisoners held by the South. The North seemed willing to compromise, so Kissinger notified the president that he was satisfied. Nixon approved.

The following day, October 18, Kissinger flew from Paris to Saigon. There the deal fell apart. President Thieu was not happy with the terms of the agreement or with Kissinger, whom he thought had betrayed him. The real problem, as Kissinger saw it, was that "after eight years of American tutelage, the South Vietnamese simply did not feel ready to confront Hanoi without direct American involvement. Their nightmare was not this or that clause but the fear of being left alone. Saigon's leaders could not believe that Hanoi would abandon its implacable quest for the domination of Indochina. In a very real sense, they were being left to shape their own future; deep down, they were panicked by the thought and too proud to admit it. And they were not wrong."[1]

Thieu had 129 textual changes he wanted made to the agreement, but the big one was that he wanted the DMZ recognized as an international border and South Vietnam as a sovereign state. This demand put the United States in a tight spot. Seven years earlier, on April 7, 1965, President Lyndon B. Johnson said, "Since 1954 every American President has offered support to the people of South Vietnam. We have helped to build, and we have helped to defend. Thus, over many years, we have made a national pledge to help South Vietnam defend its independence. . . . To dishonor that pledge, to abandon this small and brave nation to its enemies, and to the terror that must follow, would be an unforgivable wrong."[2]

Unforgivable or not, the American public now wanted out, and South Vietnamese independence was the price it was willing to pay to fund the journey home. In his elegant English, Dr. Kissinger remarked, "It was not Thieu's fault that America had simply come to the end of the road—largely as a result of its domestic divisions."[3]

While Kissinger hurried off to Washington, completing his aerial circumnavigation of the globe, both North and South took to the airwaves with altered versions of the agreement. Trying to reassure North and South of American sincerity, Kissinger now made a mistake. In his first White House press conference before television cameras on October 26, 1972, he used the unfortunate words, "We believe peace is at hand," unintentionally echoing Prime Minister Neville Chamberlain on his return to London after signing the Munich Agreement with Adolf Hitler in 1938.

Well, it wasn't. South and North wanted changes to the agreement, and diplomatic wrangling continued in Paris. Now North Vietnamese concessions previously granted were taken back. The talks broke down, with Hanoi refusing to set a date for their resumption.

Polls showed that 60 percent of the American voters were heartily sick of the Vietnam War and wanted the United States out. Kissinger's phrase "peace is at hand" had raised the public's expectations and given the administration's political enemies more ammunition, which they were quick to fire at President Nixon. Kissinger said, "Two main lines of attack developed: that the whole thing was a fraud to help Nixon win the election, which, on the evidence of the polls was nonsense; and that the same terms had been attainable four years earlier, which was untrue."[4]

The American election came right on schedule in early November. President Nixon won handily by 62 percent of the vote, yet Democrats gained solid majorities in both houses of Congress. The North Vietnamese must have realized that the American electorate had handed them a partial victory.

Hanoi agreed to a date of November 20 for further negotiations in Paris. The talks stalemated again, partially because President Thieu was postponing the evil day when South Vietnam had to face the Communists alone. Whipsawed between Hanoi and Saigon and a divided America, the US government could not force a reasonable settlement. The talks broke down on December 14 because the North Vietnam politburo believed the political winds were blowing their way.

Although the new Congress wouldn't meet until January 3, 1973, President Nixon wanted the Vietnam mess solved before the Democrats legislated an end to the war. Dollars were also involved. The massive augmentation of US air forces for Linebacker had cost $14 billion by mid-autumn, so the military needed more money. Secretary of Defense Melvin Laird wanted a new appropriation from Congress, one the administration was unlikely to get. All of this was covered at great length in the American press and was undoubtedly known by the politburo gamblers in Hanoi.

Kissinger's take was that the North Vietnamese had overplayed their hand: "The North Vietnamese committed a cardinal error in dealing with Nixon: They cornered him. Nixon was never more dangerous than when he seemed to have run out of options."[5]

President Nixon decided to shove everything into the pot and try to bomb the North Vietnamese back to the Paris negotiating table before

Congress met. The winter monsoon in Vietnam limited the use of LGBs to rare clear days, and American fighter-bombers with an all-weather capability, A-6s and F-111s, could carry only limited amounts of dumb bombs. Nixon called for the B-52s.

Boeing Stratofortresses had been used before to bomb Viet Cong staging areas in South Vietnam and Laos, the "Arc Light" strikes, with overall good results. Designed to deliver nuclear weapons from great altitudes above any weather, these huge, eight-engine strategic bombers were equipped with radar navigation and bombing systems. If they weren't carrying nukes, they could carry massive amounts of dumb bombs that they laid down in "carpets," obliterating everything and everyone in the target area.

The new bombing campaign was called Linebacker II, which the press quickly dubbed "The Christmas Bombing." The targets were the industrial heartlands of Hanoi and Haiphong. In his 1968 third-party campaign for vice president, with Alabama's prosegregation Governor George Wallace at the top of the ticket, retired Air Force chief of staff General Curtis LeMay had bluntly advocated bombing North Vietnam "back into the stone age" and was castigated for it. Without any other cards to play, now Nixon and the Air Force were going to give it a try.

The B-52 is designed to fly as high as 50,000 feet. With eight engines arranged in four pods, two pods beneath each wing, the B-52 is huge, 159 feet, 4 inches long, with a wingspan of 185 feet. Officially the Stratofortress, the plane is known everywhere except in Air Force PR offices as the Buff, for big ugly fat fucker. The B-52 entered service in June 1955, and its final version, the B-52H, is still operational at this writing, sixty-three years later. The Air Force currently plans to retire the last of the B-52Hs in 2045, *ninety* years after the airframe entered service.

The B-52D was the most common model used during the Vietnam War. Modified to carry as much as thirty tons of ordnance loaded both internally and externally, the Buff could still fly eight thousand or so nautical miles unrefueled. During Linebacker II, the Christmas Bombing, B-52Gs, with a lesser ordnance capacity, were also used. The Buffs were staged from Andersen AFB on the island of Guam and from U Tapao Airfield in Thailand. The planes from Guam had to be aerial refueled once to complete their missions and return to base; the Thailand Buffs could make it to North Vietnam and home unrefueled.

On the night of December 18, 1972, the B-52s launched against the Hanoi-Haiphong industrial heartland of North Vietnam. The first night forty-two Stratoforts bombed. Among the hard targets were rail facilities, bridges, ferries, POL and storage depots, SAM sites, and previously off-limits MiG bases. On subsequent nights as many as twice that number of the huge, high-flying planes formed the bomber stream. Navy Iron Hand and Air Force Wild Weasels were in the air to suppress SAM radars, and Air Force F-111 Aardvarks and Navy A-6 Intruders ran in low to find and knock out SAM sites just moments before they could fire at the Buffs flying high in the stratosphere. The big black bombers came in waves for twelve consecutive nights.

The urban hearts of Hanoi and Haiphong were not targeted. Still, the carpet bombing caused stupendous damage in the areas that were targeted. It was not in Hanoi's interest then to confirm how badly the B-52s had hurt them, nor was it in America's interest to publicly suggest how bloody the Christmas Bombing might have been.

Long after the war an official Communist history claimed that in the Hanoi area 2,380 people were killed and 1,355 were wounded. The North Vietnamese took full credit for keeping the bombers from pulverizing the hearts of the two cities and falsely claimed, "The American imperialists were still not able to pressure our Government into making concessions." These were the same people who claimed that eight hundred American airplanes had been shot down over Haiphong during the war, a massive inflation of the true number.[6]

In what may ultimately prove to be the last great air battle America will ever fight, the heavy bombers flew into North Vietnamese airspace invisible in the night sky. The SAM sites that were still operational launched their SA-2 Guideline missiles, which rose on pillars of fire into the heavens. Shrikes and Standard ARMs streaked earthward.

Bombs marched across SAM sites, and high in the sky missiles missed or exploded against the bombers.

MiG-21s were the only fighters the Communists had that could intercept at the B-52s' altitude, and they were there, slashing in, trying to find and shoot down Buffs. American F-4s hunted the MiGs in the darkness. As the bombs plummeted down, smashing industrial and storage areas like the fist of God, B-52s were hit by SAMs and shot up by fighters. On fire, high in the night sky amid the stars, some bombers flamed fiercely as they broke up and fell. B-52 crews announced in laconic, weary voices that their planes had been fatally hit. The crewmen rode their ejection seats into the cold, thin air to fall over seven miles to earth, where they faced possible death and, if they survived that, certain captivity.

What a tableau it was in the clear night sky above the monsoon clouds. A million stars flung against the universe, fire trails of missiles rising and missiles descending and the occasional small gleam of flame against the stars as a B-52 was hit and began to burn. All while the trip-hammer flashes of exploding bombs strobed the clouds below. The men who saw it and lived carried that vivid scene of war aloft with them the rest of their days.

Despite the best efforts of the North Vietnamese, the B-52s came night after night.

In twelve nights the Buffs flew 729 sorties and dropped 15,237 tons of bombs, literally smashing the heart out of North Vietnam's war capacity. Ten Buffs were shot down in North Vietnam, five crashed in Thailand or Laos, and others were damaged. Twelve tactical aircraft also were lost. Forty-three US airmen were killed in action and forty-nine parachuted into captivity. The United States claimed six MiG-21s destroyed in the campaign, including two by B-52 tail gunners. Oddly, the North Vietnamese said that three MiG-21s were destroyed by the big bombers' quad .50-caliber tail guns. Hanoi claimed eighty-one Yankee aircraft shot down, including thirty-four Buffs and four F-111 Aardvarks.

American critics of the Vietnam War were outraged over the tightening of the military screw. Critics abroad were incensed. Even the prime minister of Australia, an American ally whose soldiers had fought for years in South Vietnam, squawked loudly, which soured US-Australian relations until that prime minister departed in 1975.

Regardless of the spin they would put on it a generation later for Vietnamese consumption, after twelve nights of relentless bombing, the Communists had reached their limit. The diplomats returned to the bargaining table in Paris and a ceasefire was set for January 27, 1973. A political accord was quickly reached, written, and signed. The Americans promised to get their troops out of South Vietnam within sixty days. This time President Thieu went along, persuaded by letters from Richard Nixon pledging American support if the North Vietnamese proved perfidious.

But Thieu should have known better. Almost every American who lived through those years knew the United States would not send troops back to Vietnam unless the Communists exploded a nuclear weapon on Los Angeles, and maybe not even then. In February 1973 the North Vietnamese released the American POWs, and the Chinese released their lone American, the Navy's Robert J. Flynn, now a lieutenant commander.

★

With the troops home, in America the Watergate scandal became the national focus. President Nixon resigned on August 9, 1974. Vice President Gerald Ford took over the presidency.

In December of that year, ignoring all their promises and guarantees to the contrary, the North Vietnamese again invaded the south. Then they paused and waited to see what the Americans would do.

President Ford asked Congress to approve a $722 million aid package for South Vietnam, which the Nixon administration had promised; Congress by a wide margin flatly refused. Senator Jacob K. Javits echoed the mood of the nation when he said, "Large sums for evacuation, but not one nickel for military aid." Congress gave the Communists a green light.[7]

The Communists had won the battle for American public opinion, or more accurately, the Kennedy-Johnson arguments for a conventional war in Vietnam had become obsolete. The world no longer looked the same as it did in the early years of the Kennedy administration when the Soviet Union and China seemed likely candidates for nuclear war with the United States and its allies.

The NVA military machine resumed its march southward. President Thieu resigned on April 21, 1975, blaming the fall of his nation on the treacherous Americans. Two days later President Ford made a speech at Tulane University in which he said that the Vietnam War was over "as far as America is concerned."[8]

Despite Congress's refusal of military aid, the Americans did mount the largest helicopter rescue operation in history and evacuated almost all US citizens and military personnel remaining in Saigon, along with tens of thousands of South Vietnamese civilians—about fifty thousand people altogether, mostly by C-141 Starlifters and C-130 Hercules. Saigon fell on April 30, 1975. Laos and Cambodia soon followed.[9]

The Communists renamed Saigon Ho Chi Minh City and consolidated the country under their rule, which had been their goal since the Japanese left in the closing days of World War II. Everywhere they went, the victorious Communists took bloody revenge on their enemies.

One might argue, as many did at the time, that the strife in Vietnam was really nothing more than a nasty civil war. Had the Soviets and Communist Chinese not fed arms and ammo to the Hanoi regime as a means to bolster the red flag at home and abroad—and, of course, to embarrass and bleed the Americans—perhaps the Kennedy and Johnson administrations would have left South Vietnam to its fate. It was almost as if the great global political struggle between the titans had to be violently acted out in that fetid, mosquito-infested backwater that only the people born there cared about. And over the Dragon's Jaw.

★

Fifty-eight thousand Americans lost their lives in Southeast Asia during that war. Their deaths in a cause the nation ultimately abandoned still rankles. Veterans of that conflict came home to a nation that blamed them for the whole mess, for causing it, for joining the military or being drafted and obeying orders, and for all the angst and guilt felt by those who evaded or defied the draft. All in all, Vietnam was a low point in America's vision of itself, a realization that sacrifice, valor, and good intentions are not enough to cure the ills of the world.

What grew from the ashes of that great tragedy was a new geopolitical order that eased the global tensions of the Cold War and, ultimately, in the 1990s, caused the collapse of Communism and breakup of the old Soviet Union as well as the transformation of China into something resembling a free-market autocracy. Vietnam, like China, remained a nominal Communist dictatorship but allowed capitalism and foreign trade to flourish, which gradually improved its citizens' economic lot manyfold.

After Vietnam the American military continued to develop smart weapons. By the end of America's involvement in Vietnam, twenty-seven thousand PGMs (precision-guided munitions) had been released in Southeast Asia, which was two-tenths of one percent of the 3.5 million bombs expended, but the PGMs recorded an average miss distance of twenty-three feet. More than half the smart bombs were scored as direct hits—ten times the figure for conventional ordnance. They had a bull's-eye CEP.

As a natural outgrowth of its space endeavors, America developed the global positioning system (GPS) based on satellites. Weapons designers married GPS sensors to guided missiles and free-falling bombs, and the result was ordnance with phenomenal accuracy without the necessity for daytime, clear-air delivery, thereby revolutionizing war in the air. No longer would tactical or strategic aircraft need to expend tens or hundreds of tons of conventional ordnance to destroy one target. One warhead would be enough, day or night, in any weather. And it could be launched from well outside the envelope of defending weapons; indeed, from hundreds of miles away.

The world saw the result in the 1991 Gulf War, Operation Desert Storm, which freed Kuwait, and the 2003 Iraq war that buried the Saddam Hussein regime.

Still, weapons that create military victory are not enough. Henry Kissinger spoke the truth: unless they lead to a political settlement that will endure, military victories are essentially meaningless. Perhaps that is the ultimate lesson of Vietnam.

The dream of airpower prophets since the horrors of World War I was that aviation would somehow save lives by reducing the necessity of mass armies of foot soldiers fighting, bleeding, and dying to bring wars to a successful conclusion. World War I ended in an armistice, and the political infrastructure that resulted soon fractured. With the help of air power, World War II solved the problem of European fascism and Japanese militarism once and for all. In the last half of the twentieth century, nuclear weapons prevented the final military battle between Communism and the great democracies. How the struggle between fundamental Islam and the secular worlds of East and West will play out remains to be seen. Only one thing is certain: there will be future wars. As military thinker Ralph Peters once said, "War may be what man does best."

★

After their victory, the Vietnamese Communists began rebuilding the Dragon's Jaw Bridge at Thanh Hoa. The AAA guns and SAMs were eventually removed. Additional spans were added downstream in subsequent years, the latest constructed by a Japanese firm.

Today those structures carry commerce north and south across the muddy Song Ma . . . and the skies above them contain only the eternal clouds and mist.

APPENDIX

US Aircraft Known Lost on Thanh Hoa Bridge Missions

Date	*Aircraft*	*Unit/Base**	*Crew*
April 3, 1965	F-100D	401 TFW/Danang	Smith (KIA)
April 4, 1965	F-105D	18 TFW/Korat	Harris (POW)
April 4, 1965	F-105D	355 TFW/Korat	Bennett (KIA)
April 4, 1965	F-105D	355 TFW/Korat	Magnusson (KIA)
April 4, 1965	A-1H	1131 SAS/TSN	Draeger (KIA)
April 4, 1965	A-1H	RVNAF SAS/TSN	Vu Khac Hue (KIA)
May 7, 1965	F-105D	355 TFW/Korat	Lambert
May 31, 1965	F-105D	35 TFS/Takhli	Peel (POW)
Aug. 2, 1965	F-105D	18 TFW/Korat	Dauthtry (POW)
Aug. 26, 1965	F-4B	VF-21/Midway	Franke & Doremus (POW)
May 30, 1966	C-130E	61 TCS/Danang	Case, Zook, etc (8 KIA)
May 14, 1967	F-4B	VF-114/Kitty Hawk	Southwick & Rollins (POW)
April 21, 1972	F-4E	8 TFW/Ubon	Brown & Peters
June 16, 1972	RF-8G	VFP-63/Midway	Ringwood

Totals

KIA/MIA	13	F-105s	6	C-130	1
POW	7	F-4s	3	RF-8	1
Recovered	4	A-1s	2	F-100	1

*Unit and Base abbreviations:

SAS: Special activities squadron
TCS: Troop carrier squadron
TFS: Tactical fighter squadron
TFW: Tactical fighter wing
TSN: Tan Son Nhut, Saigon
VF: Navy fighter squadron
VFP: Navy reconnaissance squadron

NOTES

CHAPTER 1. "WE WILL PAY ANY PRICE . . ."

1. Gary Wayne Foster, emails to Tillman, January 2016.

2. H. R. McMaster, *Dereliction of Duty: Lyndon Johnson, Robert McNamara, the Joint Chiefs of Staff, and the Lies That Led to Vietnam* (New York: HarperPerennial, 1997), 23.

3. Ibid., 51.

4. Ibid., 101.

5. Ibid., 61.

6. Ibid.

CHAPTER 2. A DAMNED TOUGH NUT TO CRACK

1. James B. Stockdale and Sybil Stockdale, *In Love and War: The Story of a Family's Ordeal and Sacrifice During the Vietnam Years* (Annapolis, MD: Naval Institute Press, 1990), 23.

2. H. R. McMaster, *Dereliction of Duty,* 125.

3. Wayne Morse comments: Denny Freidenrich, "50 Years After Wayne Morse, 40 After Mark Felt," *The Hill,* August 15, 2014, http://thehill.com/blogs/congress-blog/homeland-security/215150-50-years-after-wayne-morse-40-after-mark-felt.

4. McMaster, *Dereliction of Duty,* 94.

5. Cyrus Vance quoted in McMaster, *Dereliction of Duty,* 62.

6. David Halberstam, *The Best and the Brightest* (Bridgewater, NJ: Baker and Taylor, 2008), 250.

7. John T. Correll, *The Air Force in the Vietnam War* (Arlington, VA: Aerospace Education Foundation, 2004), 5.

8. Istvàn Toperczer, *MiG-17 and MiG-19 Units of the Vietnam War* (Oxford: Osprey Publishing, 2012), 16.

9. "Mikoyan-Gurevich MiG-17," Wikipedia, https://en.wikipedia.org/wiki/Mikoyan-Gurevich_MiG-17.

10. Ibid.

11. Cheng Guan Ang, *The Vietnam War from the Other Side: The Vietnamese Communists' Perspective* (Hoboken, NJ: Taylor and Francis, 2013), 96.

12. A. J. C. Lavalle, ed., *The Tale of Two Bridges and the Battle for the Skies over North Vietnam* (Washington, DC: Office of Air Force History, 1985), 50.

13. Walter Boyne, "Route Pack 6," *Air Force* magazine, November 1999.

14. Gary Wayne Foster, *Phantom in the River: The Flight of Linfield Two Zero One* (Ashland, OR: Hellgate Press, 2010), 10.

15. Dinh Khoi Sy, *History of the 228th Anti-Aircraft Artillery Regiment* (1998), 45, translated for the authors by Merle Pribbenow.

16. Ibid., 55–56.

17. Gary Wayne Foster, *Phantom in the River: The Flight of Linfield Two Zero One* (Ashland, OR: Hellgate Press, 2010), 87.

18. Enemy Forces, www.enemyforces.net / artillery / zu23.htm.

19. "Russian Army Light-Heavy Weapons," Army Recognition, www.army recognition.com / russia_russian_army_light_heavy_weapons_uk / m1939_61-k_37mm_anti-aircraft_gun_technical_data_sheet_specifications_description_pictures_video.html.

20. Barton Meyers. "Vietnamese Defense Against Aerial Attack," Center for the Study of the Vietnam Conflict, 1996, www.vietnam.ttu.edu / events / 1996_Symposium / 96papers / meyers.php.

21. Steve Gray, "First Combat Use of the Walleye Weapon," *A-4Ever Skyhawk Association Journal* (Fall 2014): 9–10.

CHAPTER 3. THE FIRST HAMMER BLOW

1. McCrea and Center for Naval Analyses, *U.S. Fixed Wing Aircraft Losses in Southeast Asia.*

2. W. H. Plunkett, 34th TFS Attacks on Thanh Hoa Bridge, www.34tfsthuds.us.

3. Ibid.

4. Ibid.

5. "George C. Smith," POW Network, www.pownetwork.org/bios / s / s038.htm.

6. Colonel Ivy J. McCoy, via email from Ron Rowen, March 2017.

CHAPTER 4. "HE DID NOT WANT ANY MORE MIGS SHOT DOWN"

1. Pham Ngoc Lan, quoted in Roger Boniface, *MiGs over North Vietnam: The Vietnamese People's Air Force in Combat, 1965–1975* (Manchester: Crecy Publishing, 2015), 4.

2. "They Were Warriors," Forgotten F-105 Warriors, www.forgottenf-105warriors .com / Pilots.html.

3. Toperczer, *MiG-17 and MiG-19 Units,* 30–31.

4. Magnusson missing: "Magnusson, James A. Jr.," POW Network, www.pow network.org / bios / m / m007.htm.

5. Jack Graber, email to Bob Laymon, April 2005, Shared by Laymon with authors.

6. Peter Davies, "F-100—MiG Encounters of the First Kind," *The Intake,* Spring 2012.

7. Ibid.

8. Don Kilgus: Robert F. Dorr, "F-100 Versus MiG-17: The Air Battle Nobody Told You About," Defense Media Network, April 18, 2014, www.defensemedianetwork.com/stories/f-100-versus-mig-17-the-air-battle-nobody-told-you-about.

9. Ibid.

10. Byron E. Hukee, *USAF and VNAF A-1 Skyraider Units of the Vietnam War* (Botley, Oxford: Osprey Publishing, 2013), 60.

11. See also Jack Broughton, *Thud Ridge: F-105 Thunderchief Missions over Vietnam* (Manchester: Crecy Publishing, 2006).

12. Jacob Van Staaveren, *Gradual Failure: The Air War over North Vietnam, 1965–1966* (Washington, DC: Air Force History and Museums Program, 2002), 107.

13. Van Staaveren, ibid., 108.

CHAPTER 5. A GRIM BUSINESS

1. John Prados, "The '65 Decision: Bombing Soviet SAM Sites in North Vietnam," *VVA Veteran*, January–February 2006, www.vva.org/archive/TheVeteran/2006_01/featuresSAM.htm.

2. Colonel James Bassett, emails to Tillman, June 2014.

3. John T. Correll, "Take It Down! The Wild Weasels in Vietnam," *Air Force* magazine, July 2010.

4. John B. Nichols and Barrett Tillman, *On Yankee Station: The Naval Air War over Vietnam* (New York: Naval Institute Press, 2013), 58.

5. Davies, *F-105 Thunderchief Units*, 8.

6. Ibid., 26.

7. Robert L. LaPointe, *PJs in Vietnam: The Story of Air Rescue in Vietnam as Seen Through the Eyes of Pararescuemen* (Anchorage, AK: Northern PJ Press, 2001), 111–112.

8. "Martin ASM-N-7/GAM-83/AGM-12 *Bullpup*," Directory of U.S. Military Rockets and Missiles, www.designation-systems.net/dusrm/m-12.html.

9. Robert S. McNamara, *In Retrospect* (New York: Vintage Books, 1996), 185.

10. Lavalle, *Tale of Two Bridges*, 42.

11. Ibid., 42.

12. Robert Peel, phone interview with Tillman, June 27, 2015.

13. "395 F-105 Combat Losses," www.burrusspta.org/395_Combat.pdf.

14. Lavalle, *Tale of Two Bridges*, 44.

15. J. L. Maienschein, *Estimating Equivalency of Explosives Through a Thermochemical Approach* (Lawrence Livermore National Laboratory, 2002).

16. Michael M. McCrea, Center for Naval Analyses, *U.S. Navy, Marine Corps, and Air Force Fixed-Wing Aircraft Losses and Damage in Southeast Asia (1962–1973)* (Arlington, VA: Center for Naval Analyses, 1976).

17. Robinson Risner, *The Passing of the Night: My Seven Years as a Prisoner of the North Vietnamese* (Duncanville: World Wide Printing, 1999), 9. See also http://34tfsthuds.us/resources/Pictures/G-K/Jones_Eddward_L.pfd.

18. The History of the Joint Chiefs of Staff, 1960–1968, vol. II, 25–26, http://webdoc.sub.gwdg.de/ebook/p/2005/dep of state/www.state.gov/www/about_state/history/vol_iii/050.html.

CHAPTER 6. ENTER THE NAVY

1. Wally Schirra, conversation with Tillman, 1994.

2. Derived from unpublished US Navy Southeast Asia Statistical Summary, Office of Naval Aviation History, no date.

3. A-7s Greek retirement: www.airforce.gr/cms/.

4. Rear Admiral Denny Wisely, USN (Ret.), conversation with Tillman, 2004.

5. "Klusmann Charles Frederic," POW Network, www.pownetwork.org/bios.

6. Richard W. Schaffert, email to Tillman, February 2015.

7. "Air War in North Vietnam (Vol. I) in United States–Vietnam Relations 1945–1967," Department of Defense anthology, www.dod.mil/pubs/foi/International_security_affairs/vietnam_and_southeast_asiaDocuments/290.pdf.

CHAPTER 7. "UNLIMITED LOSSES IN PURSUIT OF LIMITED GOALS"

1. Robert K. Wilcox, *Scream of Eagles: The Real Top Gun: How They Took Back the Skies over Vietnam* (London: Phoenix, 2011), 23.

2. Michael O'Connor, *MiG Killers of Yankee Station* (Friendship, WI: New Past Press, 2003), 28.

3. Ibid., 29.

4. Toperczer, *MiG-17 and MiG-19 Units,* 20.

5. O'Connor, *MiG Killers of Yankee Station,* 30.

6. Jeremiah Denton, *When Hell Was in Session* (WND Books, 2009), np.

7. Jack Woodul, email to Tillman, February 19, 2015.

8. "Franke, Fred Agustus," POW Network, www.pownetwork.org/bios/f/f052.htm.

9. Fred A. Franke, email to Tillman, March 29, 2015.

10. Franke loss: McCrea and Center for Naval Analysis, *U.S. Fixed-Wing Aircraft Losses in Southeast Asia.*

11. Wynn F. Foster, *Captain Hook: A Pilot's Triumph and Tragedy in the Vietnam War* (Annapolis, MD: Naval Institute Press, 1992), 68.

12. Barrett Tillman, "Tailhook '88," *The Hook,* Fall 1988, 99.

CHAPTER 8. THEY NEEDED A BIGGER BANG

1. Foster, *Captain Hook,* 99.

2. Ibid., 103.

3. Thomas F. Brown, emails to Tillman, February 2015.

4. The US Navy continued to improve its steam catapults, making them longer

and giving them more capacity. By the time USS *Nimitz,* the second nuclear-powered carrier, entered service, its catapults were so powerful that it could not launch lightly loaded F-8s unless the ship had a negative wind over the deck. Coonts participated in one of the F-8 evolutions aboard *Nimitz,* launching Naval Reserve Crusaders from NAS Dallas in the spring of 1976 as the ship backed down into the wind.

5. Stockdale and Stockdale, *In Love and War.*

6. Foster, *Captain Hook,* 105.

7. James Stockdale, conversation with Tillman, 1983.

8. "Vice Admiral James Bond Stockdale," http://a4skyhawk.org/3e/va163/stockdale.htn.

9. Dinh Khoi Sy, *History of the 228th,* 62–63.

10. Lavalle, *Tale of Two Bridges,* 46.

11. W. H. Plunkett, 34th TFS Attacks on Thanh Hoa Bridge.

12. "Vietnam—Escalation of the War," Global Security, www.globalsecurity.org/military/ops/vietnam2-escalation.htm.

13. "Vietnam War Statistics," www.shmoop.com/vietnam-war/statistics.html.

14. "Defense Spending in the 20th Century," U.S. Government Spending, www.usgovernmentspending.com/spending_chart_1900_2015USp_XXs1li011mcn_30f_Defense_Spending_in_20th_Century.html.

15. Ang Chen Guan, *The Vietnam War from the Other Side* (UK: Rutledge Surzon, 2002), 97. See also McCrea and Center for Naval Analyses, *U.S. Navy, Marine Corps, and Air Force Fixed-Wing Aircraft Losses and Damage in Southeast Asia.*

CHAPTER 9. PAYING THE PRICE

1. Samuel L. Sayers, conversations with Coonts, 2016. Like all new weapons systems, the A-6 had its problems, all of which were eventually solved. The A-6 electronic systems were continually updated and remained state of the art until the airplane's retirement from Navy and Marine service in 1997. The A-6 remains one of the few aircraft the United States never exported, even to allies.

2. McCrea and Center for Naval Analysis, *U.S. Fixed-Wing Aircraft Losses in Southeast Asia.*

3. Captain Sam went on to command VA-34, then VA-42 (the east coast A-6 training squadron). He served as program manager (chief engineer) for A-6/EA-6 aircraft, then program manager for the Advanced Tactical Aircraft (ATA). He retired in 1986. His wife, Janet, died of cancer in 1989. He was the technical adviser on the movie *Flight of the Intruder,* based on the novel by Stephen Coonts. He remarried Mary (Salkeld) Sayers and was enjoying a well-earned retirement when he unexpectedly passed away in May 2017 at the age of eighty-two. Discussing the Vietnam War, Coonts asked him, "Knowing all you know about naval aviation and the war, would you sign up to do it again?" Sam's quick answer: "Hell, yes." One suspects he spoke for most Navy and Air Force Vietnam-veteran flight crewmen.

CHAPTER 10. FOOLS, DRUNKS, AND LOST FIGHTER PILOTS

1. Correll, *The Air Force in the Vietnam War,* 16.

2. Ang Chen Guan, *Vietnam War from the Other Side,* 96. If the Russians ever bothered to use Vietnamese-speaking Russians as instructors, Ms. Ang never mentions it. Cultural snobbery?

3. Van Staaveren, *Gradual Failure,* 263–264.

4. *Chicago Tribune,* "Any Bombs to Sell?" March 14, 1966, http://archives.chicagotribune.com.

5. R. W. Schaffert, email to Tillman, February 2015.

6. Philip D. Chinnery, *Air Commando: Inside the Air Force Special Operations Command* (New York: St. Martin's Press, 1997), 74.

7. "MCARA War Stories: Skyknight Down!," MCARA, www.mcara.us/skyknight_down.php.

8. Ibid.

9. Ibid.

10. Peter E. Davies, *F-105 Wild Weasels vs. SA-2 "Guideline" SAM, Vietnam 1965–73* (Oxford: Osprey Publishers, 2011), 50.

11. Rick Morgan, emails to Tillman, April 2017.

CHAPTER 11. CAROLINA MOON

1. Chinnery, *Air Commando,* 74.

2. Ibid.

3. Joseph Trevithick, "America Builds Massive Floating Bombs," War Is Boring, December 15, 2014, https://warisboring.com/america-built-massive-floating-bombs-to-blast-a-vietnamese-bridge.

4. Ibid. See also "Operation Carolina Moon," Global Security, www.globalsecurity.org/military/ops/carolina-moon.htm.

5. Carolina Moon summary provided by Lynn O. Gamma AFHRO, Maxwell Air Force Base, Alabama, March 2017.

6. Joseph Moore, conversation with Tillman, 1982.

7. Lavalle, *Tale of Two Bridges,* 52–54.

8. Staaveren, *Gradual Failure,* 258–259. See also "Carolina Moon May Through June 1966," research paper provided by USAF Historical Research Agency, March 2017.

9. Dinh Khoi Sy, *History of the 228th,* 73–74.

10. Troy Hayward, email to Tillman, March 2017.

11. Bear Taylor, "Rolling Thunder Remembered . . . 31 May 1966 . . . Carolina Moon," Rolling Thunder Remembered, www.rollingthunderremembered.com.

12. Ibid.

13. Lavalle, *Tale of Two Bridges,* 56.

14. Author analysis of CAN list of USAF in-flight losses, May 31, 1966. The F-4

loss, on an armed recon mission, is listed at 1815, versus 2100 for the C-130. Additional insight provided by Commander Ken Davis, USN (Ret), emails to Tillman, May 2017.

15. Troy Harworth, emails to Tillman, March 2017; moon phase chart for May 1966, www.calendar-12.com/moon_calendar/1966/june.

16. Nguyen Xuan Mai, ed., *Memories of Defending the Skies over the Fatherland* (Peoples Publishing House, 2013, translated for the authors by Merle Pribbenow.

17. "Quả thủy lôi 'tối mật' của Mỹ để đánh cầu Hàm Rồng," Soha News website, March 25, 2013, http://soha.vn/quan-su/qua-thuy-loi-toi-mat-cua-my-de-danh-cau-ham-rong-20130325155418936.htm, translated for the authors by Merle Pribbenow.

18. Robert McNamara's book, *In Retrospect,* makes it crystal clear that he had no hope whatsoever that the war would end in 1967; indeed, he had no hope that it could be won militarily.

19. John Darrell Sherwood, *Afterburner: Naval Aviators and the Vietnam War* (New York: New York University Press, 2004), 269.

20. David C. Richardson, email to Tillman, July 7, 2010.

21. Ronald J. Zlatoper, emails to Tillman, April 23, 2017.

22. Richardson email, July 7, 2010.

CHAPTER 12. THE THANH WHORE BRIDGE

1. Jeremy Taylor, email to Tillman, February 2015.

2. Stephen R. Gray, *Rampant Raider: An A-4 Skyhawk Pilot in Vietnam* (Annapolis, MD: Naval Institute Press, 2017), 203–204.

3. "Martin Marietta AGM-62 *Walleye*," Directory of U.S. Military Rockets and Missiles, www.designation-systems.net/dusrm/m-62.html.

4. "VA-212 Rampant Raiders," A-4 Skyhawk Association, http://a4skyhawk.info.

5. Steve Gray, "The First Use of the Walleye Weapon," *A-4ever Skyhawk Association Journal* (Fall 2014), 9–10.

6. Lavalle, *Tale of Two Bridges*, 59.

7. Gray, *Rampant Raider*, 205–206.

8. Sherwood, *Afterburner*, 269.

9. "Smith, Homer Leroy," POW Network, www.pownetwork.org/bios/s/s105.htm.

10. Stephen Gray, emails to Tillman, June 2015.

11. Jim Winchester, *Douglas A-4 Skyhawk: Attack and Close-Support Fighter Bomber* (Barnsley: Pen & Sword Aviation, 2005), 112–113; Kenneth P. Werrell, "Did USAF Technology Fail in Vietnam?," *Airpower Journal* (Spring 1998), www.airpower.maxwell.af.mil/airchronicles/apj/apj98/spr98/werrell.html.

12. CHECO Report, "The War in Vietnam, Jan–Jun 1967," April 29, 1968, 106, part of PACAF Rolling Thunder briefing to CINCPAC for the period of February 20–March 19, 1967, cited in Plunkett Papers.

CHAPTER 13. THE BRIDGE CLAIMS ANOTHER VICTIM

1. "A Massive Effort to Turn the Tide," in *Intelligence and Vietnam: The Top Secret 1969 State Department Study,* National Security Archive, www2.gwu.edu/~nsarchiv/NSAEBB/NSAEBB121.

2. Craig M. White, "F-105 Days," http://vimeo.com/163954955.

3. John Holm, email to Tillman, May 5, 2016.

4. "Southwick, Charles Everett," POW Network, www.pownetwork.org/bios/s/s108.htm.

5. "Rollins, David John," POW Network, www.pownetwork.org/bios/r/r042.htm.

6. Gary Wayne Foster, *Phantom in the River: The Flight of Linfield Two Zero One* (New York: Midpoint Trade Books, 2011), 135–139.

7. Ibid., 132.

8. "Rolling Thunder Remembered . . . 15 May 1967 . . . 'Phantom in the River,'" Rolling Thunder Remembered, www.rollingthunderremembered.com/?p=5432.

9. R. W. Schaffert, email to Tillman, February 2015.

10. Plunkett Papers, 12.

CHAPTER 14. "WE ARE MIRED IN A STALEMATE"

1. Military spending, www/usgovernmentspending.com.

2. Vietnam War Casualty Statistics. www/archives.gov. Military Personnel in Southeast Asia, www.edu/colleges/ . . . /MilitaryPersonnelinsoutheastasia.doc.

3. Draftees, www.sss.gov/induct.htm.

4. Correll, *Air Force in the Vietnam War,* 9.

5. Ibid., citing Momyer.

6. Desert Storm aviators reported much the same situation in 1991. The politicians and brass pulled decision making up the ladder, apparently on the theory that if they were going to be held responsible for every bomb dropped and every airplane lost, they might as well run the show. The initiative and responsibility of subordinates was squeezed from the system. This was and is no way to run a military . . . or a war. The scars of Vietnam run very deep.

7. 355th TFW History, January–March 1968, vol. III, OPREP-4/146/RT57A189, Microfilm N0464, frame 0525; also, Microfilm N0463, frames 1620 and 1651–1652, courtesy of W. H. Plunkett.

8. Pete Purvis, "That Damn Bridge Again," *Flight Journal* (August 2007), 66–70.

9. Plunkett Papers, "34th TFS Attacks on the Thanh Hoa Bridge," printed May 3, 2014, 13.

10. "Kenneth W. Mays, F-105 History," unpublished memoir, cited in H. W. Plunkett Papers, April 25, 2011.

11. Plunkett Papers, "34th TFS Attacks on the Thanh Hoa Bridge," 14.

12. McCrea and Center for Naval Analyses, *U.S. Fixed Wing Aircraft Losses in Southeast Asia.*

13. H. W. Plunkett Papers, 15, citing 355th TFW History, January–March 1968, OPREP-4/146/RT57A189, Microfilm N0464, frame 0525; see also microfilm N0463, frames 1620 and 1651–1652.

14. Lavalle, *Tale of Two Bridges,* 63.

15. Hoang Ngoc Lung, *The General Offensives of 1968–69* (McLean VA: General Research Corporation, 1978), 9.

16. William J. Luti, "Did Fake News Lose the Vietnam War?" *Wall Street Journal,* January 30, 2018, www.wsj.com/articles/did-fake-news-lose-the-vietnam-war-1517270406.

17. Ibid.

18. "Walter Cronkite's 'We Are Mired in a Stalemate,'" https://facultystaff.richmond.edu/~ebolt/history398/cronkite_1968.html.

19. Johnson's announcement, March 31, 1968, as quoted on the LBJ Presidential Library website: www.lbjlib.utexas.edu/johnson/archives.hom/speeches.hom/680331.asp.

20. Henry Kissinger, *White House Years* (New York: Simon & Schuster, 2011), 983. In his book *Ending the Vietnam War: A History of America's Involvement in and Extraction from the Vietnam War* (New York: Simon & Schuster, 2003), 46, Kissinger goes further: "The Tet offensive turned into a major psychological victory for Hanoi. One can reflect with some melancholy on the course of events had, in its aftermath, American leaders stepped up pressure on the North Vietnamese regular combat units, which were now deprived of their guerilla shield. Had Johnson done so, it is probable that he would have achieved the unconditional negotiations he was so desperately seeking, and maybe even an unconditional cease-fire. This is suggested by the rapidity—maybe less than seventy-two hours—with which Hanoi accepted Johnson's renewed offer to negotiate, which was coupled with a unilateral partial bombing halt based on the San Antonio formula."

CHAPTER 15. "COURAGE IS FEAR THAT HAS SAID ITS PRAYERS"

1. McNamara, *In Retrospect,* 209–212.

2. John Clark Pratt, ed., *Vietnam Voices: Perspectives on the War Years, 1941–1975* (Athens: University of Georgia Press, 2010), 275.

3. "Neil Armstrong," Wikipedia, https://en.wikipedia.org/wiki/Neil_Armstrong.

4. "Buzz Aldrin," Wikipedia, https://en.wikipedia.org/wiki/Buzz_Aldrin.

5. "U.S. Civilian Plane Shot Down Near Cuba," CNN, February 24, 1996, www.cnn.com/US/9602/cuba_shootdown/25.

6. Risner, *The Passing of the Night,* 175.

7. Colby Itkowitz, "How Jane Fonda's 1972 Trip to North Vietnam Earned Her the Nickname 'Hanoi Jane,'" *Washington Post,* September 18, 2017, citing an Associated Press report in April 1973, which quoted an interview Fonda gave to KNBC-TV in Los

Angeles. On July 4, 2018, *Colorado Springs Gazette* columnist David Ramsey had this to say: "Fonda offers a cautionary tale for those outraged by the strange turns of American politicians. She traveled to North Vietnam . . . on what she called a peace mission but got lost on the journey and declared war on her own countrymen. . . . Her once-idealistic opposition to [the] war—a war most Americans now believe was misguided—soured into loss of sight. Enraged by evil on one side, she failed to see evil on the other."

8. *Washington Post*, September 18, 2017.

9. "Peel, Robert Delaney," POW Network, www.pownetwork.org.bios/p/p058.htm.

10. "Merritt, Raymond James," POW Network, http://pownetwork.org/bios/m/m127.htm.

11. Will Dunham, "The POW Who Blinked 'Torture' in Morse Code During TV Interview Has Died," *Huffington Post*, March 28, 2014, www.huffingtonpost.com/2014/03/28/jeremiah-denton-dies_n_5050132.html.

12. Stockdale and Stockdale, *In Love and War*, 248–249.

13. Franke conversation with Tillman, 1987.

14. Risner, *The Passing of the Night*, 116–117.

15. "Vice-Admiral James Bond Stockdale," http://a4skyhawk.org/3e/va163/stockdale.htm.

16. Stockdale and Stockdale, *In Love and War*, 169.

17. Larry Smith, *Beyond Glory: Medal of Honor Heroes in Their Own Words* (New York: W. W. Norton, 2000), 351–353.

18. Stockdale and Stockdale, *In Love and War*, 94.

19. Ibid., 168.

20. Jennifer Abbey and Margaret Aro, "Three Vietnam POWs Mark 40 Years of Freedom," ABC News, May 28, 2013, http://abcnews.go.com/US/vietnam-pows-mark-40-years-freedom/story?id=19275515.

21. Flynn obituary, *Pensacola News Journal*, May 23, 2014.

CHAPTER 16. NIXON AND KISSINGER

1. University of Virginia, www.millercenter.org/president/Nixon/foreign-affairs.http.

2. Ibid.

3. "Henry Kissinger," Wikipedia, Wikipedia.org/wiki/Henry Kissinger.

4. Ibid.

5. Ibid.

6. Kissinger, *Ending the Vietnam War*, 75–90.

7. Ibid., 76.

8. Ibid., 90.

9. "China and the United States: Nixon's Legacy After 40 Years," Brookings-Tsingua, February 23, 2012, www.brookings.edu/up-front/2012/02/23/china-and-the-united-states-nixon's-legacy-after-40-years/http.

10. Author analysis, *U.S. Fixed-Wing Losses in Southeast Asia*.

11. Correll, *The Air Force in the Vietnam War,* 14.

12. John T. Correll, "Lavelle," *Air Force* magazine, November 2006, www.airforce mag.com.

13. Wayne Thompson, *To Hanoi and Back: The U.S. Air Force and North Vietnam, 1966–1973* (Washington, DC: Smithsonian Institution Press, 2010), 203.

14. G. H. Turley, *The Easter Offensive, Vietnam 1972* (Annapolis, MD: Naval Institute, 2010), 307.

15. Kissinger, *Ending the Vietnam War,* 268–283.

16. Ibid., 255.

CHAPTER 17. "YOU AIN'T HIT THE TARGET YET"

1. "Bombs for Beginners," www.globalsecurity.org/military/systems/munitions/into-bombs.htm.

2. Tom Clancy and John Gresham, *Fighter Wing: A Guided Tour of an Air Force Fighter Wing* (New York: Berkley Books, 1995), 151.

3. Peter deLeon, *The Laser-Guided Bomb: A Case History of Development* (Santa Monica, CA: Rand, 1974), v.

4. Paul G. Gillespie, *Precision Guided Munitions: Constructing a Bomb More Potent Than the A-Bomb,* dissertation, Air Force Institute of Technology, 115.

5. "Weldon Word," *People* magazine archive, May 30, 1991, http://people.com/archive/weldon-word/http.

6. Clancy and Gresham, *Fighter Wing,* 155.

7. Thomas G. Mahnken, *Technology and the American Way of War Since 1945* (New York: Columbia University Press, 2010), 293.

8. Brockway McMillan, Henry G. Booker, et al., *Radiation Intensity of the PAVE PAWS Radar System* (Washington, DC: National Research Council, 1979).

9. Mahnken, *Technology and the American Way of War,* 293.

10. "We Were Dropping a Cadillac," www.sgspires.tripod.com/Paveway_History/Usage/usage.html.

11. Donald J. Blackwelder, *The Long Road to Desert Storm and Beyond: Development of the Precision Guided Bombs* (Maxwell AFB: Air University, 1992), 25.

12. Tails Through Time, December 1, 2009, www.tailsthroughtime.com/2009/12/first-laser-designation-system-used-on.html.

13. Clancy and Gresham, *Fighter Wing,* 190.

14. Dr. Carlo Kopp, "Smart Bombs in Vietnam," *Defense Today,* September 2009, www.ausairpower.net/PDF-A/MS-PGMs-in-NVN-Sept-2009.pdf.html.

15. Blackwelder, *The Long Road to Desert Storm and Beyond,* 26–27.

16. Failor, cited in Gillespie, *Precision Guided Munitions,* 168.

17. "Cadillacs over Southeast Asia," http://sgspires.tripod.com/usage.html.

18. John Clark Pratt, *Vietnam Voices: Perspective on the War Years, 1941–1975* (Athens: University of Georgia Press, 2010), 195–196.

19. Captain Lonny McClung, USN (Ret), conversation with Tillman, 2015.

CHAPTER 18. BACK TO NORTH VIETNAM

1. "Vietnam War Casualty Statistics," National Archives, www.archives.gov/research/military/vietnam-war/casualty-statistics.html.

2. Turley, *The Easter Offensive*, ix.

3. Ron Rowen, emails to Tillman, March 2017.

4. Spencer C. Tucker, ed., *The Encyclopedia of the Vietnam War: A Political, Social, and Military History* (Santa Barbara, CA: ABC-CLIO, 1998), 233.

5. "Brigadier General Carl. S. Miller," U.S. Air Force, www.af.mil/AboutUs/Biographies/Display/tabid/225/Article/106212/brigadier-general-carl-s-miller.aspx.

6. Richard Hilton, *There Are No Sundays: A Youngster from Oklahoma Finds a Home in Jet Fighters* (Phoenix, AZ: Privately printed, Alphagraphics, 2014), 319; Richard D. Hilton, email to Tillman, April 4, 2017.

7. Author analysis of Air Force victories credited in Southeast Asia 1965–1968; Dr. Frank Olynyk, *United States Credits for Destruction of Enemy Aircraft in Air-to-Air Combat Post–World War 2* (privately printed, 1968).

8. Richard D. Hilton, emails to Tillman, March–April 2017.

9. James D. Franks, email to Tillman, April 17, 2017.

10. Harry Edwards to Phillip Chinnery, *Full Throttle: True Stories of Vietnam Air Combat, Told by the Men Who Lived It* (New York: St Martin's Press, 1988), 276.

11. William Thaler, email to Tillman, May 4, 2017.

12. Ibid.

13. Ibid.

14. HC-7 website.

15. Thaler, email to Tillman.

CHAPTER 19. POUNDING THE NORTH

1. "Transcript of President Nixon's Address," *New York Times*, May 9, 1972, www.nytimes.com/1972/05/09/archives/transcript-of-president-nixons-address-to-the-nation-on-his-policy-in.html.

2. John Darrell Sherwood, *Fast Movers: Jet Pilots and the Vietnam Experience* (New York: St. Martin's, 2001), 85–86.

3. Mark 20 Rockeye was a free-fall, unguided cluster weapon weighing about 480 pounds. The clamshell dispenser contained 247 dual-purpose, armor-piercing bomblets weighing 1.3 pounds each. When the dispenser opened after a preset number of seconds, the bomblets dispersed into an oval pattern. Each bomblet, shaped like a dart, contained a shaped-charge warhead of .4 pounds of high explosive capable of penetrating up to seven and a half inches of armor. If the bomblet hit a soft target, it detonated as an antipersonnel device, spraying shrapnel. The pattern

density could be doubled by dropping two at a time and elongated by training off multiple weapons. Rockeye was very effective against AAA, tanks, trucks, ammo and fuel dumps, and SAM sites. The weapon became operational in 1968. "MK-20 Rockeye," Global Security, Globalsecurity.org/military/systems/munitions/mk20.htm.

4. Randy Cunningham with Jeffrey L. Ethell, *Fox Two: The Story of America's First Ace in Vietnam* (Mesa, AZ: Champlin Fighter Museum Press, 1984), 100.

5. Ibid., 108.

6. Ibid., 110.

7. Steven Ritchie, interview with Coonts, 1995. See also Stephen Coonts, "The Last Ace," from *War In the Air* (New York: Pocket Books, 1996).

8. Clancy and Gresham, *Fighter Wing,* 150.

9. Lavalle, *Tale of Two Bridges,* 85.

10. Richard Hilton, emails to Tillman, March–April 2017.

11. Ibid.

12. Eighth Tactical Fighter Crew Assignments of May 13, 1972, compiled by Dean Failor.

13. Author's transcript of May 13 mission tape, provided by Colonel Richard Hilton, 2017.

14. Melvin F. Porter, *Linebacker: Overview of the First 120 Days* (Headquarters: Pacific Air Forces, September 1972), 50, https://archive.org/stream/projectcheco-ADA487179/ADA487179_djvu.txt.

15. Hilton, emails to Tillman, April 2017.

16. Hilton, *There Are No Sundays,* 318.

17. Porter, *Linebacker,* 51.

18. Bart Flaherty and Russ Ogle, emails to Tillman, January 2016.

CHAPTER 20. "WE DROPPED THE BRIDGE"

1. Paul Ringwood, emails to Tillman, March 2016.

2. Ibid.

3. Ibid.

4. John T. Smith, *The Linebacker Raids: The Bombing of North Vietnam, 1972* (London: Cassell, 2000), 75.

5. James E. Wise, *At the Helm of USS America: Its 23 Commanding Officers, 1965–1996* (Jefferson, NC: McFarland & Company, 2014), 128.

6. Norman Birzer and Peter Mersky, *U. S. Navy A-7 Corsair II Units of the Vietnam War* (Oxford: Osprey, 2004), 75.

7. Leighton Smith, interview with Tillman, April 29, 2017.

8. Sherwood, *Afterburner,* 280–281.

9. Smith, interview with Tillman, April 29, 2017.

10. Ibid.

11. Joseph Satrapa, phone conversations with Tillman, April 19 and 22, 2017.

12. Smith, interview with Tillman, April 29, 2017.

13. Leighton W. Smith Jr. Distinguished Flying Cross citation, 1972, provided to authors by Smith.

CHAPTER 21. THE VIOLENT CRESCENDO

1. Kissinger, *Ending the Vietnam War,* 354.

2. "Lyndon B. Johnson: Address at Johns Hopkins University: 'Peace Without Conquest,'" The American Presidency Project, www.presidency.ucsb.edu/ws/?pid=26877.

3. Kissinger, *Ending the Vietnam War,* 354.

4. Ibid., 379.

5. Ibid. p. 409. In his books *White House Years* and *Ending the Vietnam War,* Kissinger discussed Nixon's personality at numerous places. Kissinger was brilliant, a master negotiator, and highly skilled at reading people. Nixon was paranoid, secretive, and didn't work well with people. He avoided confrontation wherever possible. His obsessions led to Watergate and his resignation, yet America owes him a great deal. Nixon had the moral courage to use every diplomatic and military means to extract America from a tragic war. Lyndon Johnson, for all his bluster, never had the backbone to accomplish it.

6. Hiep Son et al., *The Capital, Hanoi: History of the Resistance War Against the Americans to Save the Nation, 1954–1975* (Hanoi: 1991). Translated for the authors by Merle Pribbenow, by permission.

7. Michael Yarvitz, "Pics: The Day the Senate Told Ford No More War in Vietnam," MSNBC, June 13, 2014, www.msnbc.com/rachel-maddow-show/pics-the-day-the-senate-told-ford-no-more-war-vietnam.

8. Andrew J. Bacevich, "A Requiem for Vietnam," *American Conservative,* February 7, 2018, www.theamericanconservative.com/articles/a-requiem-for-vietnam.

9. "Vietnam Evacuation: Operation Frequent Wind," https://media.defense.gov/2012/Aug/23/2001330098/-1/-1/0/Oper percent20Frequent percent20Wind.pdf.

BIBLIOGRAPHY

Ang Chen Guan. *The Vietnam War from the Other Side: The Vietnamese Communists Perspective*. New York: Routledge-Curzon, 2002.

Attinello, John S., et al. *Air to Air Encounters in Southeast Asia. Volume II: F-105 Events Prior to 1 March 1967*. Arlington, VA: Weapons System Evaluation Group, September 1968.

Bell, Kenneth H. *100 Missions North*. Washington, D.C.: Potomac, 1993.

Boniface, Roger. *MiGs over North Vietnam. The Vietnam People's Air Force in Combat, 1965-75*. Mechanicsburg, PA: Stackpole Books, 2010.

Boyne, Walter J. "Breaking the Dragon's Jaw." *Air Force Magazine*, August 2011.

Broughton, Jack. *Going Downtown: The Air War Against Hanoi and Washington*. Pacifica, CA: Pacifica Military History, 1988.

Center for Naval Analyses. *U.S. Navy, Marine Corps, and Air Force Fixed-Wing Aircraft Losses and Damage in Southeast Asia (1962-1973)*. Arlington, Virginia, August 1976.

Clancy, Tom, John Gresham, and Barrett Tillman. *Fighter Wing: A Guided Tour of an Air Force Combat Wing*. New York: Berkeley Books, 2004.

Colvin, John. *Twice Around the World: Some Memoirs of Diplomatic Life in North Vietnam and Outer Mongolia*. London: Leo Cooper, 1991.

Correll, John T. *The Air Force in the Vietnam War*. Arlington: Air Force Association, 2004.

Crabtree, James D. *On Air Defense*. Westport, Connecticut: Praeger Publishers, 1994.

Davies, Peter E. *F-105 Thunderchief Units of the Vietnam War (Osprey Combat Aircraft #84)*. Oxford, UK: Osprey Publishing Ltd, 2010.

____. *F-105 Wild Weasel vs SA-2 "Guideline" SAM, Vietnam 1965-1973*. Oxford, UK: Osprey Publishing Ltd, 2011.

____. "F-100—MiG Encounters of the First Kind." *The Intake*, Spring 2012.

deLeon, Peter. *The Laser-Guided Bomb: A Case History of Development*. RAND Corporation. Santa Monica: 1974.

Ethell, Jeffrey and Alfred Price. *One Day in a Long War*. New York: Berkeley Books, 1989.

Fey, Peter. "The Effects of Leadership on Carrier Air Wing Sixteen's Loss Rates During Operation Rolling Thunder, 1965–1968." Fort Leavenworth: Army Command and General Staff College, 2006.

Foster, Gary Wayne. *Phantom in the River: The Flight of Linfield Two Zero One*. Ashland, OR: Hellgate Press, 2010.

Foster, Wynn. *Captain Hook: A Pilot's Triumph and Tragedy in the Vietnam War*. Annapolis: Naval Institute, Press, 1992.

Gray, Steve. "The First Combat Use of the Walleye Weapon." *The A-4Ever Skyhawk Association Journal*. Fall 2014.

Gillespie, Paul G. "Precision Guided Munitions: Constructing a Bomb More Potent than the A-bomb." Doctoral dissertation. Bethlehem: Lehigh University, June 2002.

Halberstam, David. *The Best and the Brightest*. New York: Random House, 1989.

Hiep Son, et al. *The Capital, Hanoi: History of the Resistance War Against the Americans to Save the Nation, 1954-1975*. Hanoi: People's Army Publishing House, 1991.

Hilton, Richard. *There Are No Sundays: A Youngster from Oklahoma Finds a Home in High-Performance Jet Fighters*. Phoenix: Alphagraphics, 2014.

Hone, Thomas C. *Case Studies in the Achievement of Air Superiority*. Edited by Benjamin Franklin Cooling. Washington, D.C.: Center for Air Force History, 1991, p. 506.

Hukee, Byron E. *USAF and VNAF A-1 Skyraider Units of the Vietnam War*. Oxford, UK: Osprey Publishing Ltd, 2013.

Karnow, Stanley. *Vietnam: A History*. Second edition. New York: Penguin Books, 1997.

Kopp, Dr. Carlo. *Almaz S-75 Dvina/Desna/Volkov Air Defence System. Airpower Australia*. Technical report APA-TR-2009-0702, updated April, 2012. http://www.ausairpower.net/APA-S-75-Volkhov.html.

LaPointe, Robert. "PJs in Vietnam: The Story of Air Rescue in Vietnam as Seen Through the Eyes of Pararescuemen." Translated by Merle Pribbenow. Northern PJ Press, 2001.

Lind, Michael. *Vietnam: The Necessary War*. New York: Simon and Schuster, 2003.

McNamara, Robert Strange, with Brian Van De Mark. *In Retrospect: The Tragedy and Lessons of Vietnam*. New York: Vintage Books, 1996.

McMaster, H.R. *Dereliction of Duty: Johnson, McNamara, the Joint Chiefs of Staff, and the Lies that Led to Vietnam*. New York: Harper Perennial, 1998.

Mahnken, Thomas G. *Technology and the American Way of War Since 1945*. New York: Columbia University Press, 2008.

Mersky, Peter. *U.S. Navy and Marine Corps A-4 Skyhawk Units of the Vietnam War*. Oxford, UK: Osprey Publishing Ltd, 2007.

Meyers, Barton. "Vietnamese Defense Against Aerial Attack." Center for the Study of the Vietnam Conflict, 1996. Accessed March 10, 2015.

Momyer, General William W. *Air Power in Three Wars*. Washington, D.C.: Department of the Air Force, 1978.

Nalty, Bernard. *The War Against Trucks: Aerial Interdiction in Southern Laos, 1968–1972*. Washington, D.C.: Air Force History and Museums Program, 2005.

Nguyen Sy Hung, et al. *Air Engagements in the Skies over Vietnam (1965-1975)*. Translated by Merle Pribbenow. Hanoi: People's Army Publishing House, 2013.

Nichols, John B. and Barrett Tillman. *On Yankee Station: The Naval Air War over North Vietnam*. Annapolis: Naval Institute Press, 1987.

O'Connor, Michael. *MiG Killers of Yankee Station*. Friendship, WI: Ne Past Press, 2003,

Porter, M. F. "Linebacker: Overview of the First 120 Days." Headquarters Pacific Air Forces. Directorate of Operations Analysis. September 27, 1973. https://archive.org/stream/projectcheco-ADA487179/ADA487179_djvu.txt

Powell, Robert R. *RA-5C Vigilante Units in Combat*. Oxford, UK: Osprey Publishing Ltd, 2004.

Pratt, John Clark. *Vietnam Voices: Perspectives on the War Years, 1941–1975*. Athens, GA.: University of Georgia Press, 1999.

Pribbenow, Merle, translator. *History of the 228th Anti-Aircraft Artillery Regiment*. Headquarters and Party Committee. Colonel Dinh Khoi Sy. Hanoi: People's Army Publishing House, 1998.

___. Colonels Nghiem Dinh tich and Pham trung Xuyen. *History of the Air Defense Missile Troops 1965–2005*. Hanoi: People's Army Publishing House, 2007.

Purvis, Samuel M. "That Damn Bridge Again." *Flight Journal*, August 2007.

Risner, Robinson. *The Passing of the Night: My Seven Years as a Prisoner of the North Vietnamese*. Old Saybrook, CT: Konecky & Konecky, 1973.

Robinson, William A. *The Longest Rescue: The Life and Legacy of Vietnam POW*. Lexington: University Press of Kentucky, 2013.

Sherwood, John D. *Afterburner: Naval Aviators and the Vietnam War*. New York: NYU Press, 2004.

___. *Fast Movers: Jet Pilots and the Vietnam Experience*. New York: Simon & Schuster, 2001.

Smith, Larry. *Beyond Glory: Medal of Honor Heroes in Their Own Words*. New York: W.W. Norton, 2000.

Stockdale, Jim and Sybil Stockdale. *In Love and War*, Annapolis: Naval Institute Press, 1990.

Taylor, Keith (2014 edition), *Voices from the Second Republic of Vietnam (1967–1975)*. New York: Southeast Asia Program Publications.

Thompson, Wayne. *To Hanoi and Back: The U.S. Air Force and North Vietnam 1966–1973*. Washington, D.C.: Smithsonian Press, 2000.

Torpezer, Istvan. *MiG-17 and MiG-19 Units of the Vietnam War*. Oxford, UK: Osprey Publishing Ltd, 2001.

___. *MiG 17/19 Aces of the Vietnam War*. Oxford, UK: Osprey Publishing Ltd., 2016.

Turley, G.H. *The Easter Offensive*. Novato, CA: Presidio Press, 1985.

Van Staaveren, Jacob. *Gradual Failure: The Air War over North Vietnam 1965–1966*. Washington, DC: Air Force History and Museums Program, 2002.

Wilcox, Robert. *Scream of Eagles*. New York: Pocket Star Books, 2005.

Winchester, Jim. *Douglas A-4 Skyhawk: Attack and Close-Support Fighter Bomber*. Barnsley, UK: Pen and Sword, 2005.

Wise, James E. *At the Helm of USS* America*: Its 23 Commanding Officers, 1965–1996*. Jefferson, NC: McFarland & Company, 2014.

CONTRIBUTORS

James R. Bassett, USAF
Pete Batcheller, USN
Walter J. Boyne, USAF
Thomas F. Brown, III, USN
George Cannelos, USN, USAF
Brig. Gen. Dan Cherry, USAF
Richard Davies
Kenneth J. Davis, USN
Dave Dollarhide, USNR
David Dungan, USN
Bill Egen, USMC
Bart Flaherty, USNR
Wayne Foster
Wynn F. Foster, USN
Fred A. Franke, USN
James D. Franks, USAF
Jim Glendenning, USN
Jack L. Graber, USAF
Stephen R. Gray, USN.
Richard P. Hallion
Troy Harworth
Mark Hasara, USAF
Richard D. Hilton, USAF
Hoang Tran Dung
John Holm, USN
Bryon E. Hukee, USAF
Randy Kelso, USN
Carlo Kopp
Bob Krone, USAF
Robert C. Laymon, USAF
Lonny K. "Eagle" McClung, USN
Ivy McCoy, USAF
J. Michael McGrath, USN
George Mellinger
Ronald Milam, USN
Rick Morgan, USN
Mike Najim
John Nicholson, USN
Russ Ogle, USN
Christina Olds
Robert D. Peel, USAF
Timothy Pham
Charles Plumb, USN
Howard Plunkett, USAF
David C. Richardson, USN
Robert R. "Boom" Powell, USN
Merle Pribbenow
Samuel M. Purvis, III, USN
Hugh Replogle, USN
Paul Ringwood, USN
James Rotramel, USAF
Ron Rowen, USAF
Sam Sayers USN
Richard W. "Brown Bear" Schaffert, USN
Jim Schueckler (Virtual Wall website)
D.D. Smith, USN

Leighton "Snuffy" Smith, USN
John Stiles, USAF
James B. Stockdale, USN
Jeremy "Bear" Taylor, USN
William B. Thaler, USAF
Ron Thurlow, USAF
Istvan Toperczer
Theo van Geffen
David Webb
H. Wayne Whitten, USMC
Glenn Winter
Dennis Wisely, USN
Jack Woodul, USN
R. J. "Zap" Zlatoper, USN

For archival support, thanks to Dr. Daniel Haulman and Ms. Lynn Gamma of the Air Force Historical Records Agency and to John Darrell Sherwood of the Navy History and Heritage Command. Our great thanks, also, to Rear Admiral Christopher Murray and Kallie Rose of the Naval Safety Center.

INDEX